SYSTEMS-CENTERED PRACTICE

SYSTEMS-CENTERED PRACTICE

Selected Papers on Group Psychotherapy (1987–2002)

Yvonne M. Agazarian

Foreword by

Malcolm Pines

Routledge
Taylor & Francis Group
LONDON AND NEW YORK

First published 2006 by Karnac Books Ltd.

Published 2022 by Routledge
2 Park Square, Milton Park, Abingdon, Oxfordshire OX14 4RN
605 Third Avenue, New York, NY 10017

Routledge is an imprint of the Taylor & Francis Group, an informa business

First issued in hardback 2019

British Library Cataloguing in Publication Data

A C.I.P. for this book is available from the British Library

ISBN: 978-1-85575-309-9 (pbk)
ISBN: 978-0-367-32729-3 (hbk)

Edited, designed, and produced by Communication Crafts

Deep acknowledgment and gratitude
to all the theoreticians upon whom this work is founded,
and to my friends, mentors,
and all the members of training groups
without whom there would be
no theory of living human systems
or its systems-centered practice

CONTENTS

FOREWORD

Malcolm Pines

My happy and fruitful connection with Yvonne Agazarian began in 1980 at the International Congress of Group Psychotherapy in Copenhagen. Among the many papers, hers was outstanding for its clarity and originality. I then encouraged her and her collaborator, Richard Peters, to expand their work into a book. This was done amazingly quickly. When Yvonne came to London with the draft chapters, she could re-write overnight to improve style and content.

Since then, Yvonne has continued and deepened her search to explore and explain "what happens to people in groups". In this book, we can follow her search for a language "that applies to individuals, groups, organizations, nations".

It is fascinating to see the evolution of the convent girl, struggling to explain the most fundamental issues of our lives, the existence of God, the afterlife, war, poverty, injustice, unkindness, knowing what others are feeling, into the psychological scientist. Psychoanalysis, Lewinian theory, group-analytic and Tavistock theory have all been deeply studied for what of value can be extracted and integrated: Yvonne, miner of the deep.

I am glad that we can follow her explorations, leading to the bold conclusions: the present is the only area in which problems are solved; human energy can shift away from the anguish, the wishes and fears of the past, present, and future, into present reality. Those of us who have participated in her workshops know how well she plans and carries out these aims.

New innovations attract adherents who share the excitement of discovery, who practice amongst themselves these new ways of understanding the life we live in groups. Yvonne's work has significantly changed our understandings of sociality, and her contributions are receiving their well-merited recognition. I am glad for this book.

December 2005

SYSTEMS-CENTERED PRACTICE

Author's note

For reasons of confidentiality, the names of all patients and members of groups have been changed. The genders of all unspecified persons have been left as in the original papers; the author feels that the masculine pronoun is generic for all human beings.

Introduction

Developing a theory of living human systems

The chapters in this book are selected to represent some of the steps along the way to developing my theory of living human systems, which, when put into practice, has introduced into the field some different ways of influencing human dynamics. I claim the theory as a metatheory, which adds a different but complementary view to the theories that guide the practices in psychology and sociology (Agazarian, 1997).

The book covers various stages in my attempts to solve the problem represented by the fact that, though group dynamics are different from the dynamics of individuals, yet group is often defined as the sum of individual dynamics. Even the descriptive language dichotomizes groups and individuals, defining groups in terms of group dynamics and individuals in terms of psychodynamics.

The first chapter (1987) offers my first attempt at a solution, which was to suggest "role" as an intervening variable between individuals and groups. The last chapter (2002) summarizes the practice of systems-centered therapy, which provides a systems language that applies to individuals, groups, organizations, nations, and so on.

I began theorizing at school in the convent, when I desperately tried to understand where evil came from if God was all good. I came up with several explanations, only to be told that I had re-invented several heresies. My theorizing went underground. I would lie in bed through long sleepless nights, trying to explain things: not only God, but death, the afterlife, the war, the poor, injustice, the sense of knowing what others were feeling, the unkindness of some nuns. When, as an undergraduate, I discovered philosophy, I felt I had found others who, like me, couldn't leave any explanation well enough alone. Later, studying Freud, I found myself "inventing" his second theory of instincts while I was still reading his first. Always, however, there was a central unease in me that remained unsatisfied. It was not until graduate school, when I was introduced to the scientific method, that I discovered a mental discipline that helped me not only to be clear about theory but also to think about how to put it into practice.

It was also in graduate school that I had my first experience of being mentored. David Jenkins, the head of the department, who had studied with Lewin, became interested in the way I thought and set up a once-a-week tutorial for me in which we studied Lewin and life and in which I learned to be clear about my thinking. To this day, I am filled with gratitude and some awe at how deeply he influenced my life. At that time, I was also training at a psychoanalytic institute, deeply involved in understanding Freud and the Freudian approach to life and treatment. The competing approaches of Freud's theory of instincts and Lewinian Field Theory did not sit well together, but each seemed to address a fundamental question. Freud's "Unconscious" was a better explanation than any I had discovered so far in understanding human behaviour. Lewin, on the other hand, offered a way of formulating explanations into equations so that they could be tested and researched. Out of this dilemma came what was to be my life's work: How to solve the dichotomy between group dynamic and psychodynamic explanations for human behaviour and how to research the answer. This was in 1962. By 1981 I had discovered "roles" as an intervening variable between group and individual dynamics.

The construct of role

Role as a construct solved both theoretical and practical problems. From the individual perspective, roles were an example of the repetition compulsion, in which people were doomed to repeat in the present the unresolved conflicts of the past. In theory, roles could be defined as an encapsulation of dynamics that the individual had failed to integrate. From the group perspective, the same definition could apply. Group roles could be defined as an encapsulation of dynamics that the group had failed to integrate.

Chapter 1: "Group-as-a-Whole Theory Applied to Scapegoating" (1987). In this chapter, the function of "role" for both the individual and the group is discussed, building on the work I had done of postulating role as an intervening variable between the individual and the group (Agazarian & Peters, 1981).

> The scapegoat is an excellent illustration of a member role at the individual level, and of the group-role at the group level. . . .
>
> Dynamically, at the individual level, Billy's member-role behaviour of eliciting scapegoating serves an equilibrating function for his person system. From the group-system perspective it can also be said that scapegoating is serving an equilibrating function for the group-as-a-whole and that Billy G's member-role behaviour is also serving an important group role.

Chapter 2: "Bion, The Tavistock Method and the Group-as-a-Whole" (1987). The central focus of this chapter is the impact of the idea of "roles" on the way one thinks about groups and individuals and also on how one practices. Anne Alonso invited me to be a guest lecturer at Harvard to discuss Irvin D. Yalom's "Three Reactions to a New Member" (an awesome challenge). Anne had consistently supported my work at AGPA, notwithstanding that she herself was a well-known—and well-loved—proponent of psychoanalytic thought. In preparing the talk, I was confronted with how different the implications were of practicing from a group-as-a-whole approach in contrast to Yalom's Interpersonal approach.

In 1981, I had published *The Visible and Invisible Group,* defining "roles" as an intervening variable between group and individual dynamics. Approaching group from the perspective of "roles" introduced a sharp contrast between Yalom's interpersonal interventions (encouraging the group to confront Brian as a "puppy-dog") and the group-as-a-whole intervention that would have been directed at Brian's role for the group-as-a-whole.

> . . . when Brian is being "educated" by the group not to be a "puppy-dog" [as he is in Yalom's videotape], an alternative, group-as-whole intervention would point out to the group that there is

> considerable effort and energy in the group to put the "puppy-dog" in Brian's chair, and to wonder whether it is a way of making sure that there is no trace of "puppy-dog" in any other chair in the group.

Shifting the emphasis from Brian to the group increases the possibility that the group will come to understand that it has created Brian's "puppy-dog" role to contain the rejected dependency feelings in the group.

Presenting this paper was also my first experience of how one can inadvertently promote a split in the audience. Most of the audience, Anne, and other presenters were significantly supportive of my introduction of the difference between the group-as-a-whole and the interpersonal approaches—but not all! I alienated Yalom. This, my first presentation, left me with the challenge of how to present new ideas in ways that made the differences more acceptable without obscuring them with too much similarity.

The voice of the group

Hand in hand with my exploration into roles as an intervening variable between individual dynamics and group dynamics was the idea of the "voice of the group". It was clear to me that people gave voice, not only to their own dynamics, but also to group dynamics. However simple in theory, however, it was not that simple in practice. I discovered that learning to "listen" to the voice of the group was not only revolutionary as far as group dynamics was concerned, but also often heartbreaking. It was not new to me to experience my heart going out to individuals, nor was it new to have my heart go out to the group. What was new was how heartbreaking it was to "hear" the voice of the group crying out and going unheard. This is addressed in chapter 3.

Chapter 3: "The Difficult Patient, the Difficult Group" (1987). This chapter contains my first presentation of what I heard when listening to the group voice. I prepared this paper as a presentation on a panel in which I, and other therapists, analysed a tape of a difficult group. It was in the preparation for this paper that I first clearly heard the voice of the group-as-a-whole, and I also formulated the difference it made to seeing the group from the perspective of the person as a system and the group-as-a-whole as a system. I had not yet, however, understood that the subgroup was a system that was just as fundamentally important as the other three. I introduce the subgroup in chapter 4.

Chapter 4: "Group-as-a-Whole Systems Theory and Practice" (1989). In this chapter I use the same episode as the one in chapter 3, but in this version I make the connection between the group voice and implicit subgrouping.

The episode that follows illustrates a short extract from the beginning of a group.

> The episode starts with a knock on the door. A late patient, Bess, enters, and there is much commotion as everybody makes room and they all squash their chairs together.
>
> *Miss Thera:* "... fine, come on in ..."
>
> *Dr Junior:* "... why don't you ... here, take this chair ..."
>
> *Miss Thera:* "... watch the wire ..." [*the session is videotaped*]
>
> *Bess:* "... yeah ..."
>
> *Alice:* "... move the table ..."
>
> *Edna:* "... the camera will break ..."
>
> *Alice, Bess, Clara, Edna, Glenda, Doris* [*Laughter*]
>
> *Alice:* "... it's called togetherness."
>
> [*... as they all squash their chairs together*]
>
> *Clara:* "... closeness ..."
>
> *Bess:* "... that's what we're all looking for ..."
>
> *Miss Thera:* "... all thinking ..."
>
> *Dr Junior:* "... ready? ..."
>
> *Alice:* "... Christmas ..."
>
> *Dr Junior:* "... we were just talking about the fact that Edna was seeing me individually for treatment of her depression ..."

Considering this episode again, a duet between two different subgroups can be heard.

> *The "doctor" subgroup voice:*
>
> — "Here, sit here."
>
> — "Take this chair."
>
> — "Don't trip over the wire."

— "Move the table."
— "Come on in."
— "Ready?"

The "patient" subgroup voice:

— "Come on in."
— "It's called togetherness."
— "Closeness."
— "That's what we're all looking for."
— "That's what we're all thinking."
— "It's like Christmas."

What had been particularly difficult in my presentation of this theme on the original panel was that the supervisor and the two therapists were present on the panel, and all three had their hearts on the welfare of the patients. Once again, introducing a perspective that was significantly different from their training, with such different implications on the consequences of their orientation, seemed theoretically important and in human terms unkind. (This was a clear conflict between what I later would frame as a conflict between my personal system—which I did not want to hurt anyone's feelings—and my member system—which wanted to do a good job in interpreting the tape.

These first four chapters have been focused on the differences between individual and group approaches. In fact, in attempting to find a name for my developing theory, I had called it "Group-as-a-Whole Theory", "Invisible Group Theory", "Integrational Theory", and "Maturational Theory". In chapters 5 and 6 I focus on the differences between my own group-as-a-whole approach and the group-as-a-whole traditions that had emerged from the work of Bion and the Tavistock.

Chapter 5: "The Invisible Group: An Integrational Theory of Group-as-a-Whole" (1989). In this chapter, I compare and contrast my continually developing theory with Foulkes's theory for group analysis. Again I am indebted to the support of already established figures in the field. Malcolm Pines not only introduced me to my first publisher, but also introduced me as a theoretician important to group analysis when he invited me to be the Foulkes Memorial lecturer. Foulkes's theory had the same roots as Bion's. I, on the other hand, came to group less from a psychoanalytic background and more from my training in group dynamics. The greatest difference was that Foulkes did not conceptualize group in the context of phases of development, whereas I did. This chapter, perhaps more than any other, argues that different theories lead to different outcomes.

The first example I introduce came from leading the last of four demonstration groups at an Eastern Group Psychotherapy conference. I had watched the first three groups, and through my eyes I had traced the group development from compliant cooperation, through depression, into scapegoating. The group arrived on my doorstep, so-to-speak, tired, cranky, and full of gallows humour.

— ". . . Well, at least she spelled out our task very clearly, which none of the others did . . . except X, who told us that we were going to be depressed and thus gave us some structure!"

This was followed by some wry joking about the group-as-a-whole.

— ". . . They left a hole here! . . . and we have to fill it!"

— ". . . How can we fill this hole? . . . How can we make this whole?"

— ". . . Well, at least we have the hole . . . if we have to fill it!"

(This is not so funny if one listens to the voice of the group!)

It was in this group that I put into practice the idea that group survival and development was best served by weakening the defence mechanisms that were restraining the group rather than interpreting dynamics.

Lewin's force field is a potent method for putting defence modification into practice. Lewin had demonstrated that there was a greater potential for change if one weakens the restraining forces rather than attempting to increase the driving forces (the Sisyphus approach!).

This chapter also presents a further step in observing group dynamics through the frame of subgrouping. Following "subgroup" interactions, it becomes apparent that the group begins with an "exhausted" member as a representative of a subgroup. The group understood this when I asked, "Is the group going to going to leave all the exhaustion in one chair?" This is followed by a counterbalancing subgroup that is not tired and has some energy. As this subgroup used the metaphor of a marathon, I called them the "marathon" subgroup in my mind.

The group continued to work and succeeded in integrating the two subgroups: the "marathon" subgroup stating that it would not want to work if it was going to further tire other members, and the "exhausted" subgroup claiming not to be too tired for work. My intervention at this point is an example of the combination of a group-as-a-whole and a subgroup orientation:

— "I'm wondering if, for this group, it's rather as if its run three marathons already [*referring to the three previous groups*] and that right now the group is trying to decide whether it is worth it to summon up the energy to run a fourth, knowing that it's a short one and knowing that it's going to end . . . or whether the group has earned the right to sit back, experience its exhaustion, and become aware of what it has already achieved? I sort of sense that the group's not sure whether it wants to put its energy into another marathon, or whether it wants to sit back and, in its exhaustion, process this experience."

The second example is from a demonstration group in Japan, in which I tested whether I could lead a group using clues from voice-tone and from nonverbal as well as verbal behaviour. The group spoke no English. I spoke no Japanese. My Japanese co-leader and friend, Dr. Junichi Suzuki, translated my interventions into Japanese. There were some inherent challenges. In the Japanese culture, a woman has a very different status from the man, and the group hierarchy ranged from respected and revered Japanese faculty members (including one "silenced" woman), many young female students, and two young males.

To my relief, the group did mirror familiar "new group" phenomena and needed very little intervention until, after an exchange between a male elder and a young female student, there was a sudden shift in attention away from them to another part of the group.

> It was almost as if the group had amputated part of itself in an effort to ignore whatever had just occurred. So I spoke, through Dr Suzuki, and said, "I wish to draw the attention of the group to the last few interactions" (I then retraced the group process for the group). "I wonder if the group work will be helped or hindered if the group agrees to ignore whatever it was that just happened?"

I learned later that at this point the "elders" of the group decided that I did, after all, understand Japanese!

Chapter 6: "Phases of Development and the Systems-Centered Group" (1994). This chapter is one of several in which I discuss phases of development, which are a central focus for my group work since my graduate program which oriented its "T-groups" in relation to Bennis and Shepard's theory. From early on, I recognized that the phase of development in which the group was working was a potent governor of what could and could not be achieved by the group. In other words, the phase of development was a variable as important as group leadership, group composition, group climate, and other group variables that determined what groups can do and why they can do them.

> . . . even though phases of group development have been discussed in the literature since the 1950s, they are still not a commonly accepted reality among group psychotherapists! Yet there is an evident and predictable sequence of phases in group development to be seen if the therapist knows where to look. Seen or unseen, each phase has a different and forceful impact on what happens to a group. When seen and understood, these forces can be deliberately harnessed in the service of the therapeutic goals; when not, the impact of these forces goes unidentified and unaddressed. Hence the stereotypic and repetitive creation of the roles of "identified patient" and "scapegoat" in therapist-oriented and patient-oriented—and even some group-oriented—psychotherapy groups.

This chapter was an important one for me in many ways. It meant a lot that Malcolm Pines and Victor Schermer had invited me to contribute to a book on object relations theory, thus acknowledging both my psychodynamic and my systems understanding. It also gave me an arena to introduce functional subgrouping as an alternative to the common acting-out, like scapegoating.

> In systems-centered groups it is the subgroup, not the individual member, that is required to contain different sides of predictable "splits" around difference. When the group-as-a-whole works to "contain" the conflict consciously as a working task, then it is no longer necessary to delegate conflicting differences to a scapegoat, an identified patient, or a deviant pair.

This chapter also gave me the opportunity to introduce the relationship between roles and group-system dynamics—important in that it furthered the argument that conceptualizing group in terms of systems forces rather than people made it possible to influence the development of the group in ways that are not possible from the person perspective.

> From the systems-centered perspective, the relationship between developmental forces and the developmental goals is related to systems and is manifested in "roles", not in "people". The "people" who occupy these roles are "transients" playing a part in the work of the group. . . .
>
> For example, developmental dynamics around dependency are not interpreted as a property of "dependent" or "counterdependent" *individuals* but, rather, as approach and avoidance forces. These forces are manifested in roles (Agazarian & Peters, 1981).

Chapter 7: "Reframing the Group-as-a-Whole" (1989). In this paper I had the opportunity to discuss the difference between group-as-a-whole models that did, and did not, see groups through the eyes of phases of group development. This was an important step for me, as I questioned whether or not the behaviour of A. K. Rice groups was not, perhaps, a function more of the A. K. Rice structure rather than of underlying psychopathology.

As A. K. Rice conferences had served as an irreplaceable arena for my learning about group dynamics, there was a part of me that felt disloyal as I argued that the A. K. Rice structure created the very problems that it attempted to cure. In spite of the fact that structure certainly influences function, this was an over-simplification.

> A major difference between this orientation and that of the more traditional Tavistock small group is that the task is consistently and explicitly kept in focus and related to the explicit sub-goals and to the implicit goal.

In this last quote I reference the work that I did with Harold Bridger at his conference in Minster Lovell. He pointed out the predictable differences that could be expected between groups that did have explicit goals and groups that did not. From Harold's perspective, as the Tavistock method leaves groups to intuit their own goals, the chaos that ensues is predictable and also unnecessary.

After my work with Harold, I introduced into my theory and practice the importance of clear explicit goals and the necessity of recognizing the relationship between them (the task goals) and the implicit (Basic Assumption goals). (Translating these into driving and restraining forces yielded a useful force field analysis.) As Harold was particularly unpopular among many of the leaders of A. K. Rice at that time, it reinforced my fears that I was putting my head into the lion's mouth. My fears were ungrounded.

Chapter 8: "Koinonia: From Hate, through Dialogue, to Culture in the Large Group" (1992). Another major shift in my thinking about the underlying dynamics in groups came from my work with Pat de Maré, who turned upside-down my Freudian understanding of the superego. In contrast to the work I had done with Davanloo (1987), in which he framed the superego as the root of all serious pathology, de Maré (de Maré, Piper, & Thompson, 1992) re-interpreted the superego as the potential source of creative energy.

> Whereas the small group, particularly the psychoanalytic and Foulksian group, evokes family transferences and repetition meanings in terms of the inner lives of the past, the large group requires, through the containment of hate . . . the transformation of energy into the socializing process of impersonal friendship and dialogue. [p. 98]
>
> The primary problem of large groups centres around primal hate . . . [p. 114]

At that time, I knew only too well the chaos of the large-group phenomenon and the hatred that was so easily aroused between members themselves and from members to me as the leader. Pat's work around hatred and the superego was a fundamental challenge that required transforming group hatred from a negative into a positive!

I was not to know then, but by applying the systems-centered approach that I used in small groups to large groups, the large groups also metabolized hatred into creative exploration. And this could occur, not over years, but in four 90-minute groups of 130 members in a weekend workshop!

Another debt I owe to Pat is his reinforcement of my deepening conviction that if one thought pathology and interpreted pathology in groups, that was what one got. De-pathologizing "superego" sadism led me to re-conceptualize retaliatory impulses as normal human reactions, which, when acted out, lead to hostility and sadism; when turned inward, to masochism and depression; and when explored, to simple aggression—a life force and the source not only of creativity, but of survival, development, and transformation.

> Hate, then, is not the adversary of Eros but the inevitable irreversible outcome of the frustration of Eros. [p. 62]

Chapter 9: "A Systems Approach to the Group-as-a-Whole" (1992). In this chapter I spell out, with great confidence, a summary of the theoretical developments that I had reached in 1992. I also present clear discriminations between member, subgroup, and group-as-a-whole interventions and the importance of focusing on subgroups, and I introduce the importance of boundaries.

> The appropriate level for the *systems-centered intervention* is not simply whether to intervene at the level of the subgroup, member, or group-as-a-whole, but which boundary to influence. Influencing the permeability of the boundary between, within, or among systems at any level of the hierarchy influences the balance of driving and restraining forces in relation to the goal.

It is also in this chapter that boundaries between the past, present, and future, between real time and psychological time, are introduced:

> Boundaries in time define the existence of the group, not only in space/time but also in the realities and irrealities of the psychological time that exists in the past, present, and future—all co-existing without contradiction in the unconscious—a significant determinant of the state of the system existence, experience, and productivity in the present.

All in all, this chapter presents a greater level of confidence than, perhaps, any other that I have published. It implies that understanding this theoretical perspective would make a significant difference to the field of group psychotherapy. The central issue that I was asked to address was that of the difficult patient. I approached this task by defining patients as difficult when they could not subgroup.

> A member then becomes "difficult" not because of his role salience, but because he cannot work in a subgroup. Subgrouping requires being able not to be the centre of the group: to understand that work in the group requires joining others' work and allowing them

> to join yours. It requires some understanding of the advantage of not taking things personally, volunteering to serve as a projective screen for each other, and, most important, it means being willing to give up self-defeating roles. It doesn't matter that the member who enters group cannot do any of these things, as long as he can see in them a value for him and something that he will want to learn. Without this willingness, it is inappropriate to place him in a systems-centered group.

It is in this chapter that I faced the fact of limitations of the SCT method. SCT relies on functional subgrouping for establishing a systems-centered group, and the prerequisite for being able to subgroup functionally is the ability not to take things just personally. It is through developing an awareness of oneself in context that makes it possible to subgroup. People who can only personalize cannot subgroup, therefore SCT methods will not work for them.

Chapter 10: "A Systems-Centered Approach to Individual and Group Psychotherapy" (2002). The initial paragraph of this chapter states one of the things that would make David Jenkins, my mentor, most proud.

> Systems-centered therapy (SCT) is an innovative approach to individual and group psychotherapy. It is different from most approaches to therapy in that the theory about the dynamics of systems was developed first (a theory of living human systems . . .), and the practice of systems-centered therapy developed from putting the theory into practice.

Theory itself is not the focus of this chapter, although emphasis is placed on the importance of isomorphy in understanding how system dynamics apply to all systems in the hierarchy, thus providing a single way of thinking both about groups and about individuals. And the case is made that the success of individual and group therapy depends more upon the "system" that the therapist and patient develop together than it does on either the individual patient's potential for therapy or the skills of the therapist.

The chapter's emphasis is on the reality that the present is the only arena in which problems are solved. The specific techniques enable human psychic energy to shift into present reality and away from the anguish of the wishes and fears of the present, past, and future, into present reality. The assumption is made that it is the neurological pathways that establish maladaptive thinking about the past or the future that are difficult, if not impossible, to modify. However, by diverting energy (gently) from the maladaptive patterns into curiosity and exploration of the here-and-now, new neurological pathways can become established that offer an adaptive alternative.

Techniques and methods do not, however, obviate the importance of transference. Transferences fall into four categories: the superficial transferences that are addressed in the first phase of treatment, the negative and positive transferences addressed in the middle phase, and the pervasive transference that entails the deep work in the final phase.

A detailed description, with examples, is given of the hierarchy of defence modification that paces the phases of development. The developmental phases are presented as the context that determines readiness for work and also predicts what kinds of work would be premature.

Some of the constants that characterize SCT are depathologizing; refraining instead of interpreting; leaving the locus of choice in the patient to choose which fork-in-the-road of every conflict to explore first; the emphasis on differentiating between feelings that are generated by thoughts and feelings and those that are generated from direct experience; maintaining eye contact when working; working with empathy and attunement between persons and in the subgroups; identifying and weakening the restraining forces to therapy and thus releasing the inherent drive to health.

CONCLUSION

These chapters span the years when I was still painfully aware that the theory I was developing had by no means consolidated and might at any time fall apart. Developing theory is an all-consuming world unto itself. I might never have been motivated to do more than write about its implications had not the crisis of the short-term goals of managed care aroused panic in those of us who did long-term work. It was then that I set about the task of discovering how to put the theory into a formal discipline of practice, so that when managed-care patients were assigned stop-and-start therapies in short-term segments . . . IF they returned again, they could start again where they had left off . . . IF the different therapists were using the same model . . . IF there was a clear protocol for the therapists' to follow . . . IF the protocol enabled a series of small changes that persisted over time . . . IF all the small changes added up to a complete therapy . . . IF the therapeutic results mirrored the results that can be achieved long term: a lot of very big IFs.

Many of the chapters in this book describe the methods and techniques that result in the protocol of systems-centered therapy. They seems to work! But they remain simply techniques if they are not practiced from the theoretical orientation of SCT, which means not requiring a patient to practice a technique until one has mastered it by practicing on oneself. Only then can the SCT work be done with the attunement that comes from knowing the same challenges as one's patients.

Behind all methods and techniques is a theory, either implicit or explicit. A theory of living human systems explicitly assumes (a) that the primary goal of all systems is to survive, to develop, and to transform from simpler to more complex; (b) that the single dynamic of discriminating and integrating differences is both a necessary and a sufficient condition for systems to organize energy and move along the path to these goals; (c) that functional subgrouping is the operational methodology for discriminating and integrating the information necessary for the system to move towards its goals; (d) that the path to these goals is located in the phases of system development, which move from simpler to more complex; (e) that the balance of driving and restraining forces that characterizes one phase is significantly different from those that characterize another.

All systems are dependent for their existence on their structure. System structure is defined by boundaries of space/time. In living human systems, psychological space/time boundaries are a determinant as potent as the realities of geographical space and clock-measured time. System boundaries are potentially permeable.

Energy and information are equated. The energy in the system hierarchy crosses boundaries as information. Information is organized within the system through discriminations and integrations. System boundaries are reactive to noise. Reducing the restraining force of noise in communication increases the available information that the system can organize.

Just as functional subgrouping enables system function, so the SCT hierarchy of defence modification, in the context of the phases of system development, enables system structure by increasing the permeability of the boundaries to the energy of all the systems in the hierarchy.

CHAPTER ONE

Group-as-a-Whole Theory applied to scapegoating

In this chapter I present a way of looking at groups from two perspectives: the perspective of the individual and the perspective of the "group-as-a-whole" ("Theory of the Invisible Group"—Agazarian & Peters, 1981). This theoretical framework applies practically to making interventions in groups. Choosing which level to influence can have significant impact upon the potential outcome of important therapeutic group issues. For example, interpreting scapegoating from the individual perspective will have a different impact from interpreting it from the group-as-a-whole perspective and may significantly influence the developmental potential of a psychotherapy group.

* * *

The underlying dynamic common to maturation of all human systems, be they as small as a cell or as large as society, is the functional discrimination and integration of differences, from simple to complex. This is the process that makes order out of chaos, makes the uncon-

---

Y. M. Agazarian, "Group-as-a-Whole Theory Applied to Scapegoating." Supplementary paper to the workshop on "Deviance, Scapegoating & Group Development". EGPS Annual Conference, New York, October 1987.

scious conscious, and codes information and organizes it in relation to group goals.

The development of mature problem-solving skills, whether they be by individuals or by groups, are therefore a function of the rate at which similarities and differences can be discriminated and integrated. The process is twofold: similarities and differences must be perceived—both the similarities in the apparently different and the differences in the apparently similar—and system equilibrium must be sufficiently maintained so that the work of integration can take place. Until discriminations are integrated, they are disequilibrating, chaotic. It is this chaos that the group system must contain while the work of discrimination and integration takes place.

All individuals in groups must defend against the chaos without as well as that within while they attempt to organize experience. The individual patient who enters a psychotherapy group does so because he needs therapy. But for the group to have a therapeutic meaning for that person, the group itself must be a therapeutic environment, and for it to become such an environment, it must develop mature problem-solving skills. This may sound like a contradiction in terms: that a group composed of members who had joined because they have serious developmental problems must work together to develop a healthy group. However, just as is the case with an individual, so how a particular group system develops depends less upon its genetic composition than upon the mechanisms it develops to contain chaos. And this is where the group therapist has influence.

The simplest way for a group to contain chaos is to split integratable information from non-integratable information and to contain the two kinds of information separately. This reduces the information overload, and the group can then use the information that is "similar enough" without being overwhelmed by information that is "too different". The group therapist can help the group-as-a-whole to develop good skills in managing the containment of information. It is in this aspect that a theoretical framework can be useful to the therapist. Understanding the dynamics of both the individual and the group-as-a-whole systems permit the therapist to choose the intervention that has most therapeutic meaning for therapeutic development in the group.

In the theory section that follows, two separate but complementary systems are described: the system of the individual and the system of the group-as-a-whole. These two systems are hierarchically and isomorphically related. They provide the group psychotherapist with two views of the same group event, which permit two discrete dynamic explanations and two different pathways for making a therapeutic intervention. From the individual perspective, group psychotherapy is discussed in terms of how each individual's psychodynamics are characteristically expressed in their membership behaviours, which are, in turn, modified by their interactions in the group. From the group-as-a-whole perspective, group psychotherapy is discussed in terms of how group dynamics are expressed in characteristic group-as-a-whole-role behaviours, which, by modifying the development of the group, result in modifying the individual members of the group.

Theory of the invisible group

The Theory of the Invisible Group describes the invisible inner dynamics and the visible external behaviour of living systems. When applied to groups, the individual system is defined in terms of (1A) the inner-person system and (1B) the member-role system; and the group system is defined in terms of (2A) the inner group-as-a-whole system and (2B) the subgroup-role system. Because these two systems are isomorphically related—that is, similar in structure and function—it becomes possible to explain group behaviour from two theoretical perspectives and to generate two apparently contradictory, but actually complementary hypotheses: (a) all group behaviour can be explained as a function of individual dynamics; (b) all group behaviour can be explained as a function of group dynamics.

The individual system

"Person" inner-system dynamics

From the perspective of the person, individual dynamics are understood as a function of *inner-person* psychodynamics that result from genetic inheritance, developmental history, environmental influences, and past experiences.

Person interventions focus on individual internal psychodynamics. They are designed to modify the ego defence mechanisms, both as they inhibit and as they potentiate individual problem solving. The target of a person intervention is the inner *experience* of the individual. A criterion of a successful person intervention is that the person gains insight through the physical, nonverbal *experience* of his dynamics. This is different from intellectual insight. Thus, for the individual who is the scapegoat, a successful intervention would result in the full experience of the dynamics of his masochism—not an intellectualized or verbal understanding of it.

"Member-role" behavioural dynamics

From the perspective of the member, individual behaviour is understood as a function of the interpersonal dynamics of the individual interpreted as a behavioural expression of past problem-solving role behaviours modified by the present interactions. These are usually expressed in reciprocal roles.

Member interventions focus on interpersonal dynamics and on how the tensions of internal experience are expressed or acted out in behaviour that attempts to solve internal problems by action in the outside world.

Thus for the individual in the role of the scapegoat, a successful interpersonal intervention would result in an understanding of how he had repeated in the present an old role relationship from the past, attempting to relieve current internal or external pressures by reliving old solutions (the repetition compulsion). Successful member interventions to the scapegoat lead to an understanding of how he repeatedly "volunteers" for the role and/or "coaches" a scapegoating response from the group members.

Unless patients get insight into their conflicts, they will continue to helplessly repeat them. However, the conflicts that are expressed in repetitive behaviour are frequently repressed or denied, and so for the scapegoat to get intellectual understanding of how he volunteers for the scapegoat role or how he elicits attack from others is often a useful step towards confronting denial or undoing repression and can therefore fulfil the criteria for a successful therapeutic intervention.

Group-system dynamics

"Group-as-a-whole" inner dynamics

From the perspective of the group-as-a-whole, group dynamics are understood as a function of the group composition, developmental history, environmental influence, and past experiences.

Group-as-a-whole interventions are designed to modify group-level defences. This is so both in the potentiating sense that group-level defences bind group-level chaos, and also in the inhibiting sense that the group-level defences limit problem-solving potential.

The target of the group intervention is the inner dynamics of the group. Group maturation is dependent upon the integration of differences. Splitting is a mechanism that permits the group to integrate information that is "similar enough" and to "split off" and "store" information that is "too different". This carries the potential both for maturation and for fixation. In the management of scapegoating, for example, the therapists needs to be able to recognize when the underlying dynamics of scapegoating are part of a natural maturation process of the group-as-a-whole that an intervention would interrupt and when there is the potentiality for fixation that requires an intervention.

"Group-role" dynamics

From the perspective of the group role, group behaviour is understood as a function of subgroup-role relationships that enable the group to remain in a dynamic equilibrium. Thus tensions that are experienced within the group-as-a-whole, and which give rise to group-level defences, are expressed or acted out through behaviour that attempts to discharge the tensions and permit the group to solve internal and external problems.

Just as individual member-role behaviour serves an equilibrating function for the individual system, so group-role behaviour does for the group. It is as if the group-as-a-whole delegates one or more of its members to perform group roles that will bind, contain, or express group tensions, while it assigns other members, subgroups, or facets of the whole group to roles that facilitate work.

Group-role interventions assist the group to modify group-level defences and to develop problem-solving skills. A group-role intervention is the intervention of choice when it is appropriate to interrupt group scapegoating. It is an intervention that requires the group to make conscious and integrate the differences that the group has allocated to the scapegoat role. As group-level scapegoating entails group-as-a-whole acting out and projective identification, a successful group-as-a-whole intervention makes the dynamics conscious, undoes the projection, and confronts the denial. The integration work that follows serves as a powerful stimulus to therapeutic insight and development at both group and individual systems levels.

Scapegoating

Group therapists who know only the individual level of dynamics do not have a conceptual tool that will permit them to view group dynamics as a separate and discrete—though related—phenomenon. Thus, their understanding of the group is confined to the individual level, and their decisions to influence behaviour of the group must, of necessity, be targeted through the individual. This can have a significant impact not only on the probable outcome of the individual issues that members bring to group, but also, more seriously, upon the nature and potential of the development of the group itself. This is illustrated below by two different approaches to the handling of scapegoating in the group, which reflect the two different role perspectives: the member role as it relates to the individual and the group role as it relates to the group-as-a-whole.

The scapegoat is an excellent illustration of a member role at the individual level, and of the group role at the group level. Let us take, for example, a scapegoat, "Billy G". Billy G comes into the group, and the group scapegoats him for behaving in ways that are too different for the group to tolerate. After some work, a compromise is worked out, and Billy G's unacceptable behaviour is sufficiently modified by the group for him to be accepted as a member. In the process of modifying Billy's behaviour, the group also modifies itself. There is some "give and take" on either side.

Examining the scapegoating event from the individual perspective, you will almost invariably find that Billy G's psychodynamic solution to inner-person disequilibrium was to become a target; that he was the family member who was consistently scapegoated, that he has a history of being the lightning rod for anger. Even though he may experience being scapegoated as one of life's most painful experiences, he helplessly volunteers for the role in the group, thus once again reproducing the experience. An individual interpretation to Billy G would help him to understand, in terms of his masochism, why he sets himself up in this way. An individual interpretation would carry a very good potential for doing excellent therapy against the matrix of the group at the person level, not only with Billy G, but, through resonance, with others in the group. The therapist could also point out the dynamics of the reciprocal interpersonal member behaviour. Those who attack Billy G are probably repeating their own familiar family bully roles in the group, and they also have the opportunity to gain insight into both their person and their member dynamics. Useful as it is to the individual, however, the individual system perspective does not tell the whole story.

Dynamically, at the individual level, Billy's member-role behaviour of eliciting scapegoating serves an equilibrating function for his person system. From the group-system perspective it can also be said that scapegoating is serving an equilibrating function for the group-as-a-whole and that Billy G's member-role behaviour is also serving an important group role. This understanding brings with it some important implications for group dynamic development.

A useful way of conceptualizing development, both at the individual level and also at the group level, is to think of maturation as a function of discrimination and integration. One of the attractions of conceptualizing maturation in this way is its elegant correspondence to the development of cell complexity through miosis, which results in living beings. Just as the maturation of the cells in a living being is a function of the discrimination and integration of similarities and differences of structure and function, so is the maturation of a group. However, the process of maturation of the group inevitably arouses resistance to change at the individual level. The work of perceiving and integrating differences must, by its very nature, arouse cognitive dissonance. One way of maintaining the comfortable equilibrium of homogeneity and avoiding dealing with emerging differences is to deny difference, to split off awareness, and to use a group member—usually one who volunteers for the role, as in the case of Billy G—as the container through projective identification. The group can then deal with that member as a "deviant" and bring the not inconsiderable group pressure for conformity to bear upon the deviant member. The group can maintain its norms unchanged if it either brings the member into line or excludes or extrudes him in order to "get rid" of the difference that it would otherwise have to integrate. Parenthetically, the same "containment" dynamic exists when a subgroup of the group rather than a single group member performs the group role—as, for example, when disagreement in a group is contained in a silent subgroup who do not give voice to their disagreement, or when differences in group feeling are isolated by a split, such as when the group functions at a level of intellectualized flight, with all feeling in the group denied and unavailable. There is a correspondence between these group-as-a-whole dynamics and the individual dynamics of denial, intellectualization, and isolation.

Thus, group-role dynamics represent an important step in containing, for the group, differences that it is not yet able to integrate and thus maintaining the group equilibrium. In the early phases of group development, scapegoating serves the function of containing differences that the group is not yet developmentally able to integrate.

Scapegoating occurs developmentally when group flight is giving way to group fight. During the flight phase, members solve differences through homogenous pairing: they pair for power and control—power to protect against control by others, by the leader, by the group, by unconscious forces; or power to control others, the leader, the group, unconscious forces. The fight phase introduces heterogeneity: dissimilar people fight, and in the process of resolving the fights members come to terms with differences. There are, however, differences that the group is not able to integrate, and the group solution is to project these into a deviant member who will contain them for the group. In the group communication pattern to a deviant person, the group pressures the member to conform to the group norms, to become converted, or to leave.

In the process of integrating the scapegoat, the group comes to tolerate some of the differences that had previously been intolerable, and these differences thus become available to the group as resources that would otherwise have been split of an remained unavailable had the scapegoating been resolved through conversion or extrusion.

It can now be shown clearly what happens dynamically to a group when the therapist works with scapegoating at the individual level. By targeting interventions, no matter what the content may be, at the individual level, the therapist joins the communication pattern to the deviant. This is the solution of the "identified patient" in groups—and in families, too—that maintains the group equilibrium by binding the underlying tensions in an acknowledged role that forms part of familiar role-interaction functions.

What happens when a psychotherapy group successfully works through a scapegoating phase? Two things: first, the person who is the scapegoat usually makes significant therapeutic gains; second, the group learns to tolerate differences that it would not have been able to tolerate had it not worked through a peer level. Whenever a group is unable to come to terms with differences, its potential for development and its potential for functioning as a therapeutic environment for the individual is inevitably limited. The basic dynamic of maintaining group-as-a-whole equilibrium through requiring a group-role system to contain, express, or voice dynamics of group function that are still in the process of being mastered by the group is true for each developmental phase of the group. It is therefore important for group therapists to be able to deliberately facilitate the process of differentiation and integration, which is in the service of group maturation. Facilitating work at the individual level is, therefore, best done within the context of group developmental needs that will both stimulate inner-person relevance and encourage the working-through of resolutions rather than repetitions of member roles.

SUMMARY

Understanding the differences between interpreting to an individual and interpreting to the group-as-a-whole has important implications for the therapist. For example, when the therapist makes an individual interpretation to the scapegoat, no matter how it is phrased, the therapist has joined the group communication pattern to the deviant and has thus reinforced the pattern and joined in the scapegoating!

When the therapist interprets at the group-as-a-whole level, the *group* unconscious goals can become conscious, and there is an opportunity for the individuals in the group to recognize the container function of the scapegoat for the group-as-a-whole and also to get insight into what it is that they are individually projecting into the scapegoat that they are having difficulty integrating within themselves. Thus differences can be owned and integrated at both a group and an individual level. By so doing, the group becomes able to tolerate differences and thus develop resources that would have remained unavailable had the scapegoat problem been dealt with as if it were simply an individual problem. With the shift in the dynamics of the group, there is a shift in the potential for the work of the individuals in the group environment.

Once one understands the isomorphic relationship between the group-system dynamics and individual system dynamics and can view the same event from the perspective of both the individual member and the group-as-a-whole, then one can see how the person speaks both for his own issues and also for the group. In playing his own individual member role repetitiously and even self-destructively in the short run (as the scapegoat does), he may at the same time serve in a group role, containing for the group whatever projected aspects of group life the group is unable to integrate. Thus in the long run—provided the therapist understands when it is important to focus on the group dynamic rather than on the individual dynamic—the individual may be required by the more mature group to give up the old role (whether or not he wishes to do so!) because the group no longer has any use for it.

CHAPTER TWO

Re viewing Yalom: an interpersonal tale retold from the perspective of the group-as-a-whole

Let me start by relating a true story. One sunny summer day in 1983, I was lunching with my friend George Vassiliou in his garden in Athens. We were talking about applying General Systems Theory to group psychotherapy. To illustrate a point, George threw a piece of his hamburger into the goldfish pond. One little goldfish, faster than the others, reached the hamburger first. It was too large for him to swallow, so he swam off with it in his jaws, while the other goldfish darted around him nibbling away at his prize.

George pointed to the goldfish with the meat in his mouth: "That poor little fellow is having his dinner stolen from him by the other fish, and if he is not careful, he will have nothing left to eat but the last small bite", he said. "On the other hand", said George, pointing again, "here is the whole shoal of goldfish with a large meal falling into their midst—too big a serving for any single fish to swallow; one fish holds it, while the other fish nibble at it, breaking it up into bits, which they

---

Y. M. Agazarian, "Re Viewing Yalom: An Interpersonal Tale Retold from the Perspective of the Group-as-a-Whole". Guest Lecture, Group Psychotherapy, Harvard Medical School Department of Continuing Education (sponsored by the Massachusetts General Hospital Department of Psychiatry), Boston, MA, 3–5 April 1987.

either swallow or which drop into the water for the others. Thus the meal is distributed among the whole population of the goldfish pond!"

This story illustrates two different perspectives on the same event. From the perspective of the fish in general, we see an efficient distribution and feeding system, where one fish plays a role for the whole shoal by catching the hamburger and holding it in his mouth while the whole school of fish feed. We see something very different from the perspective of the individual fish who is having his dinner stolen from him before he can swim off with it.

It is from this individual perspective that interpretations are most usually made in group psychotherapy. An event is more rarely perceived from the perspective of the group-as-a-whole. This is of major importance. When we observe a goldfish pond, how we as observers interpret the event does have an effect on the way the fish behave, but this does not hold true when we observe and interpret an event in a psychotherapy group. Even reading about the individual goldfish having its dinner stolen by the other fish elicits a response from us that is different from our reaction to reading about the group-as-a-whole's distribution of the hamburger to all the fish. From the group-as-a-whole perspective, the individual fish is not a victim of the other fish, rather, it is performing an important role for the shoal.

The individual and the group

My task in this chapter is twofold. It is to discuss the group-as-a-whole perspective as it is grounded in the Bion–Tavistock tradition and to illustrate it by reinterpreting Irvin Yalom's interpersonal, individually oriented vignette from the perspective of the group-as-a-whole. In Yalom's vignette (1970, p. 253), individual behaviour is explained in terms of individual dynamics. My task is to explain this same behaviour in terms of group dynamics and, by so doing, demonstrate that the perspective of the group-as-a-whole does more than introduce the group therapist to different ideational perceptions, interpretations, and understandings of the group process. I argue that group-as-a-whole observations and interpretations enrich the therapeutic experience both for the therapist and for the members of the group, and they also influence the therapeutic potential of the group-as-a-whole.

Three reactions to a new member

The following pages are organized around a discussion of Yalom's description of the events that followed the introduction of a new member into his therapy group. He gives a vivid example of the reactions of three members and paints an excellent picture of the dynamics of each, which give rise to their interpersonal responses. This episode is the backbone illustration that will serve for all the discussions in the pages that follow.

> A new member, Alice—a 40-year-old divorcee—was introduced at a group's eighteenth meeting. The three men in the group greeted her in strikingly different fashions.
>
> Yalom's presentation begins with the reaction of Peter, who arrived fifteen minutes late and so missed the introduction of the new member to the group. For the next hour, Peter was active in the group, discussing issues left over from the previous meeting as well as events that had occurred in his life during the previous week. He totally ignored Alice, avoiding even glancing at her—a formidable feat in a group of six people in close physical proximity. Later in the meeting, as others attempted to help Alice participate, Peter, still without introducing himself, fired questions at her in a prosecuting, attorney-like fashion.
>
> In contrast to Peter, the two other men in the group, Brian and Arthur, were preoccupied with Alice during her first meeting.
>
> Arthur, a 24-year-old homosexual who had sought therapy in order to change his sexual orientation, reacted strongly to Alice and found that he could not look at her without experiencing the most acute sense of embarrassment.
>
> Brian, on the other hand, transfixed Alice with his gaze and delivered an unwavering broad smile to her throughout the evening. The other women in the group had confronted him with "his puppy-dog presentation of self".

Two perspectives: individual and group

The first step in viewing a single episode from both individual and group-as-a-whole perspectives is to develop a common framework and language that will lead to complementary rather than divisive understanding. I have therefore used the principles of isomorphy and complementarity that are inherent in a General Systems Theory orientation (Bertalanffy, 1968). The principles of isomorphy require that when one is defining a system, the way that one talks about its structure and function will also generalize to all other systems in the hierarchy. Thus, when systems are operationally defined isomorphically, what one learns about *the structure and function of any one system in the hierarchy* can be generalized to all systems, whether they be as small as a cell or as large as society.

In this chapter, the structure and function of the individual system and the small, face-to-face group-as-a-whole system are defined and compared. Thus what can be learned from analysing the group-as-a-whole system can be generalized to the individual system, and what can be learned about the individual system can be generalized to the group-as-a-whole system. Defining the individual and the group isomorphically makes it possible to review and reinterpret the individually oriented vignette presented above from the perspective of the group-as-a-whole. The test of the usefulness of this exercise is in whether or not this reframing leads to different and therapeutically important clinical insights that offer clinicians alternate treatment strategies. It is the contention of this chapter that it does.

Peter

To illustrate this point, I will re-interpret the dynamics of this example from both the individual and group-as-a-whole system perspectives.

Individual perspective

From the individual perspective, we are told that Peter uses women as part-objects and we can guess that this is a behavioural expression of his inner-person narcissistic developmental deficiency that manifests itself in self-preoccupation. In his individual member role in the group, he is at first narcissistically gratified as he ignores the new, predictably disappointing woman. When the group withdraws attention from him and turns to Alice, his member role changes to "prosecuting attorney", in which he acts out his orally sadistic revenge for the loss of the narcissistic gratification.

Group-as-a-whole perspective

Reframing these dynamics from the group-as-a-whole perspective requires shifting our concept of Peter's individual role—which serves to act out his individual system dynamics—to the concept of Peter in a group role, which will serve both to contain and express group system dynamics. From the perspective of his group role, Peter is acting out the conflict for the group-as-a-whole by expressing the group's denied wish to ignore the new member. By re-focusing the group onto the unfinished business of last week's group and his own personal outside events, he succeeds in excluding the new member from the group.

This group-as-a-whole hypothesis is derived from the following evidence. For one hour, Peter was apparently neither discouraged nor interrupted in his avoidance of Alice and monopoly of the group, in spite of the fact that, we are told, he arrived fifteen minutes late. Now, in my experience, fifteen minutes of work is more than enough time for a group to become almost impermeable to a late member—*unless the late member is required to play some significant role for the group.* In that case the group will then use the member's arrival in the service of some conscious hidden agenda or unconscious implicit goal.

I would suggest that Peter's behaviour had more to do with the group-assigned role for him to contain and act out the unconscious group wish to behave "as if" there were no new member. Apparently the group was too polite to ignore Alice overtly, so Peter was delegated to give voice to the group wish that the group were the same as the previous week and to express the silent rage as well as the denial of the change by ignoring the new member. It is noted in the vignette that he not only ignored Alice but avoided even glancing at her: "a formidable feat in a group of six people in close physical proximity". In group-as-a-whole thinking, this is not a formidable feat for someone who is performing an important group role for the group. If six people in close physical proximity allow a new member to be treated as if she did not exist for one whole hour, might we not wonder clinically if silence was assent? And if the group cannot get the new member to disappear through denial of her presence, perhaps they can allocate a member—like Peter, the prosecuting attorney—to chew her up and spit her out. This illustrates a not unusual group reaction to new members, in which the group politely says one thing—"come in"—and behaves as if it means another—"go away".

It was the astonishing fact that groups often say one thing and behave in another way that alerted Wilfred Bion to the fact that there was something more going on in groups than could be explained by individual unconscious motivation (Bion, 1959). Freud had only just recently introduced coherent ideas about the unconscious to individual psychology, and, in spite of the promising start, he did not further develop his group-as-a-whole thinking. Jung, who turned his attention to the collective unconscious, did so in terms of society in general rather than small groups in particular. It was Bion who directed his observations and thinking towards understanding the dynamics of the group-as-a-whole.

Bion, Tavistock, and the group-as-a-whole

To discuss the group-as-a-whole perspective as it is grounded in the Bion–Tavistock approach, I start by considering first the contributions of Bion and the Tavistock to group theory, practice, and training, continue with the model derived from my own theory (Theory of the Invisible Group—Agazarian & Peters, 1981), and finish by applying group-as-a-whole thinking to the clinical task of understanding and intervening in the group process as illustrated in the vignette presented above.

Bion

Bion first started to work with groups during World War II as Director of the rehabilitation centre of a military psychiatric hospital. It was the ideas that he began to develop there and later took to the Tavistock clinic that served as the foundation of what would develop into the Tavistock approach. Bion perceived groups not in terms of individuals but as a discrete entity, which he called "the group". One thing that was quite clear to him was that while people in groups "claimed" to be working, as a group they often behaved in ways that were quite antithetical to work. It also appeared to him that the individuals in the group seemed quite bewildered by the experience—as if they were helplessly in the grip of forces that they could not account for and that Bion himself could not attribute simply to individual unconscious motivation. It was thus that Bion came to formulate assumptions about the dynamics of the group-as-a-whole (Bion 1959).

Bion observed that when the energy of the group was directed in ways that seemed to be antithetical to work, the behaviour was, in fact, not random but appeared to be organized and directional: it seemed to be purposeful. He made the assumption that the non-work behaviour that he observed was in fact a defensive organization at the group level. He asked himself what the group was defending itself from, and he postulated that the group had a terrifying psychotic-like chore.

These group-level defences seemed to him to take identifiable forms: (a) "group dependency", in which the group attempts to fashion someone—usually the group leader—into a saviour whose goodness and wisdom would protect, nurture, and save it; (b) "group fight/flight", in which an evil enemy was created who must either be attacked and annihilated or avoided and placated; (c) "group pairing", in which the group treated two of its members as the chosen couple whose union would result in the birth of a messianic rescue in the form of some solution to the group's helplessness and hopelessness. He called these three defensive solutions—dependency, fight/flight, and pairing—"Basic Assumption cultures". When Bion worked with groups, it was to these group-level issues that he addressed himself rather than to the issues of the individual.

The Tavistock

The Tavistock method as applied for some years following Bion's formulation was used to treat psychotherapy patients in groups with the therapist paying attention to the dynamics of the group-as-a-whole. While experience in applying the Tavistock method was being gained in clinical practice, the group-as-a-whole focus was also being used as a core construct in the human relations training groups, or "T-groups", which were used in different aspects of training both in England and in the United States. Two practitioners in the United States, Herb Shepard and Warren Bennis (Bennis & Shepard, 1956), observed the sequence of happenings in T-groups over several years of a university course in which students "discovered" group dynamics by the participant–observer method, which required them to observe the dynamics of the developing group as they were participating in its development. In these groups the leader followed the Tavistock method of consulting to the group-as-a-whole rather than to the individuals in the group or to the group-of-individuals. This was in the 1950s, when university professors were expected to behave in a predictably didactic fashion. When the students were confronted by a circular ring of chairs instead of the expected classroom rows and by a non-directive professor who was largely silent instead of one who manifested immediate authority, they experienced extreme cognitive dissonance. A power vacuum was immediately created, which then became the context in which, through their reactions, they discovered group dynamics.

Phases of group development

Observing a consistent and predictable sequence of events in the T-groups, Bennis and Shepard developed their Theory of Group Development (1956), using Bion's constructs of dependency, fight/flight, and pairing as their underlying framework. Bennis and Shepard divided group development into two discrete phases, separated by an important fulcrum event. The first phase was dominated by issues of power and control in which the group used all its energy to seduce the leader into being a good, nurturing protector of its dependency needs in order to defend it from the underlying chaos and the primitive competitiveness that is aroused in the work life of the group. When this was frustrated, a fight/flight culture was precipitated in which spasmodic inter-member scapegoating finally coalesced into a ritualized attack upon the leader. When this attack is successful, the group resolves its conflict about good and evil by splitting, locating "evil" in the "bad" leader and "good" in the group. This is called the barometric event in that after a successful confrontation of the leader, the group energy is freed from the absorbing struggle with the leader for power and control and is turned, instead, into issues of intimacy.

Just as in the first phase, where the manner in which the dependency and fight/flight phases are resolved is influenced by the balance of conformist, compliant, dependent members and defiant, rebellious, counterdependent members, so in the second phase, the resolution of the issues in intimacy is influenced by the balance between the enchanted overpersonal members and the disenchanted counterpersonal members. The heavier the weighting of overpersonals, the more cohesively symbiotic the group will become and the stronger the enchantment myth that the group provides something close to heaven. The more the weighting of counterpersonals, the more the group cohesiveness will be tempered by paranoid–schizoid fears of loss of identity in the group, which finally precipitates the group into a phase of disenchantment that is close to hell.

The final phase of group development is reached through the hard work of learning to reality test, and it is this work that leads to the final stage of consensual validation, in which the group develops a culture for work, with insight into the characteristic manifestations of its defensive dependency, fight/flight, and pairing dynamics.

The barometric event

The most usual fixation point for groups led by those who are not familiar with the specific requirements of leadership of a developing group is the barometric event: the fulcrum event in which the group, by temporarily freeing itself from the bondage of its projections onto authority, can cross from a group culture dominated by power politics into a culture in which relationships based on intimacy can be explored, an essential step towards being able to use information as data rather than in the service of power politics. This crossing requires both training and understanding on the part of the group therapist. Serving the group by containing the projective identification of the group hatred is not an easy task. It is, for example, very important that the therapist knows enough not to take it personally, which is hard on the self-image, and not to retaliate, which is hard on the group.

Group-as-a-Whole Theory

Coming from the framework of psychoanalysis, with its concentrated focus on individual dynamics, to group dynamics and group-as-a-whole thinking, it was of the utmost importance to me to be able to understand the difference between interpretations that led to individual insight from interpretations that led to insight at the level of the group-as-a-whole, even though I had only the haziest idea—as, indeed, had anyone in 1961!—exactly what that meant. Of one thing, however, I was certain: If insight into unconscious dynamics freed people from the compulsion to helplessly repeat destructive behaviour, then it was of the utmost importance to know how to help groups gain insight into unconscious group dynamics and thus gain some control over group destructive behaviour. In the service of this task, I worked throughout my working life to define two discrete but complementary definitions for group: one in terms of individual system dynamics and one in terms of group dynamics (see below). Much to my surprise—and delight—when I related my formulation to other group theories in the field, I found that they also fit a hierarchical model, starting with psychodynamic intrapersonal theories, through interpersonal to Group-as-a-Whole Theory. In a sense, then, I had inadvertently also developed a classification system for theories in the group field.

The advantage of the isomorphic principle of General Systems Theory (Bertalanffy, 1969) is that it requires system definitions to be made in terms of the functions and structures that they have in common. Thus what one learns about one system in a hierarchy can be applied to understanding others in the hierarchy, both when their contexts are equivalent and when they are different. Thus, what one understands about the system of the individual will help us to learn about the system of group, and vice versa: perspectives that first appear to be contradictory turn out to be simply complementary. For example, the dynamics of Bion's Basic Assumption of dependency at the group-as-a-whole level also exists in the dependency dynamics at the individual person level. Bennis and Shepard's identification of the roles that dependent compliance and counterdependent rebellion play in group development can be seen both at the group level, where subgroups perform group roles in the service of the group dynamics, and in individual member roles that serve the person's dynamics.

Group-as-a-Whole Theory applied to the vignette

Let us now return to Yalom's three reactions to a new member and explore how these same events look from the perspective of the group-as-a-whole. In a real sense, the introduction of a new member is a marker event in the life of a group. Like the phoenix, the old group dies, and a new group is reborn. Confronted by the loss of the old group and the fear of the unknown new one, the group must establish a new equilibrium and at the same time do the work of integrating a new member. Because this group is relatively young, we can expect that it has relatively unsophisticated mechanisms for containing differences. In the early phases of development groups tend to subgroup around similarities, requiring differences to be contained either in silent subgroups or in implicit and isolated deviants who then serve as potential future identified patients or scapegoats.

Integrating a new member

The mechanism for maintaining a viable equilibrium in groups can, as I have mentioned, be viewed in terms of the container function of group roles, which are located in individuals or in subgroups that serve the group by "containing" differences that the group has not integrated. These unintegrated differences may be potential resources that the group is not yet sufficiently mature to use, or they may be unconscious, repressed, or denied aspects of the group dynamics that are "split" off from the group because earlier developmental vicissitudes have resulted in developmental fixations or compromise formations.

For example, I have already made a case for fifteen-minutes-late Peter serving the group as a container for the group-level conflict about the new member. In group-as-a-whole thinking, Peter's introduction of issues left over from the previous week would be framed as the part of the group that was refusing to "arrive" in the present or to acknowledge a new group at all. He would also be voicing—first by ignoring and later by firing questions—the rage that this polite group could not.

The process of introducing a new member is an important issue in ongoing psychotherapy groups and one that requires special handling. Recognizing that the group's wish to welcome the new member is at the consciously adaptive level and is inevitably conflictual at the unconscious level, I pay a great deal of attention to the development of norms around the introduction of new members. For example, first and foremost the group is given a voice in setting the date, with the goal of assessing what current work would be best completed before the new member arrives. Assessing this work entails attending to the issues that belong within the boundaries of the group, such as coming member or therapist absences, or anniversary dates, or unfinished business that is best done before the group changes.

Before the new member arrives, the group also identifies the resistances to this specific new-member event in the here-and-now of the group. The group thus works with the fears and hopes that are centred around the new member in fantasy as well as the feelings that the reality of the new member brings. Very frequently, familiar aspects of issues with authority and confrontation of the therapist are reworked at this time.

At the first meeting, then, the new member is received by a group that has prepared itself to do membership work. In this way, new members are introduced to the working norms of the group and are encouraged to contribute to the group experience of openly working with the conflicted feelings about a real disequilibrating event in group life. As we see, these working norms did not exist for the group illustrated in the vignette, and therefore Peter's container role served as the necessary, but not sufficient, equilibrating function for the group.

Let us now continue to discuss the process by which this group succeeds in doing the requisite membership work with Alice. First we have the events of the initial fifteen minutes, about which we know little except that Peter had no trouble pre-empting. We would guess, therefore, that any membership work that took place would have been such in name only. Next we have Peter's late entrance, at which time the group elects him to express their repressed rejection of the new member and the denial of the new group, which Peter does "for the next hour" by focusing the group on the unfinished business of the week before. Then, "later in the meeting", as others attempt to help Alice to participate, Peter, still without introducing himself (an anonymous "secret agent" for the group) fires questions at her in a prosecuting, attorney-like fashion.

With the group rage towards the new member actively expressed through Peter's prosecuting group role, the group is freed to actively express its support through a reciprocal group role. Thus the positive and negative responses towards the new member no longer pose a conflict for the group, in that the negative has been split off from the group and projected into the "prosecutor" role while the rest of the group contain the positive in a "helping-her-to-participate" role. The group-as-a-whole conflict is discharged in acting-out behaviour, Peter acting out the negative side of the ambivalence and the rest of the group acting out the positive. Thus group equilibrium is regained, but without insight or development.

The puzzling role of the group

Now let us turn our attention to another interesting issue raised by the group vignette: the role of women in the group, and how Alice fits in to it. Clearly the role of the women prior to Alice's entrance was to be sexless and without identity. Note that in the narrative Alice is the only woman given a name! Women are nameless, their reactions to Alice are not mentioned, and they are presented in relation to the men: as "sisters" for homosexual Arthur and as rejecters of "puppy-dog" Brian. Thus, prior to Alice's arrival, the group's women form a subgroup that contains for the group-as-a-whole both the denied sexuality and the denied dependency. Alice, a new female member, enters the group and is perceived as "sexually attractive and available", as we are told in the narrative. In the case of sexuality, then, the group allocated non-sexuality to the women's group role, and a separate role for sexuality when Alice enters the group.

Balancing individual and group-as-a-whole interpretations

When I am working with a group as a therapist, I focus my attention at both the individual and the group perspectives and intervene at whichever level seems to be most likely to reduce defences against work. At times I understand and interpret behaviour in terms of individual dynamics, at other times in terms of the group dynamics, and as both are usually complementary, it probably does not make a great deal of difference which I choose. There are, after all, many paths to the goal. However, there are times when there seem to be too many choices. In these cases, group interpretations are the treatment of choice, and this is the issue that I address now.

My attention is drawn to the "group-as-a-whole" whenever something happens that is surprising or unexpected or puzzling. In the vignette, I was alerted to the "group-as-a-whole" when I first became puzzled by the women's role. Had I been in the group, I would have asked myself, what is the group-as-a-whole problem that the creation of a dependency-rejecting role for women is attempting to solve? I present here a hypothetical answer to this question, and this hypothesis will then serve as a frame for a discussion about interpretations and also as an illustration of when a group interpretation is not only the treatment of choice *but the only treatment that will work.*

In the case of the vignette, I would make an educated guess that the basic group-as-a-whole problem is dependency: in this group, dependency has been denied, repressed, split off, and projected. One half of the conflict is the yearning to be nurtured, and the group has assigned to Brian the "puppy-dog" role to contain it. The other half of the conflict is the hatred and rejection of the group's dependency yearnings, and this group role has been assigned to the subgroup of women. Note that even though the group assigns to Alice a sexual role that separates her from the subgroup of the non-sexual women, she is also co-opted into the rejecting role in which she "joins" the women's "confronting candour", supported by the therapist, who perceives her as "helpful" to Brian as she reveals her initial discomfort at his beseeching smile and her fears that Brian would "empty her". (The therapist is no less subject to group dynamics than are the members.)

Thus Brian is assigned to expressing the group's dependency and the women to expressing the group's rejection of it. Through projective identification a stable set of reciprocal role relations both expresses and contains the group conflict in a manner that preserves the group equilibrium. But any non-modifiable set of reciprocal group-role relationships indicates either a developmental vicissitude or fixation in group development that has consequences at both the group and the individual level. It makes sense to assume that the group, with the unconscious collusion of the therapist, has denied its dependency and has thus reached a group-as-a-whole working equilibrium. However, unless the mechanisms of splitting, denial, and projective identification can be undone, the group-as-a-whole is doomed to helplessly repeating its scapegoating solution to the denied, repressed, projected, and detested wish to "empty the nourishing breast". And if so, then this will be true for the duration of this group. Should Brian leave, the group will find another member to fill the role.

This is a good example of group-as-a-whole thinking: that without group-as-a-whole intervention, there will be a compulsion to repeat a relationship between the "discomfited, withdrawn and rejecting mother" role relating to the "extraordinarily dependent, insatiable, beseeching infant" role. This group will continue to cure Brian-now, and all future-Brians, of dependency, and the "Brians" will, in their turn, maintain the role of "beseeching puppy-dog" unless or until the group-level projective identification is resolved.

When group-as-a-whole interpretation is the treatment of choice

At the individual level, the therapist may skilfully point out that when Brian looks to Alice with his broad, unwavering smile, his hope is that she will nurture him, and that his very expression of need is doomed to fail and provokes, instead, the denigrating rejection of his "puppy-dog" needs. She can connect it to Brian's history and point out that he is helplessly repeating with Alice his relationship with his governesses and probably also with his father. However accurate these individual interpretations, the therapist's very act of focusing her interpretations towards Brian as an individual functionally joins the group in a communication pattern to the deviant and thus not only contributes to maintaining Brian in his group role, but also reinforces the scapegoating function that Brian's role serves for the group.

For the therapist for whom individual-level insight is the only way of understanding group psychotherapy, when confronted with the repetitive and cyclical character of Brian's behaviour, there are not many alternative explanations for why her interpretations fail. The individual perspective tempts the therapist to assign the therapeutic failure to Brian's developmental vicissitudes, stemming from the loss of his mother in infancy, and to conclude, tragically, that his "extraordinary dependency" is too severe to be worked with successfully in a psychotherapy group.

It requires a group-as-a-whole orientation to notice that it is characteristic of this *group* that at any time the group's dependency conflicts become aroused, Brian becomes the focus—that there is just as much of a repetition in the attempt by the group-as-a-whole to cure Brian as a solution to group discomfort with dependency. The group-as-a-whole perspective raises the question as to whether Brian's repetitive behaviour is in fact a function of a group-as-a-whole fixation and whether, in another group, there would be room for a different outcome?

From a group-as-a-whole perspective, it could be said that the group is fixated at the stage between flight and fight: the flight dynamics of dependency, typically acted out in an attempt to cure the identified patient, are pre-empted by fight scapegoating dynamics. Thus, rather than making room for the understanding of the denied wishes to be taken care of, the wish is scapegoated. When a group-as-a-whole is permitted to deny and scapegoat dependency, it has no alternative but to develop as a premature adult.

This illustrates why it is important to understand the difference between group-level and individual-level dynamics interventions. In this case illustration, no individual in the group will be able to resolve individual conflicts around dependency until the group-as-a-whole undoes the split and repossesses the denied and repressed dependency wishes in the transference.

Having described the difficulties of undoing the projective identification in a group that contains, for the group, a developmental vicissitude, let me suggest how, in this case, it might be interpreted from the point of view of the group-as-a-whole. From this perspective, one would note how the new member, Alice, has been taken into the group and assigned a sexual role. Noting that Brian's behaviour can be interpreted as "welcoming her in the hope of finding a new source of succour" and noting that Alice is "manifesting extreme discomfort at his beseeching smile", I might find the words to say something that communicates the following message:

— "I wonder if the group is voicing, through Brian, the hope that Alice will bring into the group the nurturing and acceptance and succour that the group has felt so deprived of? . . . "And I wonder whether Alice, in reaction, is feeling just like the other women in this group have felt: that she must reject dependency because otherwise the group will expect the women in the group to provide all the mothering? . . . And I wonder if this is in fact in reaction to the

> group having given up hope of getting taken care of by the therapist?"

This might make a successful interpretation because:

1. it legitimizes the behaviour of the group as a subject for discussion rather than denial;
2. it identifies Brian's beseeching smile as a message for the group;
3. it identifies Alice's reaction as a the response of a group that has given up hope;
4. it focuses the group onto an exploration of the transference relationship with the therapist;
5. it gives the group members a common bond that will potentially support their individual work;
6. it makes explicit the implicit goal of the group-as-a-whole, which potentiates de-repression;
7. it sets the stage for the individual members to make conscious what they have been projecting into Brian's smile.

This work is greatly helped by suggesting to the members that they explore whatever it is about the smile that they feel most alien to/feel they hate most/would hate most to discover in themselves. This is the mechanism that groups need to learn in order to undo their projective identifications. Once they have this knowledge, groups often use it spontaneously when they notice that they are scapegoating.

What it misses, of course, is the indefinable ring that an interpretation has when the therapist is in tune with the group-as-a-whole, and which only happens to me when my voice is also a voice for the group.

The rationale behind this chapter

I will now take the opportunity to expand on the framework that I use in conceptualizing dynamics from a group-as-a-whole perspective.

The underlying dynamic common to maturation of any human system, be it as small as a cell or as large as society, is the functional discrimination and integration of differences, from simple to complex. This is the process that makes order out of chaos, makes the unconscious conscious, and codes information and organizes it in relation to group goals.

The process of group development, then, can be understood as a function of the rate at which similarities and differences can be discriminated and integrated. The process is twofold: similarities and differences must be perceived—both similarities in the apparently different and differences in the apparently similar—and system equilibrium must be sufficiently maintained so that the work of integration can take place. Until discriminations are integrated, they are chaotic and it is this chaos that the group system must contain while the work of discrimination and integration takes place.

Thus, how far any particular group can develop is dependent upon the mechanisms that it develops to contain chaos. The newer the group, the simpler the mechanisms. The simplest way for a group to contain chaos is to split the integratable from the non-integratable and to contain them separately in subsystems of the system-as-a-whole. This reduces the information overload, and the group can then use the information that is "similar enough" without being overwhelmed by information that is "too different" to be integrated.

Thus, on the one hand, splitting is fundamental to the ability of the group to maintain the equilibrium necessary to group development, and, on the other hand, splitting potentiates group fixation. As it is important for a group to reintegrate differences when it has developed the ability to do so and thus regain problem-solving potential, it is fundamentally important that the group therapist understand when to reinforce the containment of splitting as a factor in group development and when to undo it through interpretation so that the group members can take back their projections and reintegrate the differences that have been contained.

In the service of this task, there are therefore two defensive mechanisms fundamental to group development that are important for the therapist to monitor: denial and projective identification. Both of these contribute to the group's maintenance of a functioning equilibrium, and both put the group's development at risk.

Denial is an early defence mechanism used in the service of both individual and group development. It is important to differentiate between *group denial* (the container-source of information which the group uses when it can finally give voice to something that it "knew all along") and *group projective identification*, in which the split-off information—frequently coded in affect or symbol rather than in words—is removed from group conscious awareness through repression and projected and contained in a group role (frequently perceived by the group as deviant).

There are two major group reactions to deviance. The first is a concentrated communication pattern towards the deviant in which the group pressure is to "convert" the deviant by bringing his behaviour back within group norms. When this fails, the group subgroups by splitting itself off from the deviant, in an explicit differentiation, with the deviant defined as the container of the difference. If the deviant accepts the differentiated container role, the deviant becomes, as Peter did, a group mascot or tolerated eccentric in a defined group role. But the deviant who does not contain effectively for the group is, like Brian, scapegoated. Thus the information that was originally repressed and projected is now not only disowned but attacked, as Brian's dependency was.

In the original version of scapegoating the Israeli goat is loaded with the tribal sins and driven out of the group and into the desert. This does successfully get rid of the goat but not, of course, of the basic problem. In group psychotherapy there are three common versions of this: (a) the deviant leaves the group and the group thus extrudes the difference; (b) the deviant is made into the group mascot or jester, and the containing character of his group role is thus reinforced; (c) the deviant becomes the "chosen" patient for the group. Having created a patient to cure, the group can cure him as often as it needs to distance itself from the disequilibrating information that is contained in the patient's chair. With all three of these solutions, just as in the case of Israeli goat, the basic problem remains.

The Theory of the Invisible Group

The Theory of the Invisible Group (Agazarian & Peters, 1981), builds a bridge between Lewin's theories and Group-as-a-Whole Theory. This theoretical framework applies practically to making interventions in groups, clarifying the difference that group-level interventions can make to the potential outcome of central group issues, like scapegoating. It defines the dynamics of groups from two isomorphic perspectives: (a) the individual person, and (b) the group.

The individual perspective: person and member

The definition of individual behaviour is borrowed from Lewin's (1951) equation that individual behaviour is a function of the *life space*. Lewin defined his "life space" as a person's perception of their environment, from which he postulated that perception now predicted behaviour next. In earlier work, combining psychoanalytic thinking with Lewin, I introduced the idea of personal history as an intervening variable between perception and behaviour. It could then be argued that the behaviour of an individual in the group is a function of personal history dynamics (which orients perception) and is manifested in member roles.

Thus individuals in the group are conceptualized dynamically as both persons and members: the *intrapersonal* dynamic of the person and the *interpersonal* dynamics of the member. (Psychodynamic group therapists interpret more to the intrapersonal person dynamics, interpersonal group therapists interpret more to the interpersonal member dynamics.) *Person interventions* therefore designed to focus on the intrapersonal psychodynamic experience that is being expressed in the person's behaviour.

For example, from the individual perspective, Peter's use of women as part-object reflects inner-person developmental vicissitude that threatens his system equilibrium. Interventions are labelled "personal" when therapist interactions are targeted towards Peter (either directly, or through the group), helping him to get insight into his psychodynamics—like, for example, the function that his defensive secondary narcissistic organization plays in relation to the impoverishment of his primary narcissism. However, unless this intervention is made in the context of a group that has reached the developmental phase of intimacy, the group context is unlikely to provide him with the containment of mirroring that he would almost certainly require for the separation–individuation work to take place psychodynamically.

Contrasting person and member

Whereas from the person perspective individual behaviour is understood as a function of intrapersonal psychodynamics that result from genetic inheritance, developmental history, and environmental influences, from the member perspective individual behaviour is understood as a function of interpersonal dynamics that are manifested in roles. The major dynamic in role behaviour is the repetition compulsion, which repeats in the present important roles from the past. On the one hand, this repetition is fixating and makes it difficult for the person to change; on the other hand, it in the service of keeping the person in equilibrium.

Member interventions are designed to call attention to patterns of maladaptive role behaviour with an assumption that the member is repeating in the present roles from the past.

For example, we would expect that Peter's prosecuting-attorney behaviour towards Alice reflected some earlier role relationship. We might, for example, hypothesize from what we have been told about him that his early infant experience contained some disturbance at weaning. Perhaps his mother resented his infant bite, scolding and rejecting him, feeding the oral sadistic rage in the infant Peter that he defended against by repression. Let us assume that he later went to a church school where prosecuting-attorney scolding might have been the norm, and that Peter-the-devout-Catholic defended himself by identifying with the aggressor. This role is then satisfied when Peter can interact with any member who inadvertently volunteers to be bullied.

Thus, we might say that both outside and inside the group, when Peter is confronted with a deprivation of attention, he experiences again the oral sadistic rage that was both a cause and a consequence of his original rejection. First he denies that anything is different, seeking narcissistic reparation by becoming the centre of attention; when that interaction fails, he acts out his oral sadism and does unto women what they did to him.

Successful interpretations of the member roles fuelled by the repetition compulsion are a challenge to the therapist and a major strength of the interpersonal approach. Unless patients gain insight into the conflicts that are acted out in the roles, however, they will continue to helplessly repeat. As the conflicts that are expressed in repetitive behaviour are frequently repressed, the interpretations must be *experienced* rather than intellectualized. This is, perhaps, where the interpersonal approach does not always temper the wind to the shorn lamb. Phrases like "puppy-dog", "beseeching smile", and fear of "being emptied" might well elicit defensive compliance or defiance rather than emotional insight in the person who is the target of these interventions.

There is frequently a danger of therapist superego disapproval at self-defeating behaviour, particularly when it simultaneously provokes self-defeating responses in the group. Thus interpretations of maladaptive or self-defeating behaviour are frequently experienced by patients as a punitive as well as a narcissistic assault and are thus defended against in compliance or defiance. It is for this reason that I would probably avoid interpreting Peter's behaviour at the individual member-role level, particularly at a time when his member-role behaviour is serving a group-as-a-whole function.

The group perspective: group-as-a-whole and group role

Borrowing again from Lewin (1951), his equation that behaviour is a function of the life space can be reframed, for the group, as that group behaviour is a function of the group-as-a-whole life space. Thus the behaviour of a particular group will be a function of the group-as-a-whole history, and it will be manifested in group roles. Just as individual roles served an equilibrating function for the person, so group roles perform an equilibrating function for the group. Just as interpretations of person dynamics bring understanding to the individual, so interpretations of group dynamics bring understanding to the group. Just as person dynamics can be understood as a function of the intra-person dynamics that result from a unique genetic inheritance, developmental history, and maturation experience, so can group dynamics. And just as person behaviour can be understood as a function of intra- and interpersonal dynamics, so can group behaviour be understood as a function of the intra-group and inter-group role dynamics. This is the isomorphy between individual and group.

Group-as-a-whole interventions. These are designed to focus the group on its behaviour and to modify group-level defences. There are two levels of group-level defences to modify: (a) those defences that inhibit the natural development of the group from one phase to another, and (b) the Basic Assumption defences that inhibit the work of the group.

It is not always easy to judge when and how to modify the group-as-a-whole Basic Assumption defences. On the one hand, these defences bind the underlying primitive chaos in groups; on the other hand, they limit the development of group problem-solving potential. (There is an inverse relationship between Basic Assumption defences and work.)

An example of a group-as-a-whole intervention that deflects the attention away from Peter-the-person might be something like:

— "I wonder if Peter's late arrival today, as well as the present group focus on last week, may represent the conflict that the group feels

> about entering into the work of this week?" [*the work of this week being the work that the group needs to do to form the new group as well as the membership work necessary to include the new member*]

Another group-as-a-whole intervention would be to focus the group on the function of Brian's "puppy-dog" role as the container for group dependency, as discussed below.

Group-role interventions: Central to understanding the group-role perspective is the understanding of the phenomena of projective identification and containership as formulated by Jung and by Klein. Bennis and Shepard (1956), in their "Theory of Group Development", apply these concepts to the defensive function of Bion's Basic Assumptions by describing how the group continually binds and contains the internal group chaos through fight/flight, dependency, and pairing *group roles*, while it simultaneously uses those roles to do its developmental work.

From the perspective of *group role*, group behaviour is understood as a function of *inter-group* dynamics that manifest in existing inter-group member–member, subgroup, or group facet relationships that bind aspects of current intra-group conflict by keeping the nonintegrated aspects of group dynamics contained within stereotypic group roles. Just as member behaviour serves an equilibrating function for the individual system, so group-role behaviour does for the group. It is as if the group-as-a-whole delegates one or more of its members to perform group roles that will bind, contain, or express group problems or issues while it assigns roles that will facilitate problem-solving work to other members, subgroups, or facets of the whole group. For example, the group binds dependency in the identified patient and the hatred of differences in the scapegoat. In contrast, the informal roles of task and maintenance leaders are in the service of the group's work.

Group-role interventions are designed to modify the reciprocal roles between members and subgroups of the group that express and contain group splits. Just as, for the individual, roles contain in a split those dynamics that the individual system cannot integrate, so reciprocal member or subgroup roles contain, for the group, those differences that the group is not yet ready to integrate. Thus the paradox: splitting is fundamental to the group-as-a-whole to maintain equilibrium, and undoing the splits is fundamental for the group-as-a-whole to achieve integration. For this reason it is fundamentally important that the group therapist understands when to reinforce the containment of splitting as a factor in group development and when to interpret it so that the group can take back its members' projections and reintegrate the differences that have been contained. The group-role intervention is basically the intervention of choice when the group is scapegoating; the intervention requires the group to own in themselves what they are attacking in others.

For example, when Brian is being "educated" by the group not to be a "puppy-dog", an alternative, group-as-whole intervention would point out to the group that there is considerable effort and energy in the group to put the "puppy-dog" in Brian's chair, and to wonder whether it is a way of making sure that there is no trace of puppy-dog in any other chair in the group. This intervention confronts the group with the dynamic of having created a role to contain the rejected dependency feelings in the group. In one of my groups, a member recently said to another member: "It's extraordinary, as long as I saw you as the person with all the emotion in this group, I didn't seem to feel anything. Now, after we've all talked about how we've been expecting you to have all the feelings, you are no longer feeling overwhelmed and I'm suddenly feeling a lot!" (Parenthetically, I do not "believe" that there is some kind of hydraulic system that manages the emotions in groups—but it does seem that one member's experience can feel larger than life until the group "takes back" what the member has been holding.)

This formulation of individual and group-as-a-whole as two discrete dynamic system perspectives from which to view group psychotherapy, with an emphasis on the hierarchical and isomorphic relationship between them, is perhaps my own contribution to group theory. The practical implications it has for group psychotherapy is the understanding that responding to an individual member's role behaviour should ideally be in the context of an awareness of its group-as-a-whole context. Thus therapeutic interventions are those that potentiate both individual and group development as a complementary activity, not one at the expense of the other.

CHAPTER THREE

The difficult patient, the difficult group

This chapter is written about one session of a difficult psychotherapy group, seen on videotape at the fall conference of the Eastern Group Psychotherapy Society in 1985 and discussed by a panel composed of Miss Fitzgerald, Dr Parsons, Dr Ormont, Dr Taylor, Dr Tuttman, and myself.

The original group (whose names have been changed for purposes of protecting confidentiality) consisted of six women: Mary, Gwen, Cherry, Zara, Liza and Lizzie. Shortly after the group started, two men joined the group. One man dropped out and the second, Fred, was diagnosed as having a malignant, terminal carcinoma and died.

The panel comprised the two therapists and the supervisor of the group—Miss Fitzgerald, Dr Parsons, and Dr Taylor—and three professionals in the field with three different frames of reference—Dr Ormont, Dr Tuttman, and Dr Agazarian. My own approach was that of

---

Y. M. Agazarian, "The Difficult Patient, the Difficult Group". In: Symposium: "A Discussion of the Videotapes of a Difficult Group". *Group: The Journal of the Eastern Group Psychotherapy Society, 2,* No. 4 (Winter 1987). New York: Brunner/Mazel, Inc. (copyright © 1987 from "The Difficult Patient, the Difficult Group" by Yvonne Agazarian. Reproduced by permission of Taylor & Francis, Inc., http://www.routledge-ny.com).

the group-as-a-whole. When I first listened to the tape, I was looking for live examples of the "Theory of the Invisible Group", my own formulation of group-as-a-whole thinking. I also wanted to see whether listening to the voice of this videotaped group would yield insights into the dynamics of this group that would not have been apparent if I had confined my listening to the voices of the individual members. This, for me, is the test of theory. If theory can help us to see things or do things or understand things that we could not, without theory, then theory is useful and important.

As it seems very important for us not to fight in the field about whether or not there is such a thing as the group-as-a-whole, which is different from the sum of the individual interpersonal interactions, I suggest two hypotheses as a framework for evaluating the following ideas: first, that from the individual perspective, all behaviour that occurs in a group can be explained as a function of inner-personal and interpersonal dynamics; and second, that, with equal validity, one can observe precisely the same events in the group from the group-as-a-whole perspective and explain all behaviour as a function of group roles and group-as-a-whole dynamics.

One of the most unusual and helpful foundations for this chapter was the generosity with which Dr Parsons, Dr Taylor, and Miss Fitzgerald shared their inner experience in relation to this group and the supervisory issues around it. Supervision has a major impact on the way therapists frame their experience in the group and influence their leadership behaviour. So one group system—the group of supervisor and therapists—existed both inside and outside the boundary of the therapy group and influenced the way the therapists behaved in the group, as we shall see later.

This outpatient group of psychosomatic patients must indeed have been very difficult for Dr Taylor and Miss Fitzgerald, two relatively novice group therapists, to work with. When Miss Fitzgerald read the history of the group, she quoted some of the things that the group had said in relation to Norman, one of their members who had died of cancer. I am going to present these quotes, first suggesting that probably the single most important thing to do in a group is to listen to its voice. If one listens to the voice of the group, it becomes easier to hear what is really happening and to legitimize what is being said, both overtly and covertly. Nearly always, the group voices issues that it needs to work with and will work with if the therapists legitimize them.

This is how some of the issues aroused by Norman's cancer were voiced, not only by the members for themselves, but also for the group-as-a-whole:

- "Fred was courageous in expressing anger that the doctors were not omnipotent in arresting his cancer." [*The doctors don't cure the group either!*]
- "There wasn't enough time for the members to talk about their own somatic complaints." [*Fred was too strong a competition for the group!*]
- "Suicide might be a real issue for Fred." [*A group solution for removing the competition?*]
- "Fear of anger towards the therapists for paying too much attention to Fred." [*Continuing group fear of its own anger.*]
- "Fred's dying is a burden to the group." [*An overwhelming outside reality.*]
- "Maybe he should go for a magical treatment in Mexico." [*A cure! . . . far away from here!*]

When the group speaks, it often expresses the socially unacceptable, because the group gives voice to what is usually hidden in people's thoughts and hearts. One way of hearing the voice of the group is to assume that every time a person speaks, they communicate not only for themselves, but also for the group. Sometimes the group meaning of the individual's words are not particularly significant, and the group message lies more in the subgroup themes than in the individual voice. At other times, particularly when what is said is full of feeling, tactless, or shocking, the therapist needs to be alerted to decode the group voice in the individuals' words. The underlying truth in the group's words is the only solid currency for the group-as-a-whole.

Within the boundaries of this therapy group, there are two major sources of group themes. The first is voiced by the therapists' subgroup and remains remarkably consistent, however the other themes in the group change. The second source is the patients. Different subgroups give voice to different issues voiced at times by different patient-members for different subgroups, and at other times the voice emerges from the underlying communication of the group-as-a-whole.

The next step is to define the individual and group dynamic perspectives as a framework for discriminating between the voice of the individual and the voice of the group. Following this, in a section entitled "Hearing Voices at the Group and Individual Level", episodes from the tape are used for illustration, and the implications of interpreting to the group and to the individual level are discussed.

Let me now define the individual and group dynamic perspectives.

Individual perspective

The person system

The first component is the system of the *person*. We are all familiar with explaining group behaviour from the psychodynamic perspective. For example, we could split this audience into two subgroups by putting all of us who characteristically introject as a defence into one subgroup, and all who characteristically project as a defence into the other. And we would be saying something valid about subgroup dynamics in this room and could test how these different dynamics are reflected in behaviour.

The member system

The second component is the system of the *member*. We are also familiar with explaining group behaviour from the interpersonal and social dynamics perspective. We can meaningfully talk about the way we individually behave in this room as a repetition of the earlier roles we have learned as we grew up, starting with our role in our nuclear families and continuing with roles that we learned in our interpersonal relationships as we matured.

We are also familiar with the paired character of social roles: the reciprocity between the leader and the follower, the helper and the helped, the bully and the bullied, the thinker and the feeler. In fact, if each of us reflected for a second right now, we would probably be able to identify some of our own characteristic roles and also those roles we induce in others. What is more, we know how hard it is for us to change our roles, even when we wish to do so.

From the perspective of individual dynamics there is no need to hypothesize group-as-a-whole dynamics in order to explain what goes on in this therapy group. An equivalent statement can be made about the group perspective: from the group perspective there is no need to hypothesize individual dynamics to explain what goes on in this therapy group!

Group perspective

Group-as-a-whole system

As can be seen from the group-as-a-whole system definition, a group has a genetic inheritance, composition, developmental history, and maturational experience that is similar, at a different hierarchical level of abstraction, to the person-system definition. Group behaviour is an expression of the dynamics of the group, and just as individual behaviour serves to keep the individual system in functioning equilibrium, so group behaviour serves an equilibrating function for the group. How this is accomplished is by the allocation of group differences to group roles.

Group-role system

The group-role system serves to contain the differences in the developing group that are the raw material of group maturation. Through integrating differences, the group develops differentiated resources that can then be brought to bear on solving the problems inherent in any living system.

The simpler and less sophisticated the group—either because of its basic genetic make-up or because of its phase in group development—the more rigidly roles are differentiated and fixed. The more complex and sophisticated the group, the more flexible and interchangeable are the roles. Thus the principle of isomorphy holds true for all living systems, whether they be developing cells, developing individuals, or developing groups—small groups, large groups, organizations, cultures.

Due to its genetic makeup and its fixation at an early level of development, the videotaped therapy group represents a relatively simple culture rather than a complex one. Roles are well differentiated and are, on the whole, not interchangeable. In simple cultures, the systems of behaviours are relatively predictable. (Let me remind those for whom this theoretical framework is unfamiliar that roles are a property of a group and not of individuals and are therefore not necessarily located in any one individual nor even in any one subgroup.) Because this group is a relatively simple culture, group roles tend to be stereotypic, both in performance and in location, and are thus more clearly identifiable.

A major individual influence on the way a therapist understands his role is the cognitive framework he has learned. In this case, as we know, the framework was individually oriented, derived primarily from reading and supervision and only secondarily from the *experience* in the actual living group: a not unfamiliar dilemma for therapists in training—a dilemma, however, that tends to blind the therapist to the dynamics of the particular group to which general group dynamics apply. Thus, in the necessary interdependence between individual and group dynamic forces, the therapists were less in tune with the voice of the group and more in tune with the prescriptions that motivated them from their supervision group. In other words, their outside subgroup norms had a significant influence on their behaviour.

Their role prescriptions as group therapists were medication, individual therapy, group therapy, analysis of resistance, interpretation, and maintenance of the group boundaries. The paradox of the matter is that ostensibly this is an excellent role prescription for a therapist. For example, in this group it enabled the therapists to care-take the outer skin of the group (its structural, geographical and time boundaries), without which the group would not survive, and this group had survived for five years. (The importance of this for its members is implied in Liza: "I get from Tuesday to Tuesday.") However, the therapists' understanding of group did not allow them to respond to the communications voiced by the group itself. This is, perhaps, where a cognitive framework that focuses both on the group-as-a-whole voice as well as the voice of the individual might have permitted different outcomes for this group of patients in great difficulty.

To listen to the voice of the group, the therapist needs to hear the voices of the group members as, on the one hand, communications from their individual selves, and, on the other hand, as a communication from a group role that is important to understand in terms of the group-as-a-whole. Sometimes individual voices add volume to a subgroup message, sometimes a single individual voices an important group theme. At other times communications make sense as examples of group defences—as, for example, Liza and Lizzie do by cooperatively isolating thought and feeling, Liza voicing the feeling for the group and Lizzie voicing the intellectualization.

An individual may carry a particular and important developmental role for the group. For example, a crucial and continuing maturation process in groups is the ability to integrate similarities and differences at all levels—an ongoing task of perceiving the similar in the apparently different and the different in the apparently similar. For all humans, this is a relatively painful activity. Our wish is not to have to change our perceptions; we would like to keep the map we have already to fit the territory. But the territory is changing all the time, and so our map has to be revised all the time. This is a core issue in the dynamics of a developing group.

As we know from individual therapy, when a patient is unable to integrate certain kinds of differences, there is a dynamic that we call "projective identification" by which the therapist contains for the patient what the patient has unconsciously split off and denied in order to maintain his equilibrium. At some point later in the therapy the patient re-introjects and makes conscious differences that were impossible for him before. The same phenomenon happens in a group. Sometimes the therapist contains for the group those differences that the group needs to repress and deny, at other times a member or a subgroup serves as the container. Most frequently, but not exclusively, group projective identification is expressed through the dynamics of group deviance manifested in the scapegoat and defiant roles. In the process of reintegrating the deviant, the group develops the necessary tolerance of the previously intolerable differences and thus increases its potential resources.

Understanding projective identification as a function of group dynamics allows the therapist to observe how the group role serves as the container for the group of those dynamics that are upsetting the group equilibrium. Conceptually, understanding lies in recognizing the isomorphy between member roles (individual system) and group roles (group-as-a-whole system). Thus, group roles serve an equilibrating function that maintains the viability of the group by balancing forces that might otherwise disrupt it, even though, as in this group, the very mechanisms that keep the group equilibrium also fixate it and preclude further development.

For example, the Liza and Lizzie contain the two sides of the defensive isolation that characterizes the group, with the fat Liza containing the affect and the thin Lizzie containing thought. This is typified in the following:

Liza: "You know, I spill . . . and the person who spills the most gets hurt the most."

Lizzie is puzzled: "It doesn't make sense . . . you are very intelligent . . . and . . .

Liza: "'Course I know it doesn't make sense . . .

Lizzie (suddenly understands): "So that's why . . . It's emotionally . . . I see what you mean."

This very moving little interchange is an excellent illustration of the container phenomenon at the individual level. Liza contains and expresses the "spilling over" feelings for the group, and Lizzie contains the "making sense" for the group. As a subgroup, these two also illustrate the reciprocal group-role containment of the isolation of thought and affect that serves a defensive function for the whole group.

The Liza and Lizzie also provide an excellent example of subgroup containing. Liza contains differences that the patient subgroup cannot integrate (in a sense, she plays the scapegoat role for feeling), whereas Lizzie contains differences that the therapist subgroup cannot integrate (her role is clearly that of the defiant). The antagonism felt by Dr Taylor for Lizzie is disturbingly familiar to therapists in their relationship to the "defiant" group member. As this group member contains, for the therapist, those aspects of the therapist's dynamics that the therapist has denied and repressed, the "defiant" member is experienced as an irritant, and the therapist typically feels that the group would be better off without her—an interesting parallel to the group's experience with the group scapegoat!

From the group-as-a-whole perspective, the therapists' subgroup, just like any other subgroup, must repossess the denied parts of themselves if the group is going to regain its resources. The most direct route to finding out about the denied aspects of one's own individual self is to listen to the voice of the group. Hearing it entails listening with the third ear to the unconscious, isomorphically present at both the individual and group level. Thus to hear the group is to hear a part of oneself.

Hearing both the individual and group voices

Listening at the group level permits you to help therapy happen in a way that isn't possible if you confine your listening to the individual level. To illustrate this, let us consider interventions, first from the individual level and then from the group level.

Individual interventions

Individual interpretations are better illustrated with some knowledge of the individual. Therefore, in using Liza as an example, let us first make up a history for her. Let us surmise that she's Roman Catholic, and that her religion has reinforced her predisposition to guilt, through scrupulousness in the examination of conscience and the wish to confess and be absolved. She probably comes from a large family—perhaps she is one of the older ones who would then take part in the caretaking. She has probably contained for her parent—in all probability her mother—the parental unconscious wishes and has attempted to gratify them. In doing this, she had denied herself. What is interesting (since she is the container of feeling for the group) is that she is unable to contain her own feelings. She introjects if something—like food—is pleasant, immediately experiences guilt, and then projects or acts out the unpleasure. Thus she cannot hold still inside herself. She cannot metabolize anything. She is either taking in food and knowing she shouldn't and getting guilty, or she's projecting out.

Liza is Dr Taylor's staunchest supporter, even at the expense of her own reality. And this is, I think, one of the tragedies. In repeating her family role by supporting Dr Taylor, she denies her own reality in order to maintain her relationship with him. In Liza's reality she did not know that Cherry had individual therapy. Her jealousy of Cherry, who was getting medication and individual therapy from Dr Taylor, was minor compared with her envy of Gwen, who had been taken to hospital by Miss Fitzgerald.

— "... I bet you put your arms around her or something ... Yea ... Of course you did. ... So you touched her, right?"

In this group, as we have already pointed out, Liza contains, for the group, the denied and overwhelming dependency feelings of the patients. Thus, whereas it is permissible to talk in the group about sibling jealousy of Cherry, the patient whose depression Dr Taylor is actively medicating, it is not alright for Liza to talk of her envy of Gwen, whose passive helplessness received compassionate nurturing from Miss Fitzgerald. She must not give voice to her wish for symbiosis. Her group role is to contain the group's regressive wish for fusion, their helplessness and dependency, which are intolerable to the patients themselves as well as to the therapists. Parenthetically, it is in no way unusual for even experienced group therapists to feel overwhelmed by their own helplessness in the face of the demands implicit in the depth and suffering of the difficult patient and thus be strongly tempted to ignore or deny the reality of these patients' helplessness and sometimes even to gain distance by attacking them for it.

Individual interventions to Liza would take into account understanding of her psychodynamics at the "person" level. For example, at the person level, one could work with the difficulty she has in containing her feelings, so that she might become aware of the internal experience that results when she does not complete a projection, or help her to recognize that any pleasure arouses in her overwhelming guilt.

At the sociopsychological "member" level, one could point out how she repeats her family role in the group, how her inability to express feelings that are different from Dr Taylor's, repeat her earlier relationship with her mother—fear of hurting her, threatening the relationship, separating from her. Or one could point to how she gives to Zara, as she did to her siblings, the comforting and the nurturing that she would like to have herself, and so on.

Group-as-a-whole interventions

Let us turn now to thinking about group-as-a-whole interventions. This group of difficult patients is an excellent example why group-as-a-whole interventions are essential if members of the group are going to reach some of the goals of group psychotherapy. Let us hypothesize that the most important goal for these patients is to accept the realities of their condition and to make the best adaptation they can.

The realities that these patients face are indeed difficult, both for them and for the therapists. The potential for therapeutic gain is limited by their psychological and sociological resources. Their psychosomatic symptoms are, by and large, probably a better adaptation than the deterioration that might ensue if the problems were not bound at the level of the body ego. These are the facts of this difficult group that the therapists must face if they are going to hear enough of what is going on to help the patients face their realities.

The voice of the group cries out in metaphor and simile what cannot be said in plain language. The following is an excellent example from the beginning of the group session of the group voicing its wish to communicate to the world in general and to the therapists in particular. Implicit in what they say is the cry that there is a part of the group that is not being heard and is alone and lonely. The part of the group for which "medication" is not the treatment of choice, the part for whom the act of communicating is in itself therapy. It is not a fantasy to say that this group voice speaks as much for the helplessness and loneliness of the therapists as it does for the patients.

At the beginning of this group session, the group talks about telephoning. Liza has just finished telling the group that she has sinned again, and that her son has taken her to task for talking inappropriately on the phone. "Too much telephoning", she says. The group responds:

— "It happens because you're lonely, know what I mean, and you don't have no one to talk to."
— "And you get someone on the phone, and you say, 'Let me talk.'"
— "It will happen eventually, you know, because sometimes it happens to me."
— "It's a terrible thing to be lonely."
— "Yea, terrible."
— "Yea, I never get used to it."
— "No matter who calls you, even if it's a wrong number, sometimes it's better than nothing."
— "Is this an obscene call? Huh, don't mistake my asthma for passion." [*laughs*]
— "Call the operator, and they hang up, and you give up."
— "Isn't it terrible."
— "Call back the second time, and it's the same wrong number."
— "Sometimes you could go all day without talking to no one."
— "Sometimes you wonder. Is your phone out of order?"
— "And I get kind of panicky—and they say: 'Call me back!'"

As the therapists do not attend to the group talking about the harsh facts of their loneliness outside the group and do not legitimize bringing these feelings into the group, is the group voice not saying that, in response to their call, the therapists hang up, and they give up? "Loneliness", these members are trying to say, is an important issue. Certainly for this group it is an issue that is more serious, because it is more primal, than jealousy of Cherry's individual attention from Dr Taylor—not more serious to the therapists, however, whose hypothesis from supervision was that the major group dynamic was "killing off" new members by this group. However, as jealousy is not a topic that is already cathected by the group and loneliness is, listening to the group voice is more likely to lead to work in the group that would reach the individual members.

There is indeed, some evidence that the group had more resources in relation to envy and jealousy than they are given credit for. Jealous of Cherry's individual attention or not (attention, incidentally, that is visible *in* the group through shared glances and smiles between Cherry and Dr Taylor), the group direct a supportive and empathetic response to Cherry even as they acknowledge their own wishes for special attention:

— "It's sleeping, Cherry, it's like sleeping . . . that's my way of escaping too."
— "Well, private sessions might help."
— "Might give her the attention that she needs."
— "It would be nice if we could all get a little."
— "And then . . . maybe we can bring back more into the group."

A great opening for work on what the group-as-a-whole needs! Groups often communicate to the therapists, if the latter are listening, the issues that the patients in the group need to face. Listen to this group's response to the effects of medication, spoken almost in the same breath as advice to the patient to take it.

— "Well, I sleep all the time."
— "I'm going to bed before it's even dark out."
— "Well, look, you're missing everything, then."
— "I can't even watch television."
— "Everything happens at night, too."
— "All the fun."
— "And I'm a night person."

The group has laid out both sides of the major issue that the therapists—had they heard it—could have helped them to confront: the trade-off. Both the patient and the therapist must face the reality that taking medication helps to control the thinking disorder or ameliorate depression—but at a price. They need to say: "And if you want your thought disorder controlled, you're going to have to put up with the problems. Its a trade-off. It's a reality." Particularly for the difficult patient and the difficult group it is crucial for the therapist to help the group to develop the norm of confronting the severity of the reality that cannot be modified, as well as the aspects of it that can. When the group-as-a-whole encourages taking responsibility for cooperating with medication, an important part of the therapists' work is done!

Now let us turn to a dialogue between two subgroups. It is a duet between two group voices, each carrying a subgroup theme. One voice represents the therapists' concern with the management of the group boundaries, the other represents the group's wish for a warm climate. A late member enters; the therapists stage-manage the entrance:

— "Here, sit here."
— "Move a chair."
— "Don't trip over the wire."
— "Come on in."
— [*etc. etc. etc.*]

And in counterpoint the group says, as everybody makes room for another chair and squash together:

— "It's called togetherness."
— "Closeness."
— "That's what we're all looking for."
— "That's what we're thinking."
— "Are we ready?"
— "It's like Christmas."

Next let us turn to a more complex communication between subgroups. As I have said, two conflicted subgroups are represented in this group. (a) The therapist subgroup gives voice to the remedy of medication and the issues of jealousy over individual therapy in the group. The identified patient for this subgroup is Cherry, with a medicatable depression. Dr Taylor is the most frequent representative of this subgroup, supported by Liza. (b) The patient subgroup gives voice to the fear of chaos, loneliness, dependency, and the helpless, hopeless cry to be heard. Lizzie is the loudest voice for this subgroup, "speaking for" its identified patient, Zara, the inarticulate one, who has difficulty with the language, whose voices ask her "why she is still living", and who cannot "speak up".

The whole group nurtures Zara, and Lizzie champions her cause:

— "I know that when you're very, very, very low down, it's impossible to overcome what is pushing you down, to come to the surface long enough to say, I want to be heard. You don't wait for that person who is timid to begin with the breakthrough, the cross-talk."

The therapists have not learned how to be tuned in to the group so that they could hear what these words express for the group. It would contradict their frame of reference. The therapists therefore say to the group that Zara can speak for herself, and Lizzie is told that she is displacing her concern for herself onto Zara. This response by the therapists is a clear example of how, by responding at the more familiar individual level, the group dynamic meaning of the communication is not only ignored but denied and sometimes re-repressed.

After Lizzie said: "It's impossible to overcome what is pushing you down to come to the surface long enough to say, 'I want to be heard'", and Dr Taylor has disagreed, her voice does go underground temporarily. The group agrees with the therapists that Zara is better and is not hearing voices. Then they cry out again in unison that:

— "being frightened of everything . . ."
— "of not being able to go out . . ."
— "fearing being alone . . ."
— "not being able to read or watch television . . ."
— "this is not normal . . ."

When their voice is again unheard, and they have once again agreed with the therapists' solution of private therapy, Mary says: "I'd like to talk of something . . ."—and hers is but another voice lost in the babble. She says:

— "I needn't bother talking." . . . "No, I don't care to talk any more now." . . . "No, I'm angry." . . . "I very seldom talk, and when I do, I get interrupted."

If one listens to Mary from the individual perspective, one can hear, as Cherry did, someone who is going to "sit in the garden and eat worms". If, however, one listens to Mary in the group context, one can hear the group-as-a-whole theme continued. In this context, the therapists' individually focused interpretation that Mary is "right" and she "made it clear that she was going to say something" serves as a subgroup strategy to separate her individually from the group, just as the interpretation to Lizzie separated Elizabeth. When a group voice is interpreted at the individual level, it becomes a lone voice crying in the wilderness, and the wisdom it contains for the group and the therapists goes, tragically, unheard.

SUMMARY

If the therapist knows only the individual level in a group, then that is all she can address. If the framework for understanding allows one to structure the group and pay attention to the boundaries, then one can keep a difficult group of difficult patients going—as these two inexperienced and dedicated therapists did. When they left, the group ended.

From the individual perspective, knowing psychodynamics, one can interpret to the individual dynamics and help patients get insight into their defences and motivation and their psychogenic conflicts. Knowing social-role theory, one can help the patient to recognize the repetitious nature of his behaviour as it mirrors earlier role relationships learned, so to speak, at mother's knee.

From the group perspective, knowing group dynamics, one can be aware of some of the issues in group development and can recognize the group developmental phases. One can then facilitate the growth of the group-as-a-whole, so that the group itself provides the kind of milieu that is supportive rather than destructive to therapy.

When one understands the isomorphic relationship between group system and individual system dynamics and can see the same group event from the perspective both the individual member and of the group-as-a-whole, then one can hear how the person gives voice both to his own issues and also to the group, and how, in playing his own individual member role repetitiously, and even self-destructively in the short run, he may at the same time serve the group, containing whatever projected aspects of group life the group is not able to integrate. Thus, in the long run the individual may be required by the more mature group to give up the old role (whether he wishes to or not!) because the group no longer has any use for it. It is a fact that as the group does the work of integrating, it is the group scapegoat who often makes the fastest gains in therapy! It is also a fact that it is very difficult for a member to change roles unless the group sanctions the change! Knowing these facts of group life, the therapist is better able not to interfere in the group process and to wait for the appropriate time.

Most often, role changes are best facilitated by interpreting to the group-as-a-whole-role function rather than to the individual member. Remember: interpreting to the individual reinforces rather than reduces the one-way communication pattern involved in scapegoating.

Understanding the group-as-a-whole enables the therapist to listen to the group-as-a-whole much as one listens to individual patients with the third ear. We can then talk directly to the group unconscious and help bring it into conscious reality. Particularly with difficult patients and difficult groups, it is important to allow the group to give voice to the primal wishes and fears, so that they group can learn to legitimize its unconscious and build a group reality. It is difficult for us therapists to hear, without defending, the inner experiences that difficult patients live with every day. If we listen to the group voice, however, and allow the group to develop its own equilibrium, then we are likely to facilitate the development of the group into an environment that is therapeutic for that particular group of patients, so that the important truths can be told. Then the patients can do their work, and we can do ours.

CHAPTER FOUR

Group-as-a-Whole Systems Theory and practice

Imagine yourself on a summer picnic, throwing a piece of your hamburger to the fish in a pond. Imagine one goldfish swimming off with the hamburger in his mouth, while the others dart around him, nibbling away at it.

On the one hand, you might think that the poor little fellow is having his dinner stolen from him by the other fish, and if he is not careful, he will have nothing left to eat but the last small bite.

On the other hand, taking a second look, you might think that here is a whole school of fish with a large meal falling into their midst. It's too big a serving for any single fish, one fish holds it, while others nibble away at it and the rest dart after the bits that drift away into the water. Thus all the fish are fed.

When we observe a goldfish pond, it makes no difference to the fish whether we say "the individual fish has had all his dinner nibbled away except the last bite" or whether we say "the school has developed an efficient food distribution centre".

Y. M. Agazarian, "Group-as-a-Whole Systems Theory and Practice". In: *Group: The Journal of the Eastern Group Psychotherapy Society, 13,* Nos 3 & 4 (Winter 1989). New York: Brunner/Mazel, Inc. (copyright © 1989 from "Group-as-a-Whole Systems Theory and Practice" by Yvonne Agazarian. Reproduced by permission of Taylor & Francis, Inc., http://www.routledge-ny.com).

But, anthropomorphizing, to say to a group that "this poor little fellow is having his lunch stolen from him by the rest of you" will have a very different impact from "you are solving the problem of how to feed your whole population from one otherwise indigestible lump of hamburger". One could expect the reactions, subsequent events, and indeed the future course of the group to be significantly influenced by which of the two interpretations it receives.

Coming from our cultural heritage of individualism, the therapist most easily interprets "group" events in terms of the dynamics of the individual members. Thinking about an individual's psychodynamics is as old as psychology. Thinking about group-as-a-whole dynamics is relatively new.

For the group systems therapist, the individual and the group-as-a-whole are both dynamically and hierarchically related, both separate and discrete. Once defined, system dynamics are generalizable to all levels, and the structure, function, and behaviour of the individual as a system has an equivalent structure and function in the group and subgroup systems.

This isomorphy in systems thinking is *functionally* different. It is the difference between thinking like Aristotle, who said that whatever one says a thing is, then it is—a chair is a chair is a chair—and Korzybski, who said that whatever one says a thing is, it is not—a chair is a chair is a table is a step-ladder is a bookcase is a clothes horse, etc. All it takes is a shift in the frame of reference.

Functional thinking effectively disposes of the problem of whether a group-as-a-whole "is really" just a collection of individuals or whether it "is really" something quite different. It is, of course, always both. What it "is" at any one time will depend upon the purpose for which it is being described—the perspective from which it is useful to the "thinker" to "think".

Thinking of the "individual" and the "group" as two "systems" in a hierarchy of related systems requires an additional discipline of thinking, but one that does not contradict the existing body of psychodynamic knowledge. In fact, Group-as-a-Whole Systems Theory draws heavily upon psychodynamics when it comes to the application of the theory in practice. A systems perspective does, however, provide an additional way of looking at the dynamics of both the individual and the group, so that the combined understanding of group and individual dynamics can be applied to the practice of group psychotherapy.

The additional dimension that systems thinking introduces is complementarity—a basic orientation in systems thinking. Like yin/yang, it describes the principle of always being separate/and always related! In group-as-a-whole systems thinking, things are thought about in terms of either/or *only* when dichotomizing is useful.

For example, when thinking about group psychotherapy, it is true that as the person matures, so that person interacts more maturely with the group, and as the member interactions mature, so does the group-as-a-whole. It is also true that as the group-as-a-whole matures, increased maturity is required of its members.

Traditionally, the group therapist focuses on the dynamic maturation of the individual as the most direct path to the goal of the individual members' therapy, whereas the systems group therapist focuses on the dynamic maturation of the group-as-a-whole. The systems group therapist may not look very different while working, but this is one case where differences are more actual than apparent, more real than they seem. Systems group psychotherapy is a different discipline from traditional group psychotherapy, and it requires a different way of thinking.

Theoretical overview

In building theory, it is axiomatic that it is a hypothetical mirror that, at best, reflects the real world without too much distortion. For those who are drawn to theory building, imagine my astonishment and delight in finding the following paragraph while re-reading an old issue of *Science News*:[1]

> cells "whisper together" using electrical messages . . . the signals passed between the cells are essential for regulating cell growth, altering these signals may result in . . . [change] . . . the membrane potential [boundary permeability!] acts as . . . a barrier against the outward and inward flow of signals . . . [input/output communications]. Receptors on cell surfaces are thus needed to facilitate message transfer across membranes.

The above paragraph certainly "mirrors" the group-as-a-whole concept that "group-as-a-whole system maturation is a function of the communication across boundaries . . .", and it also gives some construct validity to the group-as-a-whole hypothesis that the task of the systems group therapist is to "consult" to the boundary between systems, and by "altering" the signals "regulate the growth" of the therapeutic potential of the group. Here are few ways that illustrate the "goodness of fit!"

Group-as-a-whole systems "whisper together" by passing messages to each other in the hierarchy. These messages contain the information that permits both the system itself and the hierarchy to which the system belongs to mature from simple to complex functioning.

"The signals passed between the cells are essential for regulating cell growth." System viability depends upon the ability to continue to obtain and integrate information in such a way that the system can mature in complexity and in its ability to adapt. This information is obtained in a reciprocal communication between the system and its environment: between each system and its own subsystem components, between each system and the system above it (for which it is a subsystem component), and between systems at the same level in the hierarchy.

The "membrane potential acts as . . . a barrier against the outward and inward flow of signals . . .": In Group-as-a-Whole Systems Theory, barrier potential is conceptualized in terms of boundary permeability. Thus by changing permeability, the nature of the barriers to information flow are changed. Boundary permeability makes it possible to restrict or increase the inward and outward flow of communication, which, in turn, influences the system's integrational potential.

Noise and the system

In group-as-a-whole systems communication, boundaries are open to information and closed to noise. Boundary permeability serves to regulate noise. Systems respond to noise with a stress response. They move to avoid noise.

In Group-as-a-Whole Systems Theory, noise in the communication system is said to have two sources. One is inherent in the process itself and is the product of the amount of ambiguity, contradiction, and redundancy that exists in the information.[2]

The second source of noise arises from the relative dissonance or consonance between the information and the existing integration of information within the system.[3] Little reintegration is required when information is relatively similar to that already organized and integrated—thus it is relatively consonant and noise-free, and it creates relatively little stress. When the information is relatively different it is potentially dissonant, and more complex reintegration is required. Differences are "noisy" and always arouse more or less system stress.

When information is too ambiguous, contradictory, or redundant (the source of external stress), or too different from the system's existing integration (the source of internal stress), it either fails to cross the boundary or, if it does, is split off and projected into a "containing" subsystem with an impermeable boundary where it is "stored" until, at some future point in maturational time, the system can "use it".

Thus the actual transfer of the information contained in the communication between systems is dependent upon the system's ability to receive it and integrate it.

The process of maturation for systems is defined as the ability to discriminate and integrate similarities and differences.

Group-as-a-whole hypotheses

An important set of system hypotheses follows. It is assumed that the basic components of systems are subsystems—that at each level the system exists in the environment of the system above and serves as the environment for the system below and that there is a potential for communication at all levels. Thus a major focus for the systems group therapist is the communications between the systems.

Some assumptions are basic to this framework:

1. The basic components of systems are subsystems; at each level, the system exists in the environment of the system above and serves as the environment for the system below.
2. Communication is an input/output informational exchange within and between systems.
3. Communication is the process by which systems discriminate and integrate information.
4. System maturation is a function of a communication process that results in discriminating and integrating the similarities and differences within and between systems and subsystems.
5. System boundaries are open to information, closed to noise.
6. Increases and reductions in ambiguities, contradictions, and redundancies in information increase or reduce the noise that is inherent in the communication process itself.
7. Altering the ambiguity, contradiction, and redundancy balance in

the communication process alters the ratio of information to noise; the boundary permeability among systems; the potential for the transfer of information between systems; and the maturational potential of the system itself and its hierarchy.

8. The system's ability to receive complex inputs and to tolerate the noise that the integration of differences entails is dependent upon the development of the integrational ability of the system.
9. The development of the ability to integrate information is dependent upon the development of the system's ability to evolve from simple to complex organizations.
10. Successful therapeutic consultations decrease the contradictions, ambiguities, and redundancies in the information across the boundaries within and between systems.
11. To the extent that the boundaries between systems at all levels of the relevant hierarchy are permeable to information, to that extent is system maturation potentiated. Maturation is a function of the ability to discriminate between similarities and differences across all boundaries of the system hierarchy and to integrate these discriminations in the direction of simple to complex.
12. By changing the structure of boundaries, the potential for transferring information is changed. *Boundary* permeability determines what information the system is open to and what it is closed to. The existing organization of information determines when information is too different to be integrated and must therefore either be defended against before it enters the system or must be split off and contained separately when it does.

By observing the "communication output of the system", the system group therapist infers the internal organization of the system and judges the approach/avoidance relationship to its primary and secondary goals.[4] Primary goals are related to integrating discriminations within the system. Secondary goals are related to the system task of discriminating itself from its environment. Ambiguities, contradictions, and redundancies increase the difficulty inherent in the maturational process of integration and discrimination and are, as such, problems that the system must solve in achieving its primary and secondary goals.

The system group therapist "consults" to the boundaries in the sense of influencing the "noise" in the transactions between the subsystems, within the individual, and within the group-as-a-whole and thus affecting both the system's internal integration and its relationship to its environment; this, in turn potentiates the system's developmental adaptation from simple to complex.

Orienting to the group-as-a-whole

Group-as-a-whole systems therapists monitor the communications across subgroup boundaries to diagnose, identify, undo, and help the group to work through projective identifications and group splitting. This work is phase-specific in that interventions are fitted to the nature and function of the subgroup roles in the developmental phase that is salient for the group.

The group-as-a-whole systems therapist "consults" to the boundaries by focusing on the boundaries between systems—the boundaries where transitional transactions take place. The nature of the communication between systems makes it possible to diagnose the potential that the system has for solving problems along the path to its goal. A basic hypothesis is that there is a direct correlation between the clarity and appropriateness of group and subgroup boundaries and the ability to get work done in the group.

The primary boundary is between the not-group and the group. The moment when individual people arrive and sit together does not necessarily establish a boundary. There is definable moment when the group "feels" different, when the boundary has been crossed and the group-as-a-whole exists. Each group tends to have a characteristic style in crossing the boundary between not-group and group. Some groups do not "start" until all members are present; others need to "call the roll"; still others "become a group" as soon as the time boundary is crossed. Traditionally, "people" are the basic unit of a group. For the group-as-a-whole therapist, the basic unit is the subgroup. In the group-as-a-whole, internal boundaries are drawn and redrawn as subgroups form and reform. Subgroups come together on similarities and separate on differences.

Subgrouping around similarities helps the group to build a problem-solving environment where the chaos of the unknown is brought into some sort of order, where information that is at the edge of awareness can be brought to light, organized, and integrated. For the group-as-a-whole therapist, the development of the skills of problem-solving is more important than the content: *how* the group communicates is always more important than *what* it is communicating about! Therefore it is not until subgrouping around similarities result in stereotypic thinking that the group-as-a-whole therapist disrupts the comfortable equilibrium of the group by pointing out overlooked differences. When, on the other hand, the exploration of differences serves to fractionate the group rather than to stimulate it towards new integrations and change, then attention is drawn to overlooked similarities. For example, it may come as a surprise to members engaged in a fight that they are in the same subgroup: "the fighting subgroup"!

Each subgroup is defined by its behaviour, and each subgroup gives voice to its subgroup theme. Just as the individual has many voices speaking for different parts of his self, so does the group-as-a-whole. And the subgroup voices may be in harmony or discord.

Thus for systems group therapists, every voice is heard in relation to other voices, whether the therapist is "listening" to an individual, or to the group-as-a-whole, or to himself! For example, the therapist's own internal dialogue is "heard" as voices from the different "subgroups" within. Thus, "I want" . . . "I can have" . . . "you'll be punished if you do", is clearly an internal communication that is transmitted across the boundaries of three subgroup systems within the system of the individual.

Intra-system dynamics can be inferred from the interaction. By observing the way the system behaves in its environment, even inconsistent behaviour can be understood as a compromise between subgroup conflict—why, for example, an individual in a group, a subgroup of the group, or the group- as-a-whole itself so frequently avoids doing the obvious thing to get what it explicitly wants.

Practically, this means that the systems group therapist watches the patterns of behaviour and listens with the third ear to hear how each member's voice speaks for the subgroup dynamics of the group-as-a-whole. This requires identifying the boundaries of the subgroups and assessing when those boundaries are permeable to information, permeable *only* to selective information, and impermeable—practically, when to help an individual member, a subgroup, or the group-as-a-whole to hear how it voices its needs and what it needs in order to be able to do its work.

The theoretical constructs that provide the systems group therapist with the frame for making systems judgements and interpretations are developed at greater length after I have presented the following episode.

The voice of the group

This short excerpt from the videotape of an outpatient group of low-functioning patients led by a "Miss Thera" and a "Dr Junior" shows how the systems group therapist listens to the voices of the group and its subgroups and thinks from the perspective of the group-as-a-whole.

At the time the videotape of the group was made, Dr Senior, the supervisor, was not so very senior, either in years or in experience. Miss Thera had been the ongoing co-therapist of this difficult group for five years while Dr "Juniors" came and went with their residencies. Thus the situation was one that is familiar to anyone who has been in an outpatient clinic: a group of the hospital's most difficult patients are treated by the staff members with the least experience and status and are monitored by an overworked supervisor who is primarily concerned that the longer-term therapists do not burn out and that the new ones survive while they learn. In this sense, this episode is ideal for my purpose in that it is a microcosm of the real life of groups in an everyday setting led by co-therapists with whom it is relatively easy to identify.

Additionally, this videotape was analysed and discussed by three different therapists from three different perspectives—psychoanalytic, interpersonal, and group-as-a-whole—for a symposium on the "Difficult Patient, the Difficult Group". It was my great good fortune to be on the discussion panel not only with my colleagues, but also with Dr Senior, Dr Junior, and Miss Thera.[5] It was the moving openness of all three of them as we talked together after the symposium that encourages me to use this episode to illustrate some of the constructs of Group-as-a-Whole Systems Theory and to speculate with such freedom about its system dynamics.

The episode starts with a knock on the door. A late patient, Bess, enters, and there is much commotion as everybody makes room and they all squash their chairs together.

Miss Thera: ". . . fine, come on in . . ."

Dr Junior: ". . . why don't you . . . here, take this chair . . ."

Miss Thera: ". . . watch the wire . . ." [*the session is videotaped*]

Bess: ". . . yeah . . ."

Alice: ". . . move the table . . ."

Edna: ". . . the camera will break . . ."

Alice, Bess, Clara, Edna, Glenda, Doris [*Laughter*]

Alice: ". . . it's called togetherness."

[. . . *as they all squash their chairs together*]

Clara: ". . . closeness . . ."

Bess: ". . . that's what we're all looking for . . ."

Miss Thera: ". . . all thinking . . ."

Dr Junior: ". . . ready? . . ."

Alice: ". . . Christmas . . ."

Dr Junior: ". . . we were just talking about the fact that Edna was seeing me individually for treatment of her depression . . ."

Now let us listen again, but this time to the duet between the two subgroups, each giving voice to the subgroup theme. As the relationship between the two subgroups is very like a "doctor–patient" interaction, I have named them "the doctor" and "the patient" subgroups.

The "doctor" subgroup voice:

— "Here, sit here."

— "Take this chair."

— "Don't trip over the wire."

— "Move the table."

— "Come on in."

— "Ready?"

The "patient" subgroup voice:

— "Come on in."

— "It's called togetherness."

— "Closeness."

— "That's what we're all looking for."

— "That's what we're all thinking."

— "It's like Christmas."

Listening to the voices, the duet between the subgroups is clear: one voices concern for the caretaking task, and the management of the group boundaries, the other voices a yearning for closeness.

Thus each subgroup emerges with its own theme, and it is the music as well as the words that is different. The first marches to a task drum in the direction of an external goal: "sit! take! don't! "move! come! ready? The second sings a song of yearning for the fulfilment of an internal goal: togetherness . . . closeness . . . we're . . . all looking . . . all thinking . . . like Christmas. . . . Please note that although it is quite clear which individual voice belongs to which subgroup, subgroups are not defined by individual *people*! Miss Thera, Alice, Bess, and perhaps Edna sing more than one tune: they share both the subgroup voice for how to organize the environment and also voice the wish to reorganize the internal environment. Subgroups are defined by function. Only Dr Junior, Clara, Doris, and perhaps Edna have no overlapping memberships. "Perhaps" Edna is based on a subtle inference that would need further evidence to be a viable hypothesis, but, "perhaps" Edna is the voice for the group-as-a-whole: the voice for overt compliance with the "doctor" subgroup, and the denied hostility in the "patient" subgroup. Edna, medicated by Dr Junior, designated as an object of jealousy by Dr Junior, apparently "helping" the doctor subgroup by cautioning Bess not to "break (Dr Junior's) camera" and eliciting a whole-hearted, resonating patient subgroup laugh.

Also clear is how the state of the subgroup system is implied by the communication. From the communication behaviour one can tell whether or not there is dissonance between the inner organization of the system implied by the communication and its relationship to the task. By observing whether the system voice and behaviour approaches or avoids the explicit goal, it is possible to infer whether or not the system's implicit and explicit goals are compatible or incompatible.

The group-as-a-whole perspective

In the above episode, the two subgroup voices are in harmony. System behaviour is congruent. There is not much evidence of conflict between the internal organization of information, the communication behaviour, and the goal at which the communication behaviour is directed. The late member arrives, the group makes room for her, and Dr Junior directs it back to work.

Boundaries

A primary function of the systems group therapist is to maintain the group boundaries. Boundaries contain the tensions of the group. When there is sufficient internal equilibrium, the group-as-a-whole has access to its internal energy, organizes it into problem-solving behaviour, and directs it towards its external goals. When inner tension cannot be contained, the system discharges tension in behavioural acting out, thus serving the primary goal of survival but at the expense of the secondary environmental goals.

There is a direct relationship between how appropriate group boundaries are to the group goals and how effectively they contain, for the group, the internal conflicts within the group. The amount of working energy available to the group at any one time is that energy that the group can spare—the energy left over from managing itself and its internal conflicts and organizing itself for work. In this sense how well the systems therapist manages the group boundaries determines how possible it is for the group to work towards and reach its goals.

In the episode of the late member, there is evidence that the "doctor" subgroup successfully supports the therapist's task of maintaining group boundaries, managing the environment, and relating to the task. Boundaries are redrawn geographically: Bess is shown a chair, the circle of chairs is opened up to make room. The environment is successfully mastered—a table is moved, the wire is navigated, the camera is preserved, and the leaders' task goal is brought back into focus for the group-as-a-whole: "Ready?" "We were just talking about . . .".

Much the same can be said for the success of the patient subgroup, which takes advantage of making room for the late member to get closer. They squash their chairs together, they laugh, and they build on what each other says, thus receiving from the environment an input that gratifies their wish for closeness. In this way, although the "doctor" and "patient" subgroup goals are different, they are compatible—both goals are met within the same event.

Goals

If we look again, however, we can see that although in this episode both goals were reached, the two goals still contain an inherent incompatibility. The patient subgroup expresses an underlying emptiness and loneliness and a yearning for human contact, the doctor subgroup talks about medicating one member for depression.

Another primary function of the systems group therapist is to relate boundaries to goals. An important group-as-a-whole system hypothesis is that at all levels of the systems hierarchy there are always two levels of system goals: the explicit goal, the goal that the group "says" it has, and the implicit goal, the goal that the group behaves "as if" it has.

In defining the goals at all levels of the system, it is important to differentiate between primary and secondary goals. Basic system goals are (a) the primary goal of survival and maturation of the system itself and (b) the secondary goal of survival and maturation of the system within its environment. The primary goal requires communication between different parts of the internal system, the secondary goal requires communication between the system and its environment. When these two goals lie in the same direction, then the group can move towards them, solving the problems along the way. When these two goals are incongruent—when the words do not match the music—then the implicit goal is reached at the expense of the explicit goal.

For the doctor subgroup, the explicit goal is to treat, but the implicit goal—the goal that can be inferred by the way the subgroup *behaves*—is to maintain authority and maintain distance.

However, maintaining authority and distance are not compatible with the implicit goal of the patient subgroup, which is to be taken care of, and to be close.

A goal matrix would look like the one shown in Figure 4.1, which provides a frame for comparing the congruence between the explicit and implicit goals of different subgroups. In the above example, although the explicit goals are complementary and on the surface all looks well, it is clear that the implicit goals are incompatible and will be a source of unconscious conflict. The task of the systems group therapist is to make this implicit group conflict explicit, to make the unconscious conscious, so that this subgroup conflict does not become a fixating split that will affect the therapeutic potential of the group.

It is probably appropriate at this point to emphasize again that for the group-as-a-whole systems therapist there are always two levels of system reality: the level of the individual and the level of the group-as-

Goal	Patient subgroup	Doctor subgroup
explicit	to be treated	to treat
implicit	to be cared for and to be close	to maintain a hierarchical and impersonal distance

FIGURE 4.1. A goal matrix

a-whole. Thus the task of making implicit conflict explicit—the unconscious conscious—is as much a task for oneself the person in the therapist as it is for oneself the therapist in the group.

The individual therapist in the group-as-a-whole

The individual perspective

From the perspective of the individual, there is evidence that Miss Thera has a voice in both subgroups—and thus is in internal contradiction. She will experience her internal conflict if she is able to hear herself. But if one of her conflicting subgroup voices is silenced behind an impermeable subgroup boundary, she will be comfortable but less therapeutically useful.

In more traditional group therapy, self-analysis and countertransference analysis will be the most direct route to understanding her own conflict and her interpersonal participation in the group. She would probably look first into herself and then look again from the perspective of her co-therapist role.

Information that she gets from these sources she can use in understanding the dynamics of the group, much as she will use countertransference information in individual therapy.

From the systems perspective, analysing her own conflict in subgroup voices will aid in identifying subgroups. Every group member has many overlapping memberships both inside and outside the group. An important first distinction is the one between those aspects of inner experience that relate or resonate to the here-and-now of the group and those aspects of experience that defend against relating or resonating. Thus the first discrimination is one of perspective—the perspective that grounds her conflict where it "belongs", so that her self-analysis can also be useful to her in her group analysis. This entails differentiating between those aspects of the conflict that relate to the here-and-now in the group and those that relate across the boundaries to her overlapping membership roles in other groups.

Analysing and managing transference and countertransference reactions and using them as information in the therapeutic process is a skill that is emphasized in the training of most therapists. For a systems therapist, countertransference and personal reactions are only one source of information about the therapeutic process. The second source requires analysing all behaviour, including the therapist's own, as an expression of system dynamics. When observing behaviour from a systems perspective, the systems therapist makes inferences about what his experience (internal behaviour) and his communications (output behaviour) in the group express both for his individual system and also for the system of the group-as-a-whole.

The group perspective

From the group systems theory perspective, the co-therapists are members of more than one system in more than one hierarchy contemporaneously. They are individual systems in themselves, subgroups in the hierarchy of the clinic, and dynamically a part of the group-as-a-whole. It is easy to identify at least three subsystems in the clinic hierarchy: (a) outpatient group system, (b) co-therapy group system, and (c) supervision group system.

Thinking as a group-as-a-whole systems therapist requires thinking about oneself from different perspectives. Most familiar is oneself—a self-focused perspective from which we tend to take things personally, in which we struggle to stay open and not to defend against the impact of the group, and in which we contain all the emotional reactions that humans fall heir to and strive to make the unconscious conscious and not act out! Most abstract is to think of oneself as a "dynamic" in the group-as-a-whole. From this perspective, one's experience and behaviour is a function of group dynamics. From this perspective "one does not take things personally"! To conceptualize oneself as an individual is to defend oneself from the dynamic focus.

Role relationships

In role, therapists individually experience themselves in relation to their co-therapist and carry with them the overlapping membership issues from their co-therapy and supervision groups. Each will also experience their relationship to each one of the individual group members—Alice, Bess, Clara, Edna, Doris, and Glenda—and each will experience their relationship with themselves. In each of these individual relationships they will be differentially aware of various transference and countertransference reactions.

Parenthetically, one of the advantages of Group-as-a-Whole Systems Theory is the clarity it can contribute to the changes in goals and roles that overlapping memberships entail, and thus helps individuals both to understand and to support the changes of behaviour that are appropriate. This is particularly useful when the same people are working together on different tasks.

For example, in the co-therapy group, the goal is for the two therapists to work cooperatively together to facilitate the maturation of the therapy group. Appropriate role behaviours will be those that serve to fulfil this task. In addition, "in-group" co-therapy-role behaviours will be different from "debriefing after the group" behaviours, and different again if the co-therapists finish their debriefing over a drink after work. The behaviours of play, for example, are significantly different from those of work. Difficulties occur when interpersonal behaviours that relate to one goal are transferred into another situation even when the goal has changed.

Roles and goals

More subtle difficulties occur when the openness of communication that is appropriate for one goal is applied to another where it is not appropriate. For example, open communication is important in a co-therapy relationship. Without open communication, some of the more difficult aspects of co-therapy tend to get acted out rather than contained. "Containing" the good/bad split for the group, for example, frequently draws the therapists into opposing subgroups, and this opposition is easily acted out both in the group and outside in their other role relationships. On the other hand, communicating across the containing boundaries, with the resonance reaching deep into intrapersonal dynamics, requires the kind of interpersonal work that challenges even the closest of friends. Thus the co-therapy relationship itself both contains the need for more open communication than is typical in a professional relationship and also stimulates more resistance to it.

Once a working openness has been achieved between a co-therapy pair, it is sometimes difficult to close the boundaries that have taken so much work to open. In other roles in other groups—like, for example, in a supervision group or a staff group—openness may be a serious deviation and will arouse stereotypic responses unless the other group has norms that can absorb an open-communication subgroup. Unfortunately, that is relatively unlikely in a clinic setting.

Roles and hierarchy

A hierarchy is implied by the pseudonyms allocated in the script: "Dr Junior", Miss Thera", and "Dr Senior". It is not only group goals that affect overlapping membership role boundaries—so do changes in hierarchy. In a supervision group the goal is feedback on the effectiveness of diagnosis and consultation. Appropriate role behaviours will relate both to this goal and to the hierarchical relationship between them as co-supervisees with their supervisor. Appropriate role behaviour in the supervision group will be different from that appropriate to their co-therapy group: same people, different groups, different goals, and different appropriate behaviours. If open communication is to become a norm for the supervision group, the group-as-a-whole must make the decision!

Roles and overlapping memberships

Now let us return to "Miss Thera's" overlapping membership issue. Let us say that her conflict is personally conscious to her, and that she recognizes its source as her overlapping memberships in both the "doctor" and "the patient" subgroups. It will be relatively easy for her to recognize her identification with taking care of the group boundaries and treating patients. More difficult will be the implicit conflict between her resonance with the patients' yearning and her own wish to protect herself from it with the boundaries of her therapist role.

To surface the implicit goals of this group requires the therapists to experience the depth of their own conflicts between the wish to help and the realities of their own helplessness: the impulse to "contain" for the group the full depth of the dependency needs and the terror of the depths of their own dependency that this will inevitably arouse.

The task of the group-as-a-whole systems therapist is not only to monitor the flow of information across boundaries between systems, so that new similarities and differences can be integrated. It is also to be aware that sometimes the integration process itself must mature before the system can complete its integration work. In this case, the group-as-a-whole system therapist may serve the as the group-as-a-whole container. When neither the group-as-a-whole nor its subgroups can contain differences, the group-as-a-whole therapist can serve as a containing subsystem. It is in this sense that the therapist's boundaries need to remain permeable to differences that the group cannot integrate and both to contain and to facilitate the group's maturation until the group can.

Difficult groups are difficult, not because the group dynamics are more complex than those of easier groups—in fact the dynamics are usually simpler—but because the therapist is challenged to contain greater chaos for the group while the group is learning to confront the harshness of its reality.

An important skill for the group-as-a-whole system therapist is to be able to identify which are the boundaries that are restricting communication. If the problem lies in a conflict between subgroups and not with the group-as-a-whole, then the target boundary is between subgroups. If the problem lies within the group itself, then the target boundary will be within the group-as-a-whole.

Usually, when systems boundary conflicts are between subgroups, they are in the service of equilibrating the group-as-a-whole. On the surface, the example of the "doctor" and "patient" subgroups looks like a system-to-system communication in the environment of the group-as-a-whole system. The salient question to ask, however, is: how is this particular subgroup interaction serving the viability of the group-as-a-whole? Before answering this question, a prior determination needs to be made. Are the subgroups serving a defensive manoeuvre to keep the group in equilibrium while inner integration is taking place? Or are the subgroups a source of disequilibrium themselves?—a symptom of a difficulty that the group-as-a-whole is having in gaining the equilibrium necessary to do its integration work?

Group-as-a-whole defences

For example, a contradiction in the group that is not owned is always a signal that there is a group-as-a-whole defence operating, in that the group is paying lip-service to reality-testing but behaving "as if" it is better to ignore reality. As it only takes one group member to surface a group denial—and as it takes the cooperation of the whole group to deny, this is an example that meets the criterion of a group-as-a-whole defence. Group-as-a-whole defences require the cooperation of the group-as-a-whole, just as do group-as-a-whole problem-solving communication patterns. Group defences and group norms of communication are always the property of the group-as-a-whole.

It is important to note that this does not necessarily mean that a group-as-a-whole defence, like group denial in this case, should necessarily be addressed by the therapist. Group-level defences serve both to maintain equilibrium while the group solves the problems that arise along the path to its goals and barriers that turn the group communication away from solving other problems along the path to the goal.

Group-as-a-whole "denial", for example, serves to code "difference" and to "store" it behind a boundary that is permeable to consciousness but not to acknowledgment and is thus perhaps one of the most accessible and efficient ways that the group-as-a-whole system has of splitting and containing difference. By making this kind of judgement as to the function of the defence, the group-as-a-whole systems therapist decides when to support group defences because they are in the service of group integration and when to disrupt them because they threaten to fixate the group's development.

The interchange in the episode around the "late member" that will serve as an illustration for the above is the contradiction between Edna's caution: "the camera will break" and the hearty group laugh in response to it. Let us imagine that Miss Thera and Dr Junior had previously discussed the possibility that the group's apparent passive compliance is masking an angry disappointment for the group-as-a-whole, that the group has isolated, repressed, and turned the anger upon itself, and passive compliance is both a symptom and an expression of the compromise. In this case, group-as-a-whole rage and disappointment is a system experience, and the doctor and patient subgroups are cooperating in an "as if" interaction that keeps the rage contained. At the level of the *individuals as systems*, each individual system will have organized itself to contain the rage in its own way. From the individual perspective, Edna's mixed message will signal her own particular resolution. From the group perspective, however, Edna's is the clearest voice for the group-as-a-whole.

Let us assume that the co-therapists have decided to address this, the first judgement call will be whether or not it matters if the intervention is made by Dr Junior or Miss Thera. The criteria for answers to most questions in group-as-a-whole systems thinking has to do with similarities or differences. As the purpose of this intervention is to point out a difference in the apparently similar that the group is overlooking, then how it is pointed out will make a difference to how it will be received. Sometimes the process of disrupting an existing integration in the group calls for choosing therapeutic dissonance; in this case, however, the less dissonance, the better. As Dr Junior has no voice in the patient subgroup, it is probable that his communication would be experienced as dissonant. Miss Thera, on the other hand, has a voice in both subgroups, and she can communicate across the boundaries of the two subgroups, causing relatively little dissonance in either.

Acting out

Miss Thera thus being the co-therapist of choice, what is the boundary transaction that would be the target of choice? Again, the question is one of similarities or differences. The most powerful target boundary is that which maintains the acting out. In this case, it is at the boundary between the group-as-a-whole explicit goal: "treatment", and the conflict over the implicit goal of closeness/distance that is inherent in intimacy. The rage that such a conflict typically evokes is turned against the group-as-a-whole, and the two subgroups maintain a complementary interaction: the "patient subgroup" turns the rage in upon itself in depression, and out in passive compliance, and the "doctor subgroup" turns the rage in on itself by feeling incompetent, and out in an autocratic leadership style that is deaf to the voice of the group-as-a-whole.

Many things can be said about the "camera" as symbolic of "camera-like" therapists who watch and record. Probably most of you who are reading this will have some idea of what you would "say" and how you would address these dynamics from your perspective. The purpose is not to put words into your mouth but, rather, to share the frame of thinking that lead to deciding which boundary to consult to, and some of the criteria for the consultation itself.

The problem that lies between the doctor and patient subgroups is a particularly good example of the need to "consult" to the boundary within the group-as-a-whole. It lends itself to several relevant levels of analysis, and at least one that is generalizable in an important way to the every day experience of group therapists—and particularly to co-therapists.

When the group-as-a-whole therapist becomes aware of noise in the communication system, the question is whether or not to consult to the boundary and attempt to influence the noise-information balance. If the noise arises from redundancy or ambiguity, then the therapeutic intervention draws the group attention to disequilibrating differences. When the group's communication pattern manifests contradiction, an intervention draws the group's attention to ignored similarities.

Splitting

"Splitting" in a group serves a maturation function in that information that is "too different" to be integrated within the existing organization of the system is split off and stored in a subgroup container. Thus a functioning group equilibrium is maintained, but there is a risk. If in the maturation process the "difference" remains inaccessible behind impermeable subsystem boundaries, then there is a potential developmental fixation. It is important, therefore, for the group to "take back" and integrate split-off information at some later point in maturational time. How to influence the communication so that the natural maturational process of undoing a split, undoing the projective identification, and reintegrating differences can take place is an important skill for the systems therapist.

The task of the group-as-a-whole systems therapist is not only to monitor the flow of information across boundaries between systems so that new similarities and differences require maturation both in the systems' ability to integrate, it is also to serve as a containing subsystem when the group-as-a-whole fails to contain differences that they have split off. In this sense, the therapist's boundaries need to remain permeable to differences that the group cannot integrate, and both to contain and to facilitate the group's maturation until the group is able to do so.

It is for this reason that the therapist often serves as the scapegoat until the group has learnt how to work out the dynamics of projective identification.

Scapegoating

Group-as-a-whole scapegoating is reflected in the group-as-a-whole communication pattern and is a boundary permeability problem within the group. It is an "acting-out" of a split that is incompletely contained within the group.

The first step is to bring to the attention of the group-as-a-whole that its scapegoating behaviour has a purpose and a function. In the ensuing work of undoing a projective identification, the group's next step is to recognize, own, and support its subgroups. In groups that are familiar with group-as-a-whole concepts, great individual relief is felt when guilt over the scapegoating rage is not taken personally. When subgrouping has failed to keep a group in equilibrium, much chaotic "noise" is released, and system defences at all levels become increasingly primitive. Stabilizing the group by identifying clear subgroupings is the first step in restoring a containing equilibrium.

Once subgroups have been identified, it becomes possible to encourage the subgroup voice and to work to make explicit the implicit subgroup goals and to increase the permeability of the subgroup boundaries to the differences that have been projected into the scapegoat.

In this case of scapegoating, work at the individual systems level is often the most direct path to the group-as-a-whole system change, but not, of course, with the individual scapegoat, which would at best create an "identified patient" and at worst reinforce the scapegoating. Encouraging individuals to open themselves to what they have individually projected often releases strong, spontaneous reactions around which subgroups can form naturally on affect rather than content.

Consulting to boundaries

There are several criteria for a consultation to boundaries. First, the information itself should mirror a problem-solving communication: in other words, it should contain as little noise as possible. This is done, whenever possible, by grounding the communications in here-and-now reality that exists at both the primary and secondary goal levels.

As always in the business of building theory and testing it in reality, there is a reciprocity between ideas and experience: sometimes the ideas form ahead of the experience, sometimes the experience has not yet been framed in ideas. In this sense, this section is a "communication transaction across a boundary from a system in transition".

This section builds on a great deal of work that a colleague and I started in 1965, identifying how to recognize patterns of communication and tell the difference between the patterns of communication that increased the probability that groups would solve problems and those that increased the probability that groups would not only fail to solve problems, but also create them (see the section below headed SAVI).

Also discussed are the first formulations for applying SAVI (system for analysing verbal interaction) communication theory to group-as-a-whole systems consultations—and in this sense is both at the "what it is" and also the "how to do it" stages of development.

As this chapter appears to be the first formal introduction to the group-as-a-whole as a different discipline, with a different set of assumptions and hypotheses, it seems useful to share the process of "transactions across the boundary" as well as the result of the "system integration" after the "transition" has been made.

First, then, some hypotheses about communication: Communications are transactions across system boundaries that effect system transitions.

Group-as-a-whole system therapist consultations are acts of communication that are intended to modify transitional transactions in the system hierarchy, within and between systems at all levels:

In the Appendix, the hypotheses and assumptions that are the criteria for group-as-a-whole consultations are spelt out. They are the underlying framework intended to guide the way the group-as-a-whole therapist works, much in the same way as the Basic Assumptions, presented in the Theoretical Overview, were intended to guide the way the group-as-a-whole therapist thinks.

Maturation is a function of communication that occurs in the relationship between and within systems in the same hierarchy.

1. each system serves as the environment for the systems below it (the individual system in relation to the subsystems of the self-system);
2. each system exists as a subsystem relating to other systems (subgroups in relation to each other);
3. each system exists in the environment of the system above it (subgroups in relation to the group-as-a-whole).

Consultations as acts of communication

1. Consultations are acts of communication that are intended to *reduce the noise* in the *patterns of communication.* There is an inverse relationship between ambiguity, contradiction, and redundancy in the information conveyed in the acts of communication and,
    a. the probability that information will be transferred in the service of solving the problems related to
    b. the system's primary and secondary goals of discrimination, integration, separation, individuation, adaptation, and maturation.
2. Consultations are acts of communication that are intended to *influence the nature* of the *transactions in the environment,*
    a. by altering the patterns of communication in the environment and

   b. by reducing the noise inherent in the process of communication,
      i. as there is an inverse relationship between information and noise in the communication process, thus the less noise, the greater the potential for the transfer of information.

3. Consultations are acts of communication that are intended to *influence the nature* of the *transaction across boundaries,*
   a. by altering the *nature* of the communication inputs across the boundaries of systems,
      i. by decreasing noise, system boundary permeability to the information content is increased,
      ii. which increases the probability of information transfer.

4. Consultations are acts of communication that *influence the nature* of the *transitions within the system,*
   a. by altering the integration requirements for the system receiving the communication,
      i. by reducing the stress of noise, similarities and differences are integrated with less dissonance.
   b. by altering the nature of the transition of the system,
      i. by decreasing the stress in the change process, changes from one state of integration to another require less defensive splitting, projecting, containing.

5. Consultations are acts of communication that *result in solving the problems* relative to *primary and secondary system goals,*
   a. by potentiating system maturation through appropriate discrimination and integration of information,
   b. by reducing the stress resulting from noise within the system,
   c. by reducing the noise in the communication outputs from the system,
   d. by increasing the potential for problem solving in the hierarchy,
   e. by potentiating system adaptation to the environment and mastery in it.

The language of consultation

The language that relates to the primary goals in the here-and-now of the group-as-a-whole is the language of emotion, condensations, metaphor, and paradox. Primary goal communication organizes chaos in ways that can be integrated without isolating thought from affect. It is the language that every therapist learns, recognizes, and uses—and is very difficult to code or teach.

The language that relates to the secondary goals is the language of problem solving. This language is relatively easy to teach. This work has mainly been pioneered in the field of human relations training in the late 1950s and 1960s, where, unlike therapy, change interventions must show measurable results if the change agents are to earn a living. Thus the criteria for success became the small change that made the big difference.

As my original group training in a Lewinian centre for group dynamics was contemporaneous with my individual training in a psychoanalytic institute, I was confronted with the necessity to understand communication from two points of view: dynamically, as one does when listening to the unconscious with the third ear, and behaviourally, as one does when one is coding "acts" of verbal behaviour in order to chart change.

Several very small changes in communication behaviour made a very big difference to the purpose of the communication. For example, it was demonstrated that the most persuasive communication is a description of the real world, not an opinion about what one should do about it. This one small change, exchanging the language of opinion for the language of description, actually revolutionized both the sales style and the sales figures for one company! It can also revolutionize the climate of a group! It came as a great surprise to me find out how many of my therapeutic statements designed to be reflective and neutral where in fact a "hard sell" !

Once it became clear that much of the theory and discipline of group dynamics could be generalized to solving problems in the practice of therapy, it became of paramount interest to find how small the change in the kind of verbal behaviour could be to be effective. Take, for example, the behaviour of a question. The kind of questioning behaviour used—the input into the system—will significantly affect the outcome answer. Thus changing a personal question to one for facts or opinion will elicit different and predictable responses, and different again if one changes to a leading question. A question functions as a leadership behaviour! It leads someone somewhere. The only way a person can refuse to follow the lead is by avoiding the question. What a simple and elegant way of describing some familiar therapist–patient interactions!

SAVI: an instrument for coding communication

Defining communication in terms of verbal behavioural acts that convey information with more or less efficiency brings communication into focus in a way that is not usually at the forefront for therapists. *How to communicate* becomes at least as important as *what to communicate*. Defining communication as behaviour had at least one major conceptual advantage in that it made it possible to borrow some of Lewin's operational definitions from Field Theory, such as the "behaviour" in his definition of the "life space".[6] And this, in turn, led to thinking about verbal behaviour as a variable in influencing the balance of noise in system communication. Much of the present theory of communication presented in this chapter has its roots in the development of SAVI, a "System for Observing Verbal Interaction" that Anita Simon and I started to develop in 1965.[7]

SAVI data can be coded in ways that picture the direction of information flow and charts the behaviours that influence changes in the communication patterns at all levels of the system hierarchy. It has been an ongoing task to use SAVI to learn practical and testable methods for consulting to the boundaries of the system. Communication patterns can provide powerful information. For example, one fixated group that we studied demonstrated that no matter how individuals in the group changed the way they communicated, the pattern of the group remained the same—thus confirming the hypothesis that the implicit goal of the group-as-a-whole (to flight) was stronger than any individual goal, including the goal of the therapist, who unwittingly reintroduced flight into the communication flight pattern when the members briefly worked!

Successful consultation results in a group communication pattern that solves problems that relate to its task. The advantage of thinking in terms of communication behaviour as it is organized by SAVI is that it provides a tool for diagnosing the potential for information transfer in a communication pattern and also maps a strategy for intervention.

Reformulating what people say in group in terms of communication as behaviour and paying attention to how the group is communicating rather than what it is communicating about is another departure from the more traditional approach to group therapy. The advantage of thinking about communication patterns as well as communications is that it requires the therapist to consider the transfer of information in the context of the group and to recognize when it is useful to understand the communication pattern from the perspective of the individual, when from the perspective of the subgroup, and when from the perspective of the group-as-a-whole.

In the group-as-a-whole system therapist's task of "consulting to boundaries", communication patterns provide a guide for the particular way that a therapist can "alter the signal" that is being "whispered" and "facilitate" the transfer of the message that is essential for regulating system growth.

Group-as-a-Whole Systems Theory is *designed* to provide a frame of reference that describes the structure, function, and dynamics of all systems in the same hierarchy in equivalent conceptual terms, so that what one says about events at one system level translates to the next system level. Each system serves as the environment for the system below it and exists in the environment of the system above it. Below is a summary of similarities, differences, and complementarities between systems group therapists and traditional group therapists.

SUMMARY

Similarities, differences, and complementarity between systems group therapists and traditional group therapists

1. Traditionally, group therapists work with people, systems group therapists work with subgroups;
   a. from the traditional group therapy perspective, groups are made up of individual members,
   b. from the group-as-a-whole systems perspective, groups are made up of subgroups.
2. Traditionally group therapists interpret to people, systems group therapists intervene at system boundaries;
   a. from the traditional group therapy perspective, therapists interpret to influence the internal dynamics and external behaviour of the person through insight,
   b. systems group therapists intervene to influence system communications between subgroups and in the group-as-a-whole.

3. Both traditionally and in systems group practice therapists monitor the way the group works, but
   a. traditional group therapists influence the way the group works by influencing the way the individuals work in it, monitoring group work by monitoring the interactions between the individual and other group members,
   b. systems group therapists influence the way the group works by influencing the way the subgroups work in it, monitoring group function by monitoring the interactions between subgroups;

   attention is drawn to the boundaries between subgroups: when the group-as-a-whole behaviour becomes too homogeneous for change, attention is drawn to unacknowledged differences between subgroups and to unacknowledged similarities when too heterogeneous; subgroup communication on similarities and differences undoes stereotyping and potentiates maturation.

4. Both traditionally and in systems group practice therapists use communication as the major therapeutic tool, but
   a. the major therapeutic technique of traditional group therapy is communicating insight to the person,
   b. the major therapeutic technique of the systems group therapist is influencing the structure and function of the communication behaviour itself across the boundaries of the subgroups.

5. Both traditionally and in systems group practice therapists take responsibility for making decisions about the structure and function of the group, but
   a. from the traditional group therapy perspective, the therapist takes the responsibility for selecting the members, defining the goals, setting the fees, deciding when and where and for how long the group will meet, deciding whether and when to bring in new members and making all the rules for the group;
   b. the systems group therapist selects the members and defines the goals and initially sets the fee, but as the group develops he delegates responsibility for group management decisions to the group. For example, the group develops rules as guidelines that lead to the group goals.

6. Both traditionally and in systems group practice therapists aim to modify the dynamics of the person's inner experience and outer behaviour, but

a. from the traditional group therapy perspective, the therapist does this by interpretations to the individual person's psychodynamics and the manifestations of those dynamics in the individuals' interpersonal behaviour, whereas
b. the systems group therapist does this by interventions that influence the permeability of the boundaries between the subgroups.

7. Both traditionally and in systems group therapy the therapist has the same treatment goal—therapy of the individual—but
   a. from the traditional therapy perspective the therapist focuses on the dynamic maturation of the individual as the most direct path to the goal of therapy for the individual members,
   b. the systems group therapist focuses on the dynamic maturation of the group-as-a-whole as the major path to the goals of the therapy group: treatment of the individual members.
8 Both traditionally and in systems group practice the therapists are concerned with phases of development and look to the developmental history, environmental influences, and maturational experience to understand vicissitudes in development and their impact on dynamics, but
   a. from the traditional group therapy perspective the therapist looks to the past: to the developmental history that the individual member brings with him into the group; the source of data is outside the group and in the past, developmental issues are the material of current therapy,
   b. the systems therapist looks to the present: the current developmental issues for the group-as-a-whole and its subgroups occur as the group matures; developmental history arises from the vicissitudes that occur in the phases of group development and are the material of current group-as-a-whole problem solving; the systems group therapist has the opportunity of monitoring how the group develops in the here and now, and thus the phases in group-as-a-whole development and its phase-specific maturational challenges provide the stimulus and the context in which individual members' developmental issues are revisited.

APPENDIX

Theoretical definitions and criteria for interventions in individual and group-as-a-whole system dynamics

Because the isomorphic principle of systems theory requires that the definitions of structure and function of any one system can be generalized to all other systems in the same hierarchy, it is axiomatic that the definition of the concepts and constructs of Group-as-a-Whole Systems Theory apply to all systems in the hierarchy, from cell to society, it is relevant specifically to the individual and group systems which are the two relevant systems in the practice of group psychotherapy.

Certain constructs of Field Theory and General Systems Theory have been adapted in formulating the theoretical definitions for Group-as-a-Whole Theory.

I re-coded the life-space equation in terms that both underline the isomorphic relationship between the systems in the hierarchy, and at the same time delineates the difference between them. The life-space equation of the group and individual systems describes each as a discrete, hierarchically related system the dynamic force fields of which are similar in structure and function.

By observing behaviour (the output of the system), hypotheses can be generated about system homeostasis, or the dynamic equilibrium in which the field of force is held. Lewin (1951), in his Field Theory, defines the "life space" by the equation that behaviour is a function of the person in interaction with the perceived environment, and person locomotion (behaviour) is related to the tensions system between the inner-person dynamics and the life-space goal. Thus the behaviour of a person is governed by vector forces directed towards the goal, the strength and velocity of which is tempered by the restraining forces that impede progress.

Lewin's "force field" describes the point of equilibrium that is the resultant of these forces, and a behavioural analysis of the force field implied by the life space at any point in time, implies the relationship between the system and the system goal. Human system behaviour can, therefore, be understood as goal-directed behaviour, and the human system force field gives a dynamic picture of the state of the system in relation to its goal. It is at this point that the goals that the system is behaving "as if" it had are the best predictors of system locomotion!

Hence, all human behaviour can be conceptualized as an output or signal of the dynamic equilibrium or internal goal state of the particular human system that is being observed in its social context.

Therapist interventions can, therefore, be conceptualized as either potentiating driving forces or weakening restraining forces that affect the system's progress in relation to its goal—which in a group-as-a-whole therapy group is to potentiate system maturation.

Definitions as they apply to the history and practice of group psychotherapy are presented below. It is important to understand that from the perspective of Group-as-a-Whole Systems Theory, both the individual and the group are defined as systems, similar in structure and function, the dynamics of which mirror each other. Thus the primary goal of both the individual system and the group-as-a-whole system—just as for any system in the hierarchy of living systems—is to survive. Primary system dynamics can, therefore, be defined in terms of the dynamics of HOW the system remains in equilibrium.

The secondary goals of the system, on the other hand, are behavioural, and they are related to goals in the environment. The dynamics of system motility can be understood in terms of movement in the direction of environmental goals and the approach/avoidance characteristic of the movement as it relates to solving the problems that arise as the system moves along the path in the direction of its goal.

The *life-space equation*: "behaviour is a function of the person in interaction with the environment" is redefined as "behaviour is a function of the system in interaction with the environment". Lewin's (1951) life-space equation can thus be re-coded in terms that both underline the isomorphic relationship between systems in the hierarchy and at the same time delineate the difference between them.

Each system in a hierarchy is both the environment for the system below it and exists in the context of the system above it; thus there is communication both "within" and "between" systems "within" and "between" levels in the hierarchy.

The life-space equation of the group and individual systems describes each as a discrete, hierarchically related system the dynamic field of force of which is similar in structure and function.

A "system" is defined as having boundaries of relative permeability and being in interaction with its life-space environment. Behaviour is defined as input and output informational transactions that are characterized by the organizational norms of the system and serve maintenance and task roles for the system, directionally related to the system goals.

The theoretical formulations for applying this to systems, when seen from the individual system perspective and from the group-as-a-whole system perspective, are described below:

1. the *individual* perspective describes the dynamics of the individual in terms of
   a. the internal dynamics of the system of the *person*, and
   b. the expression of the internal-person-system dynamics in *member-role* behaviour.
2. the *group* perspective describes the dynamics of the group in terms of
   a. the internal dynamics of the system of the *group-as-a-whole*, and
   b. the expression of the internal group-as-a-whole dynamics in *group-role* behaviour.

1. *Individual system dynamics*

Operational definition: the behaviour of a particular individual is a function of the history of that particular *person system* and manifested in *member-role behaviour*.

a. *Individual person intra-system dynamics*

Theoretical frame

The *person* perspective has been explained by psychodynamic and intra-personal theorists, the best-known of whom is Freud. From the perspective of the *person*, individual behaviour is understood as a function of *intra-personal* (inner-person) psychodynamics that result from genetic inheritance, developmental history and environmental influences, and past experiences.

Criteria for person interventions

Person interventions are designed to focus the individual on the internal psychodynamic experience that is expressed in the person's behaviour.

They are designed to modify the ego defence mechanisms, both as they inhibit and as they potentiate individual problem solving. The target of a person intervention is the inner *experience* of the individual. A criterion of a successful person intervention is that the person gains insight through the physical, nonverbal *experience* of his dynamics. This is different from intellectual insight. Thus, for the individual who is the scapegoat, a successful intervention would result in the full experience of the dynamics of his masochism—not an intellectualized or verbal understanding of it.

b. Individual "member-role" inter-system dynamics

Theoretical frame

The *member-role* perspective is represented by theorists like Lewin (Field Theory: 1951), Sullivan (Interpersonal Theory), and object relationists, family therapists, structural analysts, transactional analysts, psychodramatists, etc. From the perspective of the *member role,* individual behaviour is understood as a function of *interpersonal* dynamics that manifest in reciprocal roles. Thus tensions that are experienced intra-personally are expressed or acted out through behaviour that is "intended" to resolve the tensions and thus maintain the system in equilibrium.

Criteria for member interventions

Member interventions are designed to call attention to patterns of maladaptive behaviour. They focus on interpersonal dynamics and on how the tensions of internal experience are expressed or acted out in behaviour that attempts to solve internal problems by action in the outside world. Interpreting reciprocal role behaviours in a group, member-role interpretations focus on what the individual member is repeating from the past.

Thus for the individual who is the scapegoat, a successful interpersonal intervention would result in an understanding of how he had repeated in the present an old role relationship from the past, attempting to relieve current internal or external pressures by reliving old solutions (the repetition compulsion). Successful member interventions to the scapegoat lead to an understanding of how he repeatedly "volunteers" for the role, and/or "coaches" a scapegoating response from the group members.

Unless patients get insight into their conflicts, they continue to helplessly repeat them. However, as the conflicts that are expressed in repetitive behaviour are frequently repressed or denied, for the scapegoat to get intellectual understanding of how he volunteers for the scapegoat role or how he elicits attack from others is often a useful step towards confronting his denial or undoing repression, and can therefore fulfil the criteria for a successful therapeutic intervention.

2. Group system dynamics

Operational definition: the behaviour of a particular group is a function of the history of that particular *group-as-a-whole* and manifested in *subgroup roles.*

a. "Group-as-whole" intra-system dynamics

Theoretical frame

The group-as-a-whole perspective was first brought into focus by the group conceptualizers: Bion (with his Basic Assumptions), Lewin (with his group-level life space), Jung (with his collective unconscious), and the ongoing research and theory building that comes out of the work of the Tavistock, A. K. Rice, and the National Training Labs.

From the intra-system perspective of the *group-as-a-whole,* group behaviour is understood as a function of the *intra-group* dynamics that result from the unique genetic inheritance, composition, developmental history, and maturational experience of the group-as-a-group.

Criteria for group-as-a-whole interventions

Group-as-a-whole interventions are designed to focus on the group-as-a-whole and to modify group-level defences. This is so both in the potentiating sense that group-level defences bind group-level chaos (groups "store" differences that are not integrated in group roles) and also in the inhibiting sense that the group-level defences limit problem-solving potential. Thus, whereas splitting is fundamental to the ability of the group to maintain equilibrium, it also potentiates group fixation: For this reason it is fundamentally important that the group therapist understands when to reinforce the containment of splitting as a factor in group development and when to interpret it so that the group members can take back their projections and reintegrate the differences that have been contained.

The target of the group intervention is the inner dynamics of the group. Group maturation is dependent upon the integration of differences. Splitting is a mechanism that permits the group to integrate information that is "similar enough" and to "split off" and "store" information that is "too different". This carries the potential both for maturation and for fixation. In the management of scapegoating, for example, the therapists needs to be able to recognize when the underlying dynamics of scapegoating are part of a natural maturation process of the group-as-a-whole that an intervention would interrupt and when there is the potentiality for fixation that requires an intervention.

b. Group-role inter-subgroup dynamics

From the perspective of the group role, group behaviour is understood as a function of subgroup role relationships that enable the group to remain in a dynamic equilibrium. Thus tensions that are experienced within the group-as-a-whole and that give rise to group-level defences are expressed or acted out through subgroup behaviour that attempts to discharge the tensions and permit the group to solve internal and external problems.

Just as individual member-role behaviour serves an equilibrating function for the individual system, so group-role behaviour does for the group. It is as if the group-as-a-whole delegates one or more of its members to perform group roles that will bind, contain, or express group tensions while it delegates other members, subgroups, or facets of the whole group to roles that facilitate work.

Theoretical frame

Central to understanding the group-role perspective is the understanding of the phenomena of projective identification and containership as formulated by Jung and by Klein. Bennis and Shepard (1956), in their "Theory of Group Development", apply these concepts to the defensive function of Bion's Basic Assumptions by describing how the group continually binds and contains the internal group chaos through fight/flight, dependency, and pairing *group roles*, while it simultaneously uses those roles in developmental tasks.

From the perspective of *group role*, group behaviour is understood as a function of *inter-group* dynamics that manifest in inter-group reciprocal role relationships (member–member, member–subgroup, subgroup–subgroup, or group facet to group facet) that bind aspects of current intra-group conflict by keeping the non-integrated aspects of group dynamics contained within stereotypic group roles. Just as member behaviour serves an equilibrating function for the individual system, so group-role behaviour does for the group. It is as if the group-as-a-whole delegates one or more of its members to perform group roles that will bind, contain, or express group problems or issues, while it assigns roles that will facilitate problem-solving work to other members, subgroups, or facets of the whole group.

Criteria for subgroup-role interventions

Subgroup-role interventions are designed to assist the group to become *aware* of the group-level defences and to develop problem-solving skills. The most important and most challenging use of group-role interventions is to help the group to identify and work through projective identification. Group-role interventions focus on the phenomena of "group voice" and "group container" and are basically the intervention of choice when the group is scapegoating. It is the intervention that requires the group members to own in themselves what they are attacking in others.

Group-role interventions assist the group to modify group-level defences and to develop problem-solving skills. A group-role intervention is the intervention of choice when it is appropriate to interrupt group scapegoating. It is the intervention that requires the group to make conscious and integrate the differences that the group has allocated to the scapegoat role. As group-level scapegoating entails group-as-a-whole acting out and projective identification, a successful group-as-a-whole intervention makes the dynamics conscious, undoes the projection, and confronts the denial. The integration work that follows serves as a powerful stimulus to therapeutic insight and development at both the group and the individual systems.

Individual and group-as-a-whole dynamics

This formulation of individual and group-as-a-whole as two discrete dynamic system perspectives from which to view group psychotherapy, with an emphasis on the hierarchical and isomorphic relationship between them, is my contribution to group theory. The practical implication is that individual members' role behaviour takes on additional meaning when it is seen in the group-as-a-whole context. Each individual's behaviour is interpreted both as a function of group dynamics and as a function of group dynamics. Therapeutic interventions are those interventions that potentiate both individual and group development as a complimentary activity, and neither one at the expense of the other.

NOTES

1. From a report of the work of W. Ross Adey and his co-workers at Loma Linda, California. [Reported in *Science News, 133* (No. 14, 2 April 1988), p. 216.]
2. Shannon and Weaver's "information theory" assumes that there is an inverse relationship between noise (entropy) and information (negative entropy) (Shannon & Weaver, 1964).
3. Festinger's (1957) "theory of cognitive dissonance" adds a useful dimension to thinking about the relationship between communication and behaviour.
4. Howard and Scott (1965), in their "Theory of Stress", describe all behaviour as problem-solving behaviour that approaches or avoids the problems that lie along the path to a goal.
5. Papers presented at this panel were published in a special section—"The Difficult Patient, the Difficult Group"—in the 1987 winter edition of *Group*.
6. Lewin's (1951) Field Theory concept of the life space defines behaviour as a function of the person's perception of the environment. Thus to know someone's "life space" is like having a map of how a person perceives his environment and to be able to predict how he will move in relation to the perceived barriers to his goal.
7. A chapter about SAVI as an instrument that can be applied to the training and study of the discipline of group-as-a-whole system therapy appeared in *The Process of Group Psychotherapy*, edited by Beck and Lewis (2000).

CHAPTER FIVE

The invisible group: an integrational theory of group-as-a-whole

Foulkes, in his *Introduction to Group Analytic Therapy*, says:

> While having an eye on each individual member and on the effects they and their utterances have on each other, the Conductor is always observing and treating the group as a whole. The "Group as a Whole" is not a phrase, it is a living organism, as distinct from the individuals composing it. It has moods and reactions, a spirit, an atmosphere, a climate. . . . One can judge the prevailing climate by asking oneself: "What sort of thing could or could not possibly happen in this group? What could be voiced?" The Conductor can gauge his own distance to the group by asking himself "What sort of thing could I say within this situation, and what could not be said?" In fact, it is the group as a whole with which the Conductor is primarily in touch and he experiences its individuals inside this setting. He should sense what this group needs at any given moment, be it encouragement, reassurance or stimulation, steadying or exaltation. [Foulkes, 1948, p. 7]

Y. M. Agazarian, "The Invisible Group: An Integrational Theory of Group-as-a-Whole" (Twelfth Annual Foulkes Memorial Lecture). *Group Analysis: The Journal of the Group Analytic Psychotherapy*, *22*, no. 4 (1989): 74–96 (reproduced by permission of Sage Publications Ltd., London).

I was particularly lucky in that Foulkes himself was the centre of the first group conference that I attended in England. He sat in the middle of a loosely defined large group—composed, I was to learn later, mostly of the Group Analytic Society—and what struck me most was the warmth that this British group radiated towards him. Thus, it is through "the prevailing climate" that surrounded him that I first knew S. H. Foulkes.

It is the warmth of this memory that I bring with me today, as I stand before you, honoured by your invitation to give the Foulkes Lecture. I offer this chapter in tribute to Foulkes as a pioneer in understanding group as a whole. And with the opening quotation, I wish to communicate both my "feeling" about Foulkes the person, the centre of a group that surely sensed that he could give "encouragement, reassurance or stimulation, steadying or exaltation, at any given moment" and the pioneer in understanding that "The 'Group as a Whole' is not a phrase, it is a living organism, [as] distinct from the individuals composing it" (Foulkes, 1948, p. 7).

For Foulkes, his experiences in Northfield and his knowledge of psychoanalytic theory led directly into his own group-analytic understanding of the group as a whole. My understanding came, not from my psychoanalytic background, but through training in group dynamics, applying group-as-a-whole principles first in workshops and later with my individual patients, whom I brought together in a group whose model was strongly influenced by Bennis and Shepard's "Theory of Group Development" (Bennis & Shepard, 1956). (They, in turn, of course, were strongly influenced by Bion, Foulkes's colleague.)

Bibliographies are a good statement of differences. Freud, Bion, Ruesch, and Bateson I have in common with Dr Foulkes. But whereas his bibliographical references are to psychoanalysis and psychology, mine are to the literature of group dynamics and to the theory of the social sciences: Field Theory (Lewin); Cognitive Dissonance Theory (Festinger); Problem-Solving Theory (Howard & Scott); Information Theory (Shannon & Weaver); an alternative model for Instinct Theory (Bowlby) the non-Aristotelian logic of "General Semantics" (Korzybski), and General Systems Theory (Bertalanffy).

Thus whereas, like Dr Foulkes, I have spent a lifetime concentrating on putting theory into practice and practice into theory, unlike Dr Foulkes, I am not a scholar. What I seem to do is to incorporate theory, and in some sort of conceptual assimilation process I find similarities in the apparently different theories and develop an organizing principle to integrate them (Agazarian, 1987f). Dr Foulkes said that groups have their own unconscious dynamics, distinct from the unconscious dynamics of the individuals composing them. This chapter is oriented around an ongoing development of group dynamic concepts that I first presented as the Theory of the Invisible Group (Agazarian & Peters, 1981).

The Theory of the Invisible Group is an integrational systems theory that spells out the structure and function of individual and group dynamics as two discrete but related systems. Invisible group theory is "invisible" in that unconscious dynamics are deduced (Agazarian, 1983a). It is a systems theory in that these "invisible" dynamics that manifest in group and individual behaviour are conceptualized as hierarchically and isomorphically related systems (Bertalanffy, 1969), which are goal-directed and self-correcting (Bowlby, 1969). It is integrational in that it explains the dynamics that occur in the group-as-a-whole from two perspectives that co-exist simultaneously in space and time and thus permit the observer to think about individual and group systems in any series of permutations and combinations that he might wish and to maintain an integrative set of organizing principles that permit him to keep his explanations clearly related to one, the other, or both (Agazarian, 1983b).

It is important to understand that this is a non-Aristotelian, hierarchical abstraction (Korzybski, 1948) and has absolutely nothing to do with the real, visible people in the real, visible groups. It is a discipline of systematic thinking intended to provide the group therapist with a frame of reference that will help him to understand and explain what happens in a group more simply and more usefully than he could without it.[1]

Lewin (1951) said that there is nothing more practical than a good theory. Foulkes said that group psychotherapy "must develop its own concepts in its own right and not borrow them from individual psychology" (Foulkes, 1964, p. 60). In Invisible Group Theory I have defined the unconscious dynamics of the group and the individual as two discrete but isomorphically related systems of dynamics: group dynamics and individual dynamics. From the Individual Dynamic perspective, individual psychodynamics are characteristically expressed in member-role behaviours, which are, in turn, modified by interactions in the group.[2] From the group-as-a-whole perspective, group dynamics are expressed in characteristic group-as-a-whole-role behaviours, which, by modifying the development of the group, result in modifying the individual members of the group.[3] Member role and group role are basic constructs in the theory and are defined later in this chapter.

Let me first turn to the practical application of the theory and give some examples of how interventions are framed when they are oriented towards monitoring the maturation process of the group-as-a-whole.

At the First Pacific Rim Congress in Tokyo, in October 1987, I was invited by Junichi Suzuki, who had trained in group analysis in England, to give a paper on my Group-as-a-Whole Theory and present its practical applications in a workshop. Here was a unique opportunity to put theory into practice and to test it.

When I work with a group, the primary mechanism that I monitor is the group's ability to tolerate differences.[4] This is based on an understanding that maturation is a function of the ability to integrate necessary discriminations of inner and outer reality. Hypothetically then, calling the group's attention to differences that are being denied will facilitate group development. This monitoring is particularly important in a new group, in that new groups tend to split into stereotype subgroups, to emphasize similarities and to resist even acknowledging differences, let alone integrating them. The challenge then was to see if this approach, which had led to success in demonstrating group-as-a-whole maturation in European and American groups, would apply to a new group of a different culture.

With a feeling rather like jumping off a high diving board, I decided to see if I could demonstrate the theory "live" by leading a Japanese demonstration group in which I would intervene in the phenomena of containment and splitting as they were manifested in the behaviour of the group-as-a-whole. There were, however, some salient questions in my mind that made the diving-board feel very high indeed. Do Japanese groups follow the developmental sequence that is familiar to me? Would Japanese members' behaviour signal the same group-role functions that I am accustomed to identifying? Would the cultural differences be so great, would Japanese interactions be so inscrutable, that I would not recognize the nonverbal communication patterns that signal group-level denial of a split?

Dr Suzuki agreed to "co-lead" the group with me. The group would be conducted in Japanese, and I would speak to the group in English, which he would re-interpret to the group in Japanese. My understanding of the group would come, not from what was being said, as I knew no Japanese, but only from how it was said, and by whom and in what context[5]—certainly an opportunity to test theory against relatively pure group behavioural data.

The initial work required of a group is the structuring of the boundaries. I have certainly found in practice that the ability of groups to work is very closely related to the structure of their boundaries. My first step in putting theory into practice, then, was to draw clear boundaries in space and time: a tight circle of chairs with a volunteer in each chair; clear instructions to the observers on the ground rules of observer behaviour; a precise outline of the starting and stopping times and the duration of the breaks; and an explicit task statement: "to demonstrate the group-as-a-whole model by experiencing the group-as-a-whole.

The group started. To my relief, my first concerns turned out to be unfounded. This Japanese group did behave in familiar ways and did follow the developmental lines that I recognized.[6] The group initially split into the predictable stereotype subgroups of beginning group development. The first split was between the older, wiser authority of the respected "elders" or "teachers" and the younger members of the group. The initial communication was within a subgroup of three male "teachers". After a short time, it appeared that power had been negotiated and an equilibrium reached. It was "as if" the "teacher subgroup" designated a representative who then talked to the young woman sitting next to him, with the nonverbal behaviour characteristic of a teacher–student interaction: he benign, looking down, "instructive", she bowing her upper body so that she could look up at him, smiling and respectful. Throughout the life of the group, this particular teacher–student interaction repeated itself, perhaps whenever there needed to be a representation of the cultural status quo. It was as if "he" represented the "elder" subgroup, the authority of the old tradition, and "she" represented the women in the group, their traditional role of deference to male authority.

However, as the group continued, it appeared that this young woman also seemed to serve a mediating role between the "elder" subgroup and the "female" subgroup. She alternated between interacting with the younger female members, who became increasingly verbal, and the "elder" beside her. Was she the "mouthpiece", as Dr Foulkes would say, for the younger subgroup? After one such interaction, there was a sudden, long group silence. The silence was then followed by an abrupt shift of attention, as if the whole group had "turned its back" on what had just happened.

Until then, the group had developed much as a traditional hierarchical group develops. Higher-status members spoke to other higher-status members, lower-status members spoke to higher-status members, and occasionally there was some sanctioned lower-status interaction. The brief apparent negotiation between the three higher-status men who formed the "teacher" subgroup had seemed to me to have the character of an approved delegation of authority rather than of a concealed fight, and thus had appeared to me to be an integrational move for the group, which I would not want to disrupt. Intervening when the group is in the process of solving its integrational problems is to intervene in the group's natural maturational process and is liable to foster group dependency. It is in this sense that diagnosing the difference between splitting that is part of the natural maturation process and splitting that is part of a defensive and potentially fixating process is important.

The sudden shift of group attention, however, did not seem to be a facilitative split. It felt to me almost as if the group had amputated part of itself in an effort to ignore whatever had just occurred. So I spoke, through Dr Suzuki, and said: "I wish to draw the attention of the group to the last few interactions." I then retraced the group process for the group. "The lady on my left spoke to the gentleman beside her. This was followed by a group silence. Then, whereas the group had been intensely focused this way (pointing to the teacher–student subgroup), the group suddenly turned its attention away from here to there (pointing). I wonder if", I continued, "the group work will be helped or hindered if the group agrees to ignore whatever it was that just happened?"

This is an example of challenging a group when it treats an event "as if" it had not happened. It confronts a group "secret" and requires the group to struggle consciously with a conflict that it would otherwise split off and deny, repress, and render unconscious.

It is consistently astonishing how "unconscious" the group is of such an episode. When I ask a group "what just happened", it is often impossible for any member of the group to answer, and it is only after I recall the event for the group that memory returns. At other times, a subgroup of members may in fact "know" but experience themselves as either unable or unmotivated to "own up"—and again, it is not until I recall the episode that the information becomes available. There are also, of course, times when I too lose my memory and am left only with a knowledge that something had just been split off, that I had intended to call it to the group's attention, but that I do not have—and sometimes never get—recall.

The next intervention that I remember vividly turned out to be more salient than I knew. The high-status–low-status communication pattern had shifted, and everyone was talking to everyone with considerable animation; members were glancing at me frequently, and saying my name with many different kinds of emphasis. I commented "that the group seems to be experiencing some conflict with my role in that I hear my name mentioned often and members are glancing at me and apparently talking about me". Little did I know that I had spoken at the time that the "elder" had been explaining to the group that "Ybon" does not understand us at all, and she should not be leading this group. The younger members of the group were intensely involved in the issue, including the young man sitting next to me, who had, at times, looked at me with great intensity, and who had surprised Dr Suzuki (as he told me later) by addressing him as "Suzuki-San" the title of an equal, and not with the customary title of "Sensei". So much for my Japanese group that I had feared would be inscrutable, courteous, conforming, and uninvolved. It had precipitated into a classic authority issue within the first session of the group process![7]

It is particularly tempting to connect my intervention to the group about "turning its back" on the interaction between the young representative woman and the teacher and the precipitous speed with which the authority issue occurred. If indeed the group had attempted to deny and repress the non-traditional interaction that had occurred within the subgroup that represented, for the group, the traditional relationship between male teacher and young female student, then my intervention had made the conflict conscious in the group. The precipitous authority issue might represent, then, a more overt attempt to split—to split off the deviance in the group by splitting off from the deviant leader and to regain the original status quo by reasserting the authority of the male teacher.

Perhaps, therefore, in this group, the authority issue towards me, the female leader, was less representative of the traditional split between "bad leader, good group" and more dynamically related to the group effort to extrude the difference that was represented by the shift from the customary role relationship between male and female authority, particularly a female authority who appeared to have salience for the younger subgroup. Bad enough that this group served as an arena for a leadership challenge voiced for the young men[8] but worse when the group voiced a shift in the young woman's traditional role. Developmentally, of course, the maturation potential for a group that explicitly voices its authority issue is much greater than for groups who can only imply it in their defensive behaviour.

The episode I wish to discuss next occurred at the ending of this group, which had worked for a total of 60 minutes: three 20-minute work sessions and two breaks. Continued group development had taken place. After the break following the authority issue, what looked like some group-as-a-whole interpersonal work had been done between subgroups. The subgroup relationships between the men and the women had shifted. An older Japanese woman teacher who had brought back with her from America some non-Japanese outspokenness and who had originally been excluded from the "authority" subgroup had some successful interactions. The younger women, as a subgroup, had seemed to relate to me nonverbally in a special way that I did not understand (and did not interpret) but had experienced profoundly. An interaction between three of the younger women had formed a significant part of the last session, one next to me on my right, one opposite me on Dr Suzuki's right, and the one to my left who had spoken the unspeakable to the teacher.

We were close to the time boundary. Looking at my watch, I said, "It is nearly time to say goodbye to the group." The young woman beside me on my right turned to me, held out her hand, and, with tears in her eyes, said, "Goodbye, Yvonne." I, much moved, and in a gesture that is foreign to my personal leadership style, took her hand and held it, and then with my free hand, gestured to the centre of the group. There was a long, still silence. Then the young woman beside Dr Suzuki stretched out her hand towards the centre of the group, followed by the third young woman to my left. (I can only guess at the many levels of symbolism, and of system dynamics, in my physically joining with the subgroup of young women.) Gradually, in the silence, one by one, the other members of the group stretched out their hands towards the centre. There was a pause, and the "elder" joined in. Another pause, and Dr Suzuki completed the group movement. There was a moment of stillness, in which all members reached towards the centre of the group, and the group-as-a-whole crossed its final time boundary.

Thus the group ended, having given an excellent demonstration of how the group-as-a-whole expresses itself through its members and how, at certain times, behaviour in a group is better explained through understanding group system dynamics than it is through the dynamics of the individual members.[9] It had also given me a proving ground for putting theory into practice. Making conscious the group splits had certainly not slowed group development, and the group had certainly touched on the early power phases of development, had confronted the group–authority split, and had done some work in the phase of intimacy.

Theoretical discussion

Foulkes said: "Each individual patient, if we put him into the centre of our consideration, can be caught in an attempt to repeat his own neurosis and its genesis and force its neurotic pattern on the others. Yet at the same time, these individuals between them—in their complex interactional network, produce a new dynamic field" (Foulkes, 1973, p. 180).

In my Theory of the Invisible Group, I have defined this new dynamic field as a group-as-a-whole system isomorphic to the individual system. The nuts and bolts of the theory are presented below.

Human systems are hierarchical

For example, a mother–child, a nuclear family, and an extended family are a hierarchy of human systems; so are individuals, small groups, organizations, and so on. Note that each system exists in the context of the system above it and serves, in turn, as the context for the system below it: thus the nuclear family exists in the context of the extended family and is the context for the mother–child.

1. The dynamics of systems in the same hierarchy are isomorphic—similar in structure and function.[10]
2. Systems are goal-directed, self-correcting, and equilibrating.[11]

They are goal-directed in that system locomotion is not random.[12] The goal of any living system within the environment is primarily to solve the problems that arise in the normal process of survival and only secondarily to solve the problems that are environmentally generated. They are self-correcting and equilibrating in that their internal equilibrium is maintained through a process of containing and/or integrating both the familiar and the unfamiliar information that is generated by the stimuli from within and without the system. This requires an ongoing discrimination and integration of internal and external similarities and differences.[13]

3. System-role behaviour is the observable, external expression of inner-system dynamics.[14]

Just as, at the individual system level, member-role behaviour serves an equilibrating function for the individual system, so group-role behaviour does for the group system at the group system level. It is as if the group-as-a-whole delegates one or more of its members to perform group roles that will bind, contain, or express group tensions while it delegates other members, subgroups, or facets of the whole group, to group roles that facilitate work.

4. System behaviour is the outer expression of inner-system dynamics. Therefore system behaviour implies the status of the system's dynamic equilibrium and the systems' primary and secondary goals.[15]

Primary goals are related to internal system survival: system maintenance and maturation. System maintenance requires making order out of chaos, structuring the systems boundaries of inside and outside, space and time, reality and irreality. Maturation depends upon how successfully the system-maintenance-role behaviour has related to these goals.

Secondary goals are related to external survival in the environment in which the system exists and can be generated from within or without. Successful achievement of environmental goals depends upon how successfully the system-task-role behaviour is related to these goals, and how congruent the system's secondary, external goals are with the system's primary, internal goals.[16]

Therefore all system-role behaviour is characterized as moving towards or away from "solving" the discrimination problems that lie along the path to its goal (Howard & Scott, 1965). Thus all role behaviour can be analysed in terms of its vector and salience characteristics (Lewin, 1951) in relation to both its primary and secondary goals.

When system primary goals and secondary goals are incongruent, the system's behavioural vector will be directed towards the primary goals, and it is only to the extent that the primary and secondary goals lie in the same direction that the system can take a path towards the secondary goals.

Role behaviour, therefore, contains the potential for both defensive and problem-solving communications: defensive, when the implicit goal of the system is to maintain internal equilibrium by keeping certain non-integrated information separately contained (maintaining the split); problem-solving when the goal of the system is to mediate with the environment (to discriminate and integrate the input/output communications between the system and the environment) and move along the path to its explicit goal.

Role behaviour thus serves as the major bridge construct in defining the systems of individual and group isomorphically. It is in this sense that system-role behaviour signals the internal state of the system and permits the therapist to monitor the balance of defensive behaviour (which signals system homeostasis) and problem-solving behaviour (which signals system re-equilibration).

In his introduction to his 1948 monograph, Dr Foulkes said:

> The healthy organism functions as a whole and can be described as a system in a dynamic equilibrium. Dynamic means that it is never in a state of rest—has constantly to adjust activity to the ever changing circumstances, environment and conditions in which it lives. [Foulkes, 1948, p. 9]

The practical advantage of conceptualizing the system "group" from two isomorphic perspectives (each one of which is seen as a system in dynamic equilibrium, mirroring the structure and function of the other) is that not only can the group therapist deliberately influence the dynamic equilibrium at either or both of the two complementary yet discrete system levels but also his learning about system dynamics becomes cross-fertilized and multidimensional. Thus, insight into individual dynamics leads to new understandings of group dynamics and insight into group dynamics leads to new insight into individual dynamics.

For example, as an individual therapist I was accustomed to thinking about the ego equilibrating mechanisms of defence, analysing those defences that contributed to resistance, and reinforcing those defences that contributed to health. Applying this isomorphically to the group level, it came as a marvel of serendipity that as a group therapist I could think in equivalent terms. As soon as I looked for them, sure enough, defences like denial, projection, reaction formation, and isolation manifestly operated at the group system level and could be interpreted successfully to the group-as-a-whole to reduce resistance to change.[17]

Then, in rethinking defence mechanisms as a function of group dynamics, it was suddenly obvious that "splitting", commonly thought of as a pathological mechanism,[18] was in fact a primary mechanism in the service of maturation in a group. With this new understanding of splitting came the answer to a question that I had been asking for years: what were the dynamics and function of group-as-a-whole projective identification? Simple: group projective identification is a system equilibrating function and is in the service both of system goal direction and system self-correction. Dynamically, the system "splits off" the differences that it is not sufficiently mature to integrate and projects them into a subsystem. Through denial and repression, these differences are "contained" within the boundaries of the subsystem, and these boundaries remain impermeable to information exchange until, at some later point in maturational time, the system is able to decode the information and integrate it.

Formulating splitting in this way permits it to be observed functionally. Thus, splitting into opposites, like splitting good and bad, is maturationally functional; it becomes pathological only if the system does not reintegrate the split.

In short, the process of integrating differences requires change. The work of perceiving and integrating differences must, by its very nature, disrupt system equilibrium. One way of maintaining the equilibrium of homogeneity is to isolate differences: to split off awareness and create a subsystem that will function as a container for the difference and thus preserve group equilibrium. When this process is applied to individuals and groups, these subsystems can be described in terms of system-role dynamics.[19]

What the therapist must monitor, then, is the potential for communication exchange between the subsystems in the group that contain the differences that represent both the potential resources for problem-solving and the potential for developmental fixation. When subgroup roles are in a state of valid communication, there is good potential for solving the problems along the path to primary and secondary goals. When subgroup roles are not in valid communication, then certain of the systems' resources are maintained in a state of either temporary or permanent fixation.

In order to demonstrate this in practice, I will now read to you an excerpt from a group that illustrates how conflicting forces are contained in a group in unacknowledged subgroups that maintain the split. Initially, as you will hear, there is only one group voice: the voice for exhaustion. Then a "marathon" voice emerges. You will see how, as long as the "exhausted" and "marathon" subgroups contain opposing forces, the group remains in a stalemated equilibrium; when these subgroups enter into valid communication, first a disequilibrium and then a reintegration takes place.

The script that follows is taken from the fourth session of a conference demonstration group. Nine members of the conference had volunteered for the group. In the three prior sessions, the same group had worked with three different leaders, demonstrating three different leadership styles. In this fourth session I was leading the demonstration of the group-as-a-whole.

I had started the group with clear time boundaries and a task instruction "to experience the group-as-a-whole". The groups' initial response was half-appreciative, half-angry, manifested first in sarcastic joking about leaders, past and present:

— ". . . Well, at least she spelled out our task very clearly, which none of the others did . . . except X, who told us that we were going to be depressed and thus gave us some structure!"

This was followed by wry joking about the group-as-a-whole:

— ". . . They left a hole here! . . . and we have to fill it!

— . . . How can we fill this hole? . . . How can we make this whole?

— . . . Well, at least we have the hole . . . if we have to fill it!"

The excerpt that follows comes after I had interpreted some of the group's defences and reinforced the boundary between the group and the audience.[20]

A male speaks to a female: "You look so depressed."

She replies: "I'm pooped."

— "You're pooped?"

— "Exhausted."

— "This tired you out?"

— "Yea. I wonder if the group-as-a-whole [*smiles*] can resonate with that? I know I'm pooped."

[*Group silence.*]

Leader: "Is the group going to leave all the experience of being pooped in one chair?"

This intervention assumes that the "pooped" member is voicing the fixating affect for the group which she is containing in a group role. It is the first step in the process of undoing a group split in order to release the affect and restore the group's ability to work. (Incidentally, when successful, this relieves the individual member of the overload of feeling that she carries for the group, as will be seen below.) The first step is to identify the individual in the group role as a voice for a subgroup, which this intervention does. The second step is to identify the subgroup function for the group-as-a-whole. The third step is to identify the group-role relationship between the subgroups in the group. The fourth step is to deduce the group goals that these subgroups have—are they maintenance or task goals? and are they congruent or incongruent?—and the final step is to encourage the group to make a conscious decision about how to proceed, given that the conflict that the group had previously contained in a split-off subgroup-role is now consciously experienced in the group-as-a-whole.

Following the intervention, a second female member joins with the "pooped" member: No, I'm exhausted, its been an exhausting experience. I don't know how much more I have left in me.

Then a third female: I don't feel that tired. After this is over I'll probably get more tired; after yesterday I was fine, and then all of a sudden I felt tired and exhausted, so I don't feel it when it's happening. . . .

Then a male with a different voice: I don't feel tired, I feel as though I'm getting started. I feel great and ready for a marathon!"

Subgroups are becoming identified: an "exhausted" subgroup and a "marathon" subgroup.

Third female: "Are you running tomorrow?" [*the New York Marathon is the next day*]

— "No, I meant a group marathon."

Second female: "Do you mean that?"

— "Yep!"

— "Do you mean that?"

— "Absolutely!"

— "You could go on and on?"

A third male: "I don't know if I would want to if it would keep generating a feeling of exhaustion."

— "You don't want to go on?"

— "I want to go on if we feel good, I don't want to go on if we keep feeling pooped and exhausted. I figure something else better go on."

Original female: "Mm . . . you can feel exhausted and still have good feelings."

Male: "Mm . . . I got an invitation that we have to share the exhaustion somehow."

It is at this point that I make a group-as-a-whole interpretation. You will notice that as the subgroup for "exhaustion" voices good feelings, the "marathon" subgroup considers taking in some exhaustion. There are, therefore, signs both of subgroup cross-fertilization and undoing of a split and also signs of a group-as-a-whole maintenance goal that is being served by "exhaustion". The intervention that follows acknowledges the position of the two subgroups and at the same time reminds the group-as-a-whole that it has the ability to set task goals that are congruent with its maintenance needs. I say:

— "I'm wondering if, for this group, it's rather as if its run three marathons already [*referring to the three previous groups*] and that right now the group is trying to decide whether it is worth it to summon up the energy to run a fourth, knowing that it's a short one and knowing that it's going to end . . ."

Locating the group within of the reality boundaries of time:

— ". . . or whether the group has earned the right to sit back, experience its exhaustion, and become aware of what it has already achieved? I sort of sense that the group's not sure whether it wants to put its energy into another marathon, or whether it wants to sit back and, in its exhaustion, process this experience."

A male: "In an attempt to process where we've come, I feel really good that we're a lot closer to one another now than we were in the last session: there is much less antagonism, hardly any at all."

As the group had become increasingly frustrated, there had been some destructive scapegoating in the previous session.

Group: "Mm."

— "For example, there was a disagreement between Izzy and Margaret about termination, but I didn't see any antagonism. I feel very close to everyone, I guess I like the feeling of our being together as a group."

The marathon subgroup is proposing the task goal of "processing".

A fourth female: "Well, I'm exhausted, and I like the first part of what you said. I wasn't sure I was ready for the second part, which was allowing myself to experience. That's the scary part. It makes me realize how much we tire ourselves out in avoiding things, how tired I am from trying so hard. And getting permission not to try so hard, that feels like, "wait a minute—into space—flight—where's the anchor—where's something to hold on to?" But it could be, it could be all right."

Another voice from the "exhausted" subgroup is considering the marathon! This supports the impression that making the subgroup goals explicit has shifted the group equilibrium, in that each subgroup is now processing the "difference" that was previously split off and isolated in the other. The group-as-a-whole is now in a functional disequilibrium.

[*There is a long (25-second) silence.*]

Male: "Not exhausted?"

Female: "Who?"

Male: "The person behind you[?]"

The remaining male: "It's almost as if its catching, this exhaustion, and I don't want to catch it. I don't feel like I was exhausted, but there's something! I kind of feel like I have to fight it off. Its either something that I'm supposed to be, supposed to feel. If all these people are feeling exhausted, there's not much I can do about it, so I can either join them or leave [*small laugh*] . . . but maybe it doesn't have to be that way. It doesn't have to be an either/or. Maybe I can be non-exhausted and that's OK too.

The marathon subgroup is working through the experience of disequilibrium, taking back what the exhausted subgroup had contained.

Original female: "Well, I thought we had another option which is to sit back and process what's been going on and—I don't think you need to be exhausted to do that."

[*The original voice for exhaustion is experiencing relief!*]

Female: "Yea."

Original female: "You don't have to catch my exhaustion."

Male: "Mm."

Original female [*smiling*]: "I may be getting my second wind!"

This is good example of how, when the group-as-a-whole repossesses what has been split off and contained in a group role, the member who has been containing for the group experiences relief. As one member put it in another group: "I simply don't believe in a hydraulic system of group process, but it is certainly true, when the group took all that back, it was as if my feelings drained away back into the group, and I watched the groups' feelings rise."

Male: "Yea, I was aware . . . that's great."

Original female: "But I was wondering if I could rally my energy again a fourth time—because this is very stressful."

[*A group silence of 25 seconds is broken by a voice for task.*]

Male: "You're smiling, David, what are you smiling at?"

— "Well, I'm just thinking Izzy I'm very relieved to hear that you're not feeling exhausted?"

— "No!"

— "Glad to hear that, because I was beginning to think I was the only one . . ."

— ". . . Ready for a group marathon?"

— "Right. Is there anyone else beside the two of us who is not feeling exhausted?"

A fifth female: "I'm not feeling exhausted. I'm feeling like I'm just being; just kind of experiencing, kind of wondering whether other people are experiencing or not. It's OK, it just feels comfortable . . ."

This voices group work on the assigned original task of "experiencing" the group-as-a-whole.

— ". . . I feel kind of concerned about you, Pearl, because you said you were so uncomfortable and you wanted to get off the stage. And this experience is not like that for me, and I'm hoping its not going to be like that for you. I'm hoping you're going to come away with something better than just discomfort."

The group is continuing to check out its membership. The voice for the task goal is much stronger, but there is still a silent subgroup whose maintenance status is not clear. Assessing membership strength is a very important step for a group that is re-equilibrating the congruence of maintenance and task goals.

Pearl: "Oh right now I feel fine, I feel very relaxed."
— "So it's changed for you."
— "It changed."
Original female: "It's changed for me too, I think maybe getting permission not to expend all that energy changes it, some."

It is also not unusual for an individual, who has experienced relief from the pressure of "containing" for the group to "explain" why she feels relieved in terms of familiar individual dynamics.

Male: "Maybe the exhaustion has something to do with you, Marie!"

The final member is polled! "No!" she says. The group maintenance check is now complete—every member is "OK", and the group is now re-equilibrated and ready to work.

In this group, the group-as-a-whole undid the split with little help from the leader. I do, however, wish to discuss the intervention procedure when the split-off information is not so easily accessible, when the voice of the group is not so easy to hear, when the subgroup roles are not so easily identified as in the example above.

When split-off information is denied—as it is in the group relationship to deviance, for example, which occurred later in this same group—or when it repressed and projected, as it is when the group forces the deviant into a scapegoat role, then some of the current approaches in group psychotherapy not only fail at the group level but can potentially increase the danger of fixating the developmental potential of the group. It is then that it is useful to be able to recognize the danger signals.

The group communication pattern to the deviant is an unfailing signal that the group is in the process of splitting off and denying information. The success of this pattern in maintaining the split rests in the fact that by its very nature it prevents a true exchange of information between the group-as-a-whole and the role. When the group "mascot" is indulged, the group "hero" is idealized, the group "patient" is cured, or the group "scapegoat", is scapegoated, the group has successfully dealt with difference by institutionalizing it in a stereotyped role relationship. The advantage is that the system remains in homeostatic equilibrium. The disadvantage is that the development of system complexity requires the integration of differences, and maturation potential is restricted when integration does not take place.

Applying this understanding of splitting and containing at the group level led me to understand and intervene in the process by which groups "contain" deviance in a way that is quite different from my understanding and intervention style when I looked only at the individual. For example, it was a great surprise to me as a group therapist to recognize how often both the group and I created a patient to cure when I and/or the group were stuck. It was not until I understood what the dynamics were that I could recognize that we were attempting to solve one group repetition compulsion with a different repetition compulsion and could then work to exchange this repetitive solution for group problem-solving.

One of the most important applications of this theory to therapy is, perhaps, in the management of deviance and scapegoating (Agazarian, 1987d [chapter 1, this volume]). From the individual perspective, scapegoating is a pathological event—an acting out, usually repetitively, of an old role relationship, usually originating in the family group.[21] From the group perspective, scapegoating serves a maturational function in the early phases of group development, containing differences that the group is not mature enough to integrate. There is an apparent anomaly in that "acting out" scapegoating is pathological for the individual system and developmentally potentiating for the group system. However, the early stages of group development—like the early stages of individual development—are not governed by the repetition compulsion, and therefore the potential for reintegration when the system has matured remains.[22] If, however, there is a fixation in development around the scapegoating issue, then the group system will mirror the problems of the individual system in repetitively containing in a scapegoat role an attempted solution to disequilibrium. The diagnosis of a group-as-a-whole scapegoating solution to deviant information is best made through observing the communication pattern. The scapegoating pattern has three phases: In the first phase, the scapegoat is ignored: he is breaking the group norm, and the group is signalling nonverbally that ostracism is the penalty for non-conformity. The group typically avoids looking at him or addressing him, and he is responded to only cursorily, if at all. The communication pattern looks like a five-pointed star, with a sixth point that is not connected by any lines. If the scapegoat gets the message and conforms, the group has solved its problem. If his deviant behaviour continues, the second phase of scapegoating is initiated, and the group puts overt pressure on him to conform. All communications in the group focus on him: the pattern is like a fan, each rib connecting a member in the group directly with the hub of the fan, which is the position the scapegoat is in. Members support each other with glances, smiles, shrugs, nods, and whispers, while a small subgroup will take the role of grand inquisitor and pressure for a conversion, sometimes by reason, sometimes by seduction, sometimes by bullying. In the third and final phase the communication pattern looks very like the first phase: the scapegoat is ignored, isolated, treated as if he does not exist, only this time—and this is different from the first phase—the group pressure on him to "disappear" from the group is so great that he typically does, either psychologically or physically.

The second phase of scapegoating arouses many therapists to mount a rescue attempt. I well remember intervening energetically to get the scapegoat off the hook, sometimes by punishing the group for scapegoating, more often by attempting to "cure" the scapegoat by getting him to see how and why he volunteered for the role. I was often surprised at how fervently I intervened—almost as if I was trying to stuff the insight into the patient. From the group perspective, of course, my "therapeutic" fervour is now clear. Moved by the dynamics of the group, I had actively joined the communication pattern to the deviant and was serving the group role of repressing the difference that the scapegoat contained. It comes as a shock to recognize that the familiar solution of the "identified patient" in psychotherapy groups is a form of scapegoating in disguise!

The second important dynamic issue that is well illustrated in the phenomenon of scapegoating is group-level projective identification. When this is understood in the context of the dynamic function of splitting off difference and, in this case, containing it encapsulated in the scapegoat, then the therapist's intervention of choice is to address the dynamic process at the group level. In making the group conscious that the scapegoat is serving a function for the group and making each individual member conscious of what, particularly, he is projecting into the scapegoat's chair that he himself does not want to own undoes both the individual and the group dynamic of projective identification.

SUMMARY

The Theory of the Invisible Group provides an observational framework that allows the therapist to observe group behaviour from two different but complementary perspectives, to observe a behavioural sequence and make inferences about both unconscious individual dynamics and unconscious group-as-a-whole dynamics, to understand that the scapegoat both volunteers and is volunteered for the role, to infer both individual and group-as-a-whole defences, to observe the ravages of the repetition compulsion and role-locks, and to facilitate insight into projective identification at both the individual and the group-as-a-whole levels. Without insight, both individuals and groups helplessly repeat patterns of behaviour that create more problems than they solve. With insight comes the potential for solving both individual and group problems.

When the focus is on both the individual and the group-as-a-whole, each group member can get insight into the context of the here-and-now group and the individual present, as well as their there-and-then personal past. The group therapist is no exception. When he seeks to understand what he contains for the group in his group role, he has both the group and individual systems as sources of information.[23] He can understand how his own voice is both a "voice of the group" and a voice for his own individual self. Therein lies his personal growth.

What Dr Foulkes says in his preface to his *Introduction to Group Analytic Psychotherapy*, written more than fifty years ago, still speaking to the heart of the matter today:

> in making all the members of . . . group active participants in the solution of their problems . . . it is not only the Group itself which benefits, but every single Individual can best develop his own individual personality. Although the Group is the field of operation, it is the optimal degree of liberation and integration of the Individual, which is the ultimate aim of this therapy. [Foulkes, 1948, p. 10]

NOTES

1. The importance of keeping one's frame of reference in focus is well demonstrated by the paradox of the barber. The statement goes: "The barber, in a small village, shaves every man who doesn't shave himself. Who shaves the barber?" The paradox lies in the fact that the meaning of a word is dependent upon its context and that context is determined conceptually by the level of abstraction: for example, the "general" level is the context for the "particular" representative of that level. Hence, when the barber shaves other men, he is a "barber", and when he shaves himself, he is a "man". Thus "barber" exists in the context of "mankind". When the levels of abstraction are confused, so are "barber" (general) and "barber" (particular). It is the man in the barber who shaves himself, and the barber in the man who shaves everyone else.
2. Foulkes said: "Each individual patient, if we put him into the centre of our consideration, can be caught in an attempt to repeat his own neurosis and its genesis and force its neurotic pattern on the others. Yet at the same time, these individuals between them—in their complex interactional network, produce a new dynamic field" (1973, p. 180).
3. Thus the psychotherapist—and every other "member" of the group—has the choice of understanding any single event in the context of the here-and-now of the present individual and group systems, as well as his personal group and individual past there-and-then systems. The group therapist's analysis of his own voice as a "voice of the group" requires an understanding of the group's here-and-now dynamics. His analysis of himself in the role of "group container", however, requires an analysis both of the here-and-now systems—the source of his countertransference or "member" dynamics—and also of his individual there-and-then systems, which will be the source of his own "person" dynamics in volunteering for the role.
4. Theoretically, I explain system maturation as a function of the ability to discriminate and integrate the similarities and differences: both the differences in the apparently similar and the similarities in the apparently different. What happens in a group when differences are too great to be integrated into the existing system organization? Then, the system splits off the difference and projects it into a "containing" subsystem. At some later maturational point in time, when the system has developed more sophisticated integrational mechanisms, it becomes possible to reintegrate the difference contained within the subsystem. Thus, from this perspective, the mechanism of splitting is a healthy maturational defence; it becomes fixating only if the splitting is not functional. One way I monitor the process is to draw the group's attention to behaviour that I think is signalling a potentially fixating split, thus making a preconscious process conscious.

5. "It is the process of communication rather than the information it conveys which is important to us" (Foulkes, 1964, p. 11).
6. The question is sometimes raised as to whether this approach is generalizable to all groups, considering that it has been developed in the context of my experience in psychotherapy groups. Theoretically, however, group dynamics (like phases of group development, goals, norms, structure, roles, and cohesiveness) are common to all groups, be they therapy groups, demonstration groups, training groups, or task groups. The type of group in and of itself does not change the system dynamics, and primary goal developmental issues can always be seen. (Primary goals are those of system maintenance and survival). It is the secondary—task—goals and the behaviour that relates to these task goals that are determined by the "kind" of group it is. It is also important to note that task achievement in ALL groups is largely dependent upon the compatibility between primary and secondary goals. It is therefore very important in all groups to pay attention to the groups' development of the ability to tolerate differences, so that the group can develop the maturity it needs to solve the problems that arise as it moves towards its goals. It is in this sense that this approach is generalizable to groups generally.
7. Dr Foulkes identifies issues with authority as one of the two basic problems of social life (Foulkes, 1964).
8. A confrontation by a young male towards a male leader was within the tradition (although surprising to my co-leader) and could therefore be integrated into the group.
9. As Foulkes said: ". . . in this sense processes occurring in the group, though seemingly emanating from any one individual, are not strictly speaking the property of that one person. That person is reflecting, acting as the mouthpiece, for the processes which are carrying in that group-as-a-whole" (Foulkes, 1964, p. 11).
10. What the GST principle of isomorphy means practically for the therapist is the ability to listen with the third ear to a group psychotherapy session hierarchically and hear, at one level, how each member's voice gives clues to his individual dynamic equilibrium, and at another level to hear how each member's voice speaks for the dynamic equilibrium of the group. It is not the issue here to develop the hierarchy, but it is relevant to those therapists who work in more than one context—a simple example being someone who is both a group therapist and an individual therapist to some or all of the members of the group. Then an individual's voice can be heard not only in terms of their member and group-as-a-whole system dynamics, but also as a voice for the overlapping membership of the individual therapy system dynamics. And to generalize still further, for a group therapist in an institution, both the individual and the group give voice to the dynamics of the ward system and the hospital system: and so

the generalizations go on up the system hierarchy: country; hemisphere; indeed all the worlds, great and small, of humankind.

11. By observing behaviour, hypotheses can be generated about system homeostasis or the dynamic equilibrium in which the dynamic field of force is held. In Field Theory terms we are talking about the force field that results from the equilibrium reached between the driving and restraining forces in the life space. Using Field Theory as a springboard, one can argue that, because behaviour is a function of the life space, when system behaviour is observed over time, hypotheses can be generated about the system goals. Thus, system dynamics can be conceptualized as a field of force, and the behavioural manifestation can be interpreted in terms of driving and restraining forces that relate to the goal that is implied by such a force field. All human behaviour is thus framed as an output or signal of the internal state of the particular human system that is being observed in its social context.
12. In his introduction to his 1948 monograph, Dr Foulkes said: "The organism acts as if it knows its aim and had a choice as to the means to achieve this aim" (Foulkes, 1948, p. 10; 1973).
13. A distinction is made in the Theory of the Invisible Group between inner-system dynamics and system-role dynamics. Thus, at the individual level there is a distinction between person inner-system psychodynamics, which result from genetic inheritance, developmental history, environmental influences, and past experiences, and member-role dynamics, which are a function of the interpersonal dynamics of the individual interpreted as a behavioural expression of past problem-solving role behaviours modified by the present interactions. These are usually expressed in reciprocal roles and enable the individuals to remain in dynamic equilibrium at the individual system and inter-system level. When this is applied to the group system level, group-as-a-whole inner-system dynamics are understood as a function of the group composition, developmental history, environmental influence, and past experiences, and group-role behaviour is understood as a function of subgroup-role relationships that enable the group to remain in a dynamic equilibrium.
14. Role behaviour, therefore, contains the potential for both defensive and problem-solving communications: defensive, when the implicit goal of the system is to maintain internal equilibrium by keeping certain non-integrated information separately contained (maintaining the split), and problem-solving when the goal of the system is to mediate with the environment (discriminate and integrate the input/output communications between the system and the environment) and move along the path to its explicit goal. (See also Notes 11, 12, and 13.)
15. The final building block in defining the dynamics of self-correcting, goal-directed systems is the formulation of the principle of system maturation:

a function of the system's ability to discriminate and integrate its discriminations.

Maturation and all other primary goal-directed behaviour can be defined as a function of the rate at which discriminations can be made and integrated: discriminations of similarities and differences: the different in the apparently similar, and the similar in the apparently different. This is true of systems as small as a cell, where secondary goals are largely determined by the intrinsic genetic code, and as large as society, where secondary goals are largely determined by the environment.

16. I hesitated, when I was formulating the functional aspect of splitting, to use the word, because it has such a "bad" connotation and is defined so often in the literature as a defence characteristic of borderline pathology. However, as I was reframing the function of "splitting" as a characteristic of system maturation rather than redefining the word, I did not change it. I have argued that the "healthy" splitting functions so that differences that are "too different" for the system to integrate are "contained" in separate and isolated subsystems until the system has developed sufficient maturity to integrate them (which is, of course, an essential process for successful therapy with borderlines).
17. Would Dr Foulkes agree? He already sees that " . . . splitting operates by splits in the group . . . literally manifested by different members or subgroups . . ." (Foulkes, 1964, pp. 288–289).
18. Then, when I re-translated this group systems understanding to the individual system level, another serendipitous insight occurred. I found that formulating the dynamics of group-as-a-whole projective identification had increased my practical understanding of individual therapy. (In group system terms, I am the subgroup "container" for the split-off and projected difference that cannot be integrated by the group system, and "I-group role" and "he-group role" and "we-group role" maintain the group equilibrium necessary for system maturation—a slightly different understanding from the more classical analytic one, which requires the analyst to "contain" and "metabolize" the split-off and projected aspect of the patient until the patient has developed sufficiently to integrate it, but one that fitted more closely to my inner experience that something had to happen in the interactive system of "both of us" before resolution occurred. This is an example of the advantage of an isomorphic, integrative theory that applies both to group and individual dynamics.
19. These interventions are:
    - "It seems to me that the stakes are very high for this group, having recognized that there is a hole in the group, the group can only count on a funny, ineffectual, irrelevant leader to help them with the job of confronting and filling that hole."
    - "It's very hard for the group to experience the group-as-a-whole if it

remains on the understandably more comfortable level of what it might be!"

— "In my short exposure to this group it does seem that the group has developed some very useful defences that keep it safe from exploring the hole that the group is afraid it has, and intellectualization has been a very useful way of making this group experience bearable.

— "There will be no crossing of boundaries between the audience and the group."

— "Again it seems to me that the group is using its valuable and useful escape into intellectualization, an escape perhaps away from the very thing the group wishes it could experience."

— "It's possible that another way that the group is using right now to prevent the experience is by talking very fast and maybe preventing the experience that comes up when one takes a deep breath."

20. Dynamically, it is an attempt to express the disequilibrium within the system dynamics in a containing behavioural role that "acts out" the internal conflict.
21. Perhaps "acting out" in the early phases of group development functions in the same manner as playing functions for the child?
22. Scapegoating occurs when the early developmental phase of group flight is giving way to group fight. During the flight phase, members solve differences through homogenous pairing. Members pair for power and control—power to protect against control by others, by the leader, by the group, by unconscious forces; or power to control others, the leader, the group, unconscious forces. The fight phase introduces heterogeneity. People who are unlike fight, and in the process of resolving the fights, members come to terms with differences. However, there are differences that the group is not able to integrate, and the group solution is to project them into a deviant member who will contain them for the group. In the process of integrating the scapegoat, the group comes to tolerate some of the differences that were previously intolerable, and these differences thus become available to the group as resources that would otherwise have been split-off and remained unavailable had the scapegoating been resolved through conversion or extrusion.
23. This is perhaps what Dr Foulkes knew well: "The group reacts as a whole and not merely as the sum of its individual members. The transference reactions of the group as a whole are a different matter from the transference situations of the individuals concerned" (Foulkes, 1964, p. 24).

CHAPTER SIX

The phases of development and the systems-centered group

> Group development: a crucible, a relentless, uncompromising, inexorable pressure on the outer shell of defences—burning hot and cold—a ring of fire around the inner core of ash—transformation—and the many-splendoured phoenix.

Systems-centered theory approaches all living things, whether as small as a cell or as large or larger than society, by defining them as systems that are similar in structure, function, and dynamics. This then sets up a hierarchy of classes of living systems where each class, and every member in it, has a set of common factors that apply to all classes in the hierarchy; and each class, and every member of each class, is unique unto itself! The advantage of describing all living human systems isomorphically in this way is that what one learns about the dynamics of any one system says something about the dynamics of all the other systems in its hierarchy (Agazarian, 1997).

Y. M. Agazarian, "The Phases of Development and the Systems-Centered Group". In: M. Pines & V. Schermer, *Ring of Fire: Primitive Object Relations and Affect in Group Psychotherapy* (London: Routledge, Chapman & Hall, 1994), pp. 36–85 (reproduced by permission of Thomson Publishing Services, London).

It is through the discrimination and integration of similarities and differences that systems develop from simple to complex (Agazarian, 1989a). The system of the group-as-a-whole develops from simple to complex by splitting into differentiating subgroups that have the potential to remain in communication with each other across their boundaries (Agazarian, 1989a). In a systems-centered group, the basic unit is not the individual member, but the subgroup (Agazarian, 1989d).

In the systems-centered approach to the phases of development in group psychotherapy, the group is not left to develop "naturally" while the therapist "contains" the process and judiciously interprets it to make it conscious to the group, as is the case when the approach is primarily psychodynamic. Rather, group forces are deliberately exploited; certain group behaviours are deliberately encouraged, others discouraged; and all dynamics are legitimized so that they can be explored and understood (Agazarian, 1992c [chapter 9, this volume]).

Functional subgrouping

In systems-centered groups, the primary task is to develop an interdependent problem-solving system so that the work of therapy is done in the process of learning how to do the work of therapy. From the first few minutes of the very first group, members are actively discouraged from withdrawing into themselves with their pain—or into fantasy to avoid their pain: they are encouraged to work interpersonally, to talk to the group or to a particular member, and to stay connected to each other. This sets up a work style of supportive mirroring, which is the key to the therapeutic power of functional subgrouping.

The very process of learning to subgroup requires members to relate to others as well as to themselves. Members learn that there is an important difference between encouraging another member's work, paying lip service to subgroup work, and joining the subgroup with heart as well as words. When the members have difficulty working, rather than being encouraged to struggle through their resistances (as in patient-centred therapy), they are encouraged to turn to their subgroup and make space for a fellow member who has more immediate available salience for—or less resistance to—the next step. In this way, the member who starts to work "rests" without guilt when he can go no further, while others in his subgroup continue to work. Resonating with the subgroup work, the "resting" member takes his own next step when he is ready.

It is important to emphasize, however, that learning to work in subgroups is no easy task. For many members, being required to join a subgroup is experienced as a violation of individuality. Joining a subgroup is like learning a social role. It requires devoting the self to the subgroup goal, selecting from the internal range of responses those that build upon and deepen the experience that is being built and deepened by the work of the subgroup. Spontaneity in resonance with the group is an intimate and healing experience. Failures in resonance result in solo activity. At best, the solo individual relates to the group—or the self—as if to an audience, and, at worst, he recreates the experience of being forever alienated and isolated, alone. No matter how great the pain and frustration of isolation however, joining can be experienced as a compromise, or even a violation, of the essential sense of self.

Containing

"Containment" is a central concept in systems-centered group psychotherapy. Differences generate conflict, yet systems mature and transform through recognizing and integrating differences. When differences are similar enough, they are integrated with less conflict. When differences are too great, however, they are split off and projected into *containing* subsystems. This resolves one level of the conflict and creates another.

The simplest management of differences in human systems is to contain them in stereotype subsystems with stereotypical communications. This is easily done when differences are manifestly obvious, as in gender, race, age, or status. Dynamic differences cannot, however, be so easily stereotyped. The most predictable "containers" of dynamic differences, manifest at every level in the hierarchy of human systems, from individuals to societies, are the containing subsystem roles of the identified patient and the scapegoat.

In groups, there is great resonance between the delegation of containing roles like the scapegoat or the identified patient, and the individual member salience for playing the roles. Perhaps it has always been too much to expect individual group members to contain their impulses to act out, when their own conflicts in development are re-aroused and aggravated by the conflicts in the developing group.

In systems-centered groups it is the subgroup, not the individual member, that is required to contain different sides of predictable "splits" around difference. When the group-as-a-whole works to "contain" the conflict consciously as a working task, then it is no longer necessary to delegate conflicting differences to a scapegoat, an identified patient, or a deviant pair. In this way, the group learns to exploit the natural tendency to split the "like me and good" from the "not like me and bad". By *deliberately* containing the good/bad split in different subgroups, each side of the split can be explored with less conflict than when it is contained as different parts of the inner self. By employing the technique of functional subgrouping, the mechanisms of splitting and projection are utilized rather than pathologized. When these mechanisms are seen as functional, there is less pressure to deny or repress their manifestations (Agazarian & Janoff, 1993).

Psychodynamics within the systems frame

"Systems theory" is a meta-theory (Bertalanffy, 1969; see Agazarian & Janoff, 1993) Thus, framing dynamics from a systems-centered point of view adds an additional dimension to the psychodynamic framework. There is a significant compatibility between psychodynamic and systems constructs. Psychodynamic constructs of the "ego", the "id", and the "superego", for instance, can be re-defined as interdependent subsystems without changing the frame. Both psychodynamic and systems therapists would agree that therapeutic outcome results from modifications of the "communications" across the boundaries between the ego, the id, and the superego "subsystems". Dynamically, monitoring "transactions across the boundaries" results in changes in the *permeability* of the boundary between the superego and the ego, changes in selectivity in the transfer of information across the boundary between the ego and the id, and changes in the "ability" of the ego to discriminate, process, and integrate information across the boundaries within, between, and among systems at all levels of the abstraction hierarchy. Importing systems thinking imports clear guidelines for structural and functional interventions that may complement and strengthen the effectiveness of dynamic interventions.

Similarly, Anna Freud's work on the ego mechanisms of defence translates directly into the operational definitions for restraining forces at boundaries between, within, and among systems (Agazarian, 1989c [chapter 5, this volume]). Jung's "collective unconscious" is implicit in any understanding of the system of the group-as-a-whole. Melanie Klein's (Hinshelwood, 1989) important work on splitting, containing, and projective identification is fundamental both to understanding the human dynamics underlying the systems perspective and to the generalization of the systems framework to object relations theory. And, of course, Bion's (1959) Basic Assumptions of fight/flight, dependency and pairing not only generalize to, but also enrich and deepen the understanding of system dynamics as applied to systems of human beings (Agazarian, 1989e).

What the systems-centered orientation introduces to the psychodynamic approach is not a competing theory but, rather, different strategies, theoretically derived from hypotheses about how human systems function, that may well provide a more efficient way of developing the structure for regressions "in the service of the ego". However, although the psychodynamic constructs are compatible with systems constructs, they may conflict when used as a language for interpreting the development of the group system. What becomes abundantly clear is that the human tendency to discharge hostility in punitive language can find an easy expression by pathologizing normal system dynamics. In the early phases of group development almost all therapist communications, however descriptive, are experienced as superego injunctions. Inevitably, before the modification of the relationship with authority, interpretations of unconscious motives, however empathic, vastly increase group anxiety, defensiveness, and dependency. What is worse, when the members imitate the intervention style of the therapist—as all members do before they gain autonomy in the group—their interpretative style is not only an identification with the aggressor, but also an effective method of turning communication into ammunition in the power, control, and status fights of the first phase of group life (Agazarian, 1989e).

It is for this reason that systems-centered therapists talk, not in the language of pathology, but in terms of difficulties, inherent to the human condition, that are general manifestations of developmental issues aroused by the phases of group development, and dynamics that are central to the development of all living human systems. It is also for this reason that the focus of attention is not on *interpretation* but on *communication*: not on *content* but on *context*.

Context vs. content

A focus on the context and function of communication rather than its content is an acquired skill. The systems-centered therapist neither interprets individual dynamics, nor attends to the denotations and connotations of the content in the communications of the individual members. Rather, the focus of attention is on the communication transactions between subgroups. Just as in the early days of psychoanalysis it became necessary to learn how to understand communication in relation to its unconscious meanings, so now, in the early days of systems analysis, it is necessary to learn to understand communications in relation to their potential for transferring information across the boundaries in space and time: among, within and between systems in the hierarchy.

This requires understanding communications as driving and restraining forces that balance the system in relation to its goals (Agazarian, 1989a). Reducing restraining forces in communication is achieved by reducing the defences in sending and receiving. Reducing defences in the sending and receiving of transactions involves influencing the permeability of boundaries to the information contained in the communication. Influencing boundaries entails the management not only of boundaries in time and space but also those between reality and irreality. Reducing the restraining forces to communication transactions across the boundaries within, between, and among all systems in the hierarchy *is* therapeutic change!

Lewin's force field (1951) serves as an excellent model of the relationship between driving and restraining forces to communications at the boundary. Lewin recognizes these forces as "vectors" that have direction, velocity (energy), and a point of application. As a dynamic concept, he defines tension as oppositely directed vectors, which is also his understanding of conflict. Communication transactions across systems boundaries can, therefore, be understood as forces in conflict, and the drive to communicate and the defences against communication can be defined in a force field of the group's behaviour.

At the level of interpersonal communication this is isomorphic to the psychodynamic attention of managing the permeability of the boundaries between the conscious and the unconscious: increasing boundary permeability when obsessive defences predominate, decreasing permeability when there are regressive defences. Decreasing or increasing the permeability of boundaries depends upon the relationship between conflict and context. This has great significance when applied clinically to the fragile or brittle patient "as systems". When there is poor discrimination between the boundaries within the system as well as between the system and the environment, as there is with many regressive patients, it becomes important to increase the *awareness of context* before any change in the fluidity or rigidity of boundaries is made, so that internal boundary management is developed *in the context of the environment*.

It has been emphasized that transformation occurs as a function of both the system's ability to integrate discriminations of similarity and difference and the time it takes for this process to take place. In groups where boundary permeability is a major problem, the speed with which discriminations are made and integrated becomes an important factor. System goals are primary and secondary: primary goals are those of survival and development; secondary goals are those of environmental mastery. When boundary management is related to survival and developmental goals, the process of re-discrimination and re-integration takes more time.

Monitoring boundary permeability does not mean that the systems-centered approach represses the underlying primal experience of the underworld of the unconscious which arouses such annihilating terror and primitive defences in the group; but, rather than allowing the underworld to surface in the early phases of group, the systems-centered focus ensures that the group first builds a structure so that regressions are in the context of group development. In each phase a different structure is generated as a containing context for the individual confrontation of the terror engendered, both from primitive conceptions and also from the primitive defences against them.

In the first phase of development, when the group makes the transition from the good to the bad leader, the individual members also struggle with annihilating fantasies towards the therapist in the unconscious displacements to the group's identified patients and scapegoats. The primitive experiences of murderous rage towards the therapist occur in the controlled regression of the authority issue in the group-as-a-whole. The nightmare fantasies in the underworlds of human experience are brought to light in a context where they can be modified in here-and-now reality.

In the clinical field we are increasingly paying attention to the difference that our clinical orientation makes to how dynamics manifest in groups. Take, for example, the differences in approach to the "identified patient" and "scapegoat" roles. One approach will analyse the unconscious motives of the individuals, another the interpersonal repetition compulsions or the role suction, another the games people play; still another will focus on the here-and-now function of the behaviour for the developing system. As the twig is bent, so the bough grows.

Even more important to our field is the question of how we tell the difference, in our work in therapy, between when we address issues that are generic to treating human ills and when what we address are iatrogenic, regressive, or defensive constellations elicited by our own clinical interpretations (Agazarian, 1989e). In other words, when is our practice a function of our own rationalized projective identifications, which require human containers for the differences that we and our society cannot bear, and when is it a function of enabling us to cross the boundaries between our different human systems so that we can work together towards our therapeutic goals? Looking at our work through systems eyes and understanding the immutable influence of phases in the development of human group systems may be a step towards this important discrimination.

Discovering the group-as-a-whole

Bion (1959), a pioneer in thinking about the group-as-a-whole as a system independent of the people who were its members, lived at a time when either/or thinking was the norm. Bion was aware that groups dealt with different issues in relation to each other and to authority, and he observed consistent defensive responses to the internal conflicts that exist in the group, independent of the individual member conflicts. But he failed to observe that these conflicts tended to occur in a sequence. As Bion worked less than two months with groups, the marvel is not that he did not see phases of group development—although it would have been a useful influence on the development of group dynamic theory and practice if he had—but that he saw as much as he did.

In order to apply systems thinking to groups, it takes the ability not only to quantum-jump levels of abstraction, which Bion certainly must have possessed in order to formulate his Basic Assumptions as properties of the group-as-a-whole rather than the individual, but also the willingness to think about human beings beyond the psychoanalytic definitions for being human. Bion certainly possessed the background. He was acquainted with Lewin's Field Theory and Bertalanffy's General Systems Theory, each of which offers objective, dispassionate models for human behaviour. Bion, however, chose to frame his thinking about the group-as-a-whole through Klein's concepts of psychotic anxieties and the defences against them. Hence his Basic Assumptions of fight/flight, pairing, and dependency, and hence, also, his all-too-brief relationship with the dynamics of groups. Ganzarain (1989) reports Bion's rueful reply when questioned on this: "Paula Heimann and Melanie did not like analysts working with groups!" then, "That sounds pretty childish!" and "I guess I had already made my contribution . . . hence, I moved on, to explore another topic . . . psychotic thought".

The consequences for Bion and for the new group-centred paradigm in group psychotherapy was a focus on psychopathology and psychosis, in contrast to an exploration into dynamic formulations compatible with, for example, the principles of Field Theory and General Systems Theory. I was perhaps luckier than Bion in that my first analyst introduced me to Shannon and Weaver's Information Theory and thus to the concept of "noise", defined as the entropic resultant of the ambiguities, contradictions, and redundancies inherent in man's communication with man. There is an inverse relationship between the noise in the communication process and the potential for transferring information in the process (Shannon & Weaver, 1964; Simon & Agazarian, 1967). The greater the noise, the less predictive probability, and therefore the greater the chaos. Chaos, defined in terms of "noise"—random or uncoded information—is a researchable construct that reflects the universal rhythm of organization and disorganization, matter and mass, entropy and negative entropy. Noise is assumed to be inherent in the input and output communication transactions that cross system boundaries at all levels of the system hierarchy and reflect, on the one hand, the inner state of the system and the primary system goals (survival and development), and influence, on the other, the system's relationship with its environment, the environment itself, and the attainment of the systems' secondary goals (environmental mastery) (Agazarian, 1986b).

Thus in formulating the dynamics of group, I had available to me the concept of "noise" to make sense of the primal forces underlying group experience. I understood the dynamics of primal forces to be, not kin to psychosis, as they are so often interpreted, but as de-differentiated information: chaos,[1] in the sense that the manifestations of the dynamics of groups cannot be predicted, although their principles can be hypothesized. It can be assumed that man has an instinctive compulsion to "make sense" of the unknown. Primary "sense" is primitive sense: archaic, anthropomorphizing, primordial, chaotic, often experienced as psychotic. Thus each new experience arouses the terror of the unknown combined with curiosity about it, which fuels the impulse to explore, organize, and master.

Discovering phases of group development

An intensive comparison of the different theories of group development, in both social psychology and in psychology, has been made by Ariadne Beck (1981). She found that although different authors had different labels for the different events that they observed in groups, the sequences and descriptions of those events were consistent across writers. However, even though phases of group development have been discussed in the literature since the 1950s, they are still not a commonly accepted reality among group psychotherapists! Yet there is an evident and predictable sequence of phases in group development to be seen if the therapist knows where to look. Seen or unseen, each phase has a different and forceful impact on what happens to a group. When seen and understood, these forces can be deliberately harnessed in the service of the therapeutic goals; when not, their impact goes unidentified and unaddressed. Hence the stereotypic and repetitive creation of the roles of "identified patient" and "scapegoat" in therapist-oriented and patient-oriented—and even some group-oriented—psychotherapy groups.

Bennis and Shepard (1956) did the original work that resulted in the sequence of group developmental phases described in this chapter. Their work on group development was based on their observations of repeated and consistent sequences of individual behaviour that occurred in groups of university students whom they observed over a period of more than five years. They categorized these predictable sequences of events into phases of group development. Theoretically, they were influenced by Sullivan and Bion, particularly by Bion's Basic Assumptions about group defences of dependency, fight/flight, and pairing. Bion, in his turn, had been greatly influenced by his analyst, one of the pioneers in the development of object relations theory: Melanie Klein. Thus the concepts of "containment" and "projective identification" are implicit in Bennis and Shepard's (1956) group developmental theory, as are, indirectly, the underlying issues of Klein's depressive and paranoid–schizoid positions. Bennis and Shepard observed two discrete phases in group development. They called the first phase "dependence—power relations" and the second phase "interdependence—personal relations". They noted that the leader-oriented *Phase I* gave way to the group-oriented *Phase II*, separated by an important transformational "barometric event". They noted two predictable subphases in Phase I: the first a more passive phase of flight and the second a more active fight phase during which the group progresses from passive stereotyping to active scapegoating, first of each other, and then of the leader. Scapegoating the leader is not always overtly hostile. It can be manifested by covertly seducing the leader into membership or denigrating the leader as an incompetent. In fact, in therapy groups, as distinct from training groups, it is often easier for the group to covertly seduce authority than to challenge it overtly.

A group that successfully overthrows authority temporarily resolves the conflict around good and evil by splitting: locating "evil" in the "bad-leader", and "good" in the "group-as-a-whole". Bennis and Shepard (1956) called this "barometric" in that after a successful confrontation of the leader the group energy is freed from the compelling struggle with authority and is turned, instead, towards issues of intimacy. In the five years that they observed their student groups, Bennis and Shepard noted that it was not unusual for the group to remain in the first phase of development throughout the 17-week term, either failing to reach, or aborting, the direct confrontation with the leader. Unfortunately, it is not unusual for the therapy group to remain in the first phase of development throughout its entire life. In systems-centered terms, there has not been sufficient system development for the "transformation" to occur.

Individual and group development

Before describing the phases of group development from the systems-centered point of view, it is important to point out that whereas there are many similarities between the phases of the development of a group and an individual, there are also important differences.

For example, the developmental phases of a group parallel but do not correspond to the developmental phases of an individual at the manifest level. The dynamics of the human baby can be described (for instance) as characterizing, first, a paranoid–schizoid developmental position and, second, a depressive position in the important process of separating and individuating into a differentiated human being. Group dynamics can be described as manifesting behaviour more typical of the depressive position in the struggles for power and control in the first phase of group development, and moving into—regressing into—the paranoid–schizoid position in the second phase, when individuals in the group attempt to develop intimacy with each other. This does not deny that the fragmenting terror of the world of partial objects is lurking beneath the more manifest struggles for power and control. (So, too, in human development, the dynamics of the paranoid–schizoid phase lurk under the depressive in the socializing development of the child.) It is axiomatic that the terror present in the beginning moments of a beginning group is a nameless rather than an un-named dread, as is well understood by Ashbach and Schermer (1987): "The void . . . is the *absence* of information, direction, connectedness . . . which attends a situation where structure is minimal. . . ." Although the authors are referring to individuals, their words apply equally well to all human systems. Notwithstanding the presence of these dynamics in the first phase of group development, the paranoid–schizoid dynamics are not *manifest* until the second phase.

In the first phase, the group first denies its paranoid rage and, in a reaction formation familiar to every therapist, creates a patient to cure of the dependency hunger that is feared in the self. This is the solution of compliance with authority in the hope that in passive followership the self may be actualized—thus the identified patient, who contains for the group the anguished cry for someone to be able to depend upon, and who is offered up to the therapist by the group for an analysis interminable. When this solution fails, the defiant, rebellious, paranoid rage breaks through the reaction formation, targeted first towards the scapegoat and ultimately towards the therapist. It is the whole object that the group wishes to destroy. From the depths of the experience, it is true that the fantasies in the group are primal and bloody: however, the cry is that there is room for only one object: it is either you or I. When these dynamics are acted out in society, leaders are murdered, as are the followers in the ghettos; and when society's reaction formation turns its identified patients into scapegoats, the programs are directed towards society's helpless and homeless as well.

Being able to discriminate between the initial power/control phase and the later intimacy phase of a developing group can be clinically important for the individual patient. For example, insight for individual members into individual dependency and counterdependency, relationships to authority, and work with their underlying depressive dynamics all occur most easily in the first phase of group development, and insight into individual issues of interpersonal closeness and distance, love addiction, loneliness, alienation, despair, and work with the underlying paranoid–schizoid dynamics occur most easily in the second phase. When individual work is "in phase", members in the group spontaneously access memories and feelings that serve as stimuli that are relevant to the general work and specific to their own. The loss of an apparently appropriate new member, however, may well bewilder a therapist who does not "match" the member to the developing group phase. In a developing group, the dynamics of each phase of development are available as a major force that has impact upon the individual experience. Within each member, salient developmental issues are aroused that resonate with the issues that the group is in the process of mastering. Thus, groups provide the context in which individual developmental issues are revisited. Group members mature as the group learns to work and to love and to play!

The issues on the surface in the first phase of group development have to do with members' dependency upon the therapist and competition with each other. Therefore it appears that the manifest human dynamics in the first phase of group development are developmentally equivalent to the struggle for individual autonomy. Indeed, the behaviour and content in the group reflects this. The projections in the interactions between the members in the group are fully object-related, in spite of the fact that the projections also contain dynamics that are not. The creation of the identified patient and scapegoat are certainly a function of projective identification—the splitting-off from the self the unacknowledged and unconscious parts of the self, projected into another. However, the group roles themselves are a function of the repetition compulsion, and the group work with the *people* who are volunteered into these roles is object-related. The communication patterns between the group and the identified patient or deviant, for example, are *socially* stereotypic, as is the content.

Underlying system dynamics are no different, whether the "groups" observed are therapy groups, training groups, or groups of people working on a board or in committee; and no different in organizations, or even in nations! What makes the difference to the work of any group system are not group dynamics but the clarity of the relationship between the dynamics and the goals. Group structure is related to function, and group function is related to group goals. Appropriate boundaries, therefore, are boundaries that are both permeable to information and able to contain the information so that it can be organized into a driving force in relation to the group goals (Agazarian, 1992c). The major difference between training groups and therapy groups in this task is that the task of the training groups is most often to make boundaries more permeable, whereas in the therapy groups the task is often to make them appropriately permeable. The more inappropriately permeable the boundaries, the greater the danger that undifferentiated information will flood the system.

In systems-centered group therapy, therefore, group-as-a-whole boundaries are developed to *contain* the regression in the *group* before any regression in function takes place. Thus some facility in opening or closing boundaries at all system levels has been developed *before* the group works on the goals that have brought the members into therapy. Before the group addresses the issues of organizing the information stored in the chaos of the primary process, skills in information organizing have already been acquired. That this structural work in no way dilutes the experience of the primary process but, rather, increases both access and insight is illustrated later in this chapter.

Phases of development in the systems-centered group

There are many paths to a goal. The goals in systems-centered therapy are the same as those of psychodynamic therapy, but the ways of reaching them are different. The development of a group results from an interplay of the same forces that characterize the process of development of any human system: separation, individuation, integration, and transformation. All human systems move from primal dependence to independence and interdependence, and the course is determined by successive integrations of approach and avoidance forces (Agazarian, 1989c [chapter 5, this volume]). From the systems-centered perspective, the relationship between developmental forces and the developmental goals is related to systems and is manifested in "roles", not in "people". The "people" who occupy these roles are "transients" playing a part in the work of the group.

Roles as subsystems

For example, developmental dynamics around dependency are not interpreted as a property of "dependent" or "counterdependent" *individuals* but, rather, as approach and avoidance forces. These forces are manifested in roles (Agazarian & Peters, 1981). "Roles" are subsystems, characterized by boundaries and goals, that serve a dynamic system function. Roles maintain a system equilibrium while the system develops interdependence. For example, in the passive phase of *flight*, the group "identified-patient" role is created to contain the group's passive and helpless dependency, offered to the "good" leader to nurture and cherish. In the active *fight* phase, the group "scapegoat" role is created to contain the active deviance, in an attempt to bind the murderous rage so that the bad leader is not destroyed. However, which members will occupy these roles is not predetermined. Many will volunteer, but few will be chosen! Thus dependent or counterdependent forces are contained in subsystems of systems—isomorphic (similar in structure and function)—and can be observed simultaneously at the system levels of member, subgroup, and the group-as-a-whole. Compliant over-dependent and defiant counterdependence roles are a constant in the first phase of group development and perform a special containing function in the development of functional dependency. Similarly, in the second phase, containment of blind trust and fusion on the one hand and mistrust and alienation on the other are not the property of "over-personal" and "counterpersonal" individuals, but roles that are in service of functional separation and individuation.

In systems-centered groups, the norms of working not alone but always in a subgroup make it more difficult for the group to create either an identified patient or a scapegoat and easier for the group to subgroup around understanding the conflict that the group is attempting to master by setting up the roles. The identified patient, for example, contains for the group the wish both to be helped and to help, as a defence against helplessness and in the service of masochism. The scapegoat, on the other hand, contains for the group the wish both to victimize and to be a victim, as a defence against differentiating and in the service of sadism. In both cases, promoting functional subgrouping to explore the issues contained in the roles is rewarding for the members and resolving for the group-as-a-whole. This is particularly important in the case of vulnerable patients. In the containing structure of a subgroup, for example, the patient who does not yet have the ability to feel compassion either for himself or for others can be "held" while his subgroup contains the regression necessary to understand the impulses involved in scapegoating or creating the identified patient. When the vulnerable patient expresses, for example, his sadism without the expected retaliation and is, at the same time, able to listen to other members explore, compassionately, both the experience of being sadistic and being the target of sadism, the potential for future interpersonal connections is made.

In the pages that follow, I have addressed the expected course of development as outlined by Bennis and Shepard (1956) and my own earlier work (Agazarian & Peters, 1981) as well as the modifications that are introduced by the systems-centered techniques of functional subgrouping. When subgroups contain different sides of the group "splits" and the group-as-a-whole "contains" the conflict as a working task, it is no longer predictable that conflicts will be projected into a scapegoat, an identified patient, or a deviant pair. In systems-centered theory, system development results in an interplay of forces inherent in separation, individuation, integration, and transformation.

Phase I: leader-oriented

When social behaviour fails, as it must in a therapy group, the group first coalesces around creating a deviant role as a container for the projectively identified aggression. This takes the form of creating first an identified patient, and later a scapegoat, a hero, or a cause. Creating an identified patient or a scapegoat is often considered a difficult but inevitable event in group psychotherapy. Indeed, in some forms of therapy, putting people on the "hot seat" or encouraging the group to use scapegoating to promote interpersonal insight is seen as a useful form of therapy (Agazarian, 1992b). The systems approach in family therapy (Bateson, 1972) and the group-as-a-whole work in the Tavistock (Coleman & Bexton, 1975) did much pioneering work in recognizing that the system creates specific roles to serve containing functions for group projections. It is relatively easy to recognize the phenomenon when the group creates the role of scapegoat, but not so easy to recognize that the role of the "identified patient" serves the same containing function for the projective identifications of the group, and often also for the leader!

In Phase I, the preoccupation with the politics of power and control is the resultant of defensive manoeuvres that protect the system from the frustrations that are inherent in dependency and the deeper annihilation anxiety that is aroused in the separation–individuation struggle. The multidimensional dynamics of the early days of a new group are familiar to all psychodynamic therapists. Which level of regression is salient to the work of the developing group in this phase is a matter of some controversy (see discussion in this chapter under the section "Individual and Group Development").

From the systems point of view, the major force to be contended with is the flight from functional dependency into the defences against impulses to be dependent. As this dynamic flight is common to therapists as well as to patients, *dependency* is often given a bad name in groups. Indeed, Bion claims "dependency" as one of the Basic Assumptions. Few interpret his Basic Assumption of dependency as a defence against dependency; many interpret that dependency is the defence. Much work in the beginning of a systems-centered group is directed towards legitimizing dependency and the exploration of the consequences of the defences that make it difficult to depend on either the self or others. The ability to subgroup depends upon it. As is explored in much greater depth later, there is a relationship between the ability to develop some functional dependency upon the therapist and upon the process of subgrouping and how virulent the paranoid threshold will be as the group works through Phase II, and how usefully its members can use the group as a transitional space in the Winnicottian (1951) sense.

The systems-centered goal of Phase I development is, therefore, to undo the defences against dependency disappointment and restore the ability to be functionally dependent. Nothing human can be achieved unless a functional dependency can be developed among the members in relation to the therapist and to the group process, for the life and work of the group. This is well understood by others in the field, although they may not use the label "functional dependency". For example, Ganzarain (1992, p. 23) says: "this group displayed appropriate dependency, which led to the members realistically assimilating the help I offered and integrating it to foster their further emotional growth. . . ."

How painfully vulnerable the group is in its first attempts to be compliantly dependent upon the therapist is shown in the excerpt below:

Fern: "Well, I don't exactly know what you mean by work in here, can you explain that to me?"

Therapist: "So you have a question that you're not quite sure how to answer. Is anyone else in that boat?"

[*Group: silence*]

[*Fern: mum*]

[*Group: silence*]

Fern: "Well, what am I supposed to do?"

Mark: "Yeah!" [*Mark joins the subgroup*]

Fern: "What exactly am I supposed to do?"

Mark [*to Fern*]: "I want to know the answer to your question."

Annie: "Yeah!" [*Annie joins the subgroup*]

Fern: "Well, I don't have the answer."

Annie: "I don't have the answer."

Mark: "I was kind of wanting her [*therapist*] to answer. She didn't really answer." [Agazarian, 1991c][2]

Phase I: Subphase Ia. Flight and the identified patient

The flight subphase of Phase I is characterized by group behaviour that is predominantly dependent, stereotypic, and conforming. Members come together around similarities that are mainly irrelevant to the goals of the group but are highly relevant to political survival. The following doggerel caricatures the stereotype responses to authority that are obvious to the observer but not to those members who are caught up in acting them out.

- Passive compliance:

  "tell us to jump, and we'll ask you how high,
  we promise we'll never question you why."

- Active compliance:

  "we'll stand on your shoulders and speak with your voice;
  make them do what you say, without giving a choice."

- Defiance:

  "whatever you say, we will do the reverse
  and dare you to say that we are perverse."
  We'll always know better and tell everyone so,
  so "off with your head" and away we all go".

Insight into these responses comes relatively easily in subgroup work around passive compliance, but less easily in the work around active defiance. The passively compliant part of the self emerges as obedient, conforming, pleasing, adaptive, and lovingly merging with blind trust: given to flight and avoidance and "love". Members with most salience for this response recognize how easily and spontaneously they subgroup around their similarities and how difficult it is to tolerate differences. It comes as useful insight, as members explore the passive and compliant aspect of their responses to authority, how easy it is for them to volunteer as the identified patient in the group, and how often the group volunteers them. The compliant subgroup often recognizes a consistent and debilitating underlying depression that defends them against the full experience of both their disappointment and their aggression when the "identified patients" are not cured. It is more difficult for the compliant subgroup to experience the aggression that they defend against, and their tendency is to act out the aggression by sabotaging themselves, the therapist, and the group by following the letter of the law but not its spirit.

In the early phases of group development, the group-as-a-whole can suddenly turn on an active member and either scapegoat him or elect him as a surrogate leader! Most active members can tell tales of the suddenness of their rise to power, followed by an equally swift descent when their leadership did not provide the solution to the problems they had been elected to solve.

The role of the identified patient is a stabilizing solution to the tensions in the flight subphase. When it manifests, it is like a "play within a play": a pairing that both creates a patient for the therapist to cure and provides the therapy that the group feels the therapist is failing to provide. Understanding this enables the group to understand their attempt to create an isolated subgroup to act out the wish for therapy—and to do the first important learning in how to take back whatever conscious projections are available to them.

Below is a good example of how the group-as-as-whole dynamics of creating the "identified patient" are isomorphic to the individual dynamics that create the "premature adult" or "prettified child".

Maggie: "So why are you here, why are you here?"

Carrie: "Feel like, I feel scared to say it like, uh, well, its just that, its just that I'm not very happy, and I find like I work a lot, I work very hard. And, uh . . ."

Maggie: "What do you do?"

Carrie: "I do counselling, with kids, in schools."

Mark: "In schools?"

Carrie: "Yeah, I work a lot, and I just don't feel very good, about, I don't know what. And then I have times when I just don't feel like doing anything, and I wake up at night, and I can't sleep, and I really feel weird sometimes when I wake up. I don't feel very happy. And that's why I'm here."

Mark: "Mm."

Maggie: "I know what that's like." [*joins the subgroup*]

Annie: "Well, how long have you felt that way?" [*takes on the role of the authority*]

Carrie: "I don't know, my whole life."

Annie: "When you wake up, sometimes you said you felt weird. What's that like?"

Carrie: "Um, I don't know, why do you want to know?" [*resisting the role suction*]

Annie: "Well, this is a self-help group, obviously, so the best we can do is to try and help each other I think. I want to help you."

This affords an opportunity, if the climate is right, to point out to the group that the therapeutic attention to Carrie, as a potential identified patient, is at the same time a reproach to the "bad" therapist.

Carrie: "Well, that's nice."

Annie: "I don't want to put you on the spot." [Agazarian, 1991c]

Transition: from Subphase Ia to Subphase Ib: flight into fight

The transition from flight to fight is the transition from passive to active. The actively compliant subgroup learns about their identification with the aggressor and their tendencies to try to bully other members into compliance with authority. The actively and passively defiant subgroups explore the many manifestations of their overt and covert sabotage of authority.

It is commonly understood by therapists that without insight, human systems are doomed to repeat rather than to change. However, as in all human dynamics, nothing is quite that black and white. In every repetition there is the potential for development. The example below shows how spontaneous subgrouping enables the members to support each other as they move towards tentative defiance, on the brink of exploring the depth of their disappointment in the therapist.

Fern: "I'm still waiting to hear from her. I mean, how do I know just talking about my problems is the job? I've been talking about my problems for years, and nothing's ever happened."

Sally: "Yeah, right."

Annie: "Well, we can talk about her [*the therapist's*] problems, but I don't think that's going to help."

Carrie: "Whose problems?" [*giggles*]

Annie: "Her problems!"

Mark laughs.

Annie: "That's not going to help."

Adam: "Group therapy . . . we'll all be the therapists . . ."

Annie: "I love it!"

Adam: ". . . and she can be the patient!

[*Whole group laughs spontaneously.*]

Annie: "Love it!"

Sally: "This is how to have fun!"

Mark: "Pick on somebody bigger than you!"

Sally: "Bigger than you, right!"

Mark: "Fine. I like that!"

Adam: "But if we're all together, then she's not bigger."

Annie: "I'm not sure about that."

Carrie: "This makes me nervous, now, because I'm afraid we made her mad." [Agazarian, 1991c]

In the systems-centered group, the transition into the fight phase marks the transition from work that is primarily targeted at the cognitive defences against anxiety into work that targets the character defences against impulse. In the flight subphase the group learns to tell the difference between the feelings that arise from their conflicts and the symptoms that result from the defences against the anxiety, tension, and irritability that is engendered by the frustration that these conflicts arouse. It is in this phase that members learn that tantrums and acting out and depression are defensive expressions of anger, not the anger itself. That the experience of anger is quite different from the experience of anger mixed with defences against anger.

In the fight subphase, role relationships are identified. The role relationships in the first phase of development are a repetition of those originally developed in earlier struggles with authority. Typically, these role solutions fall into relationships of either compliance or defiance and occur between peers as well as with authorities. Exploring these role relationships brings to light the related character defences, like the passive-aggressive aspect of compliance, and the aggressive activity of defiance. Character defences are ego-syntonic in a way that tactical and social defences are not. In making the character defences manifest, the systems therapist also encourages the group to look at what they are likely to cost the group in its development. This is the first step in making character defences ego alien. Through subgroup work, the consequences of the compliant and defiant roles are experienced as giving power to others while keeping powerlessness for the self.

The strongest character defence against impulse is stubbornness. Stubbornness is characteristically evoked in the group whenever there is a power struggle between the group and the therapist. The tragedy of stubbornness is that, on the one hand, it saves the inner life and, on the other hand, it makes it impossible to live it. Stubbornness makes it impossible to experience any inner life relationship with either the self or the other. It is particularly important to the development of systems-centered groups that the therapist draws the group's attention (and his own!) both to the survival function of stubbornness and also to its cost. Characteristic defences unwittingly replicate, in the present of the group, the role relationships learned in the past. The work of identifying the function of the containing role of victim for the group in the first subphase leads to a better understanding of the function of the scapegoat role in the second subphase.

Phase I: Subphase Ib: fight and scapegoating

The predictable course of the subphase of fight manifests in group behaviour that is predominantly contentious, with members pairing politically for control. Defiant subgroups explore their tendencies to be rebellious, non-conforming, resistant to influence, stubborn, individualistic, contentious, and authoritarian throughout. The defiant subgroup battles consistently with the impulse to take a stand against group issues. In groups, it is the defiant subgroup that creates the safety that ultimately enables the shift from the therapist to the group.

In psychodynamic groups, relationships shift constantly as the tides change in the group. Scapegoating a member (usually initiated by the aggressive and active complaints) makes for group cohesion in relation to a common enemy—therefore the scapegoat is an integrative agent for the group in the dynamics of the fight subphase, in the same way as the identified patient was in the flight subphase. Scapegoating also serves as a trial run. The group, discovering that it can survive scapegoating and coming together as a group-as-a-whole around the resolution of scapegoating, does the necessary membership work to enable it to take on the therapist.

But group scapegoating is by no means a benign experience, even when it is used as a therapeutic tool. Anyone who has been in a group on the brink of scapegoating knows the "feel"—reminiscent of the *Lord of the Flies*. It is true that the surviving scapegoat often makes the first major strides in therapy of all the members of the group. It is also true that sometimes the scapegoat does not survive and leaves therapy.

Techniques derived from the systems-centered view provide alternatives to acting out group tensions in scapegoating. From the beginning of the first subphase of group development, systems-centered members are introduced to the idea that they project into others that which they are not able to address in themselves and have worked to "take back" their projections. They learn that it is the hurt self that is projected into the "identified patient" to be cured; that it is the unacceptable self that is projected into the scapegoat and treated as unacceptable.

Transition from Phase I to Phase II: leader-oriented to group-oriented

> "a crucible, a relentless, uncompromising, inexorable pressure on the outer shell of defences—burning hot and cold—a ring of fire around the inner core of ash—"

The barometric event

The "barometric event" is the fulcrum that marks the transition from Phase I and Phase II. In a systems-centered group, it is also the transition between the "training phase", in which the group-as-a-whole acquires the skills to undo the defences and "contain" frustration, and Phase II, in which the conflicts in primary experience are experienced and explored. Throughout this phase—and indeed, throughout the life of the group—the therapist's responsibility is to contain the group projective identifications until the group-as-a-whole can contain those dynamics itself. The therapist role serves as a container for the group-as-a-whole good/bad split while the group crosses the boundary between fantasy and reality—the fantasy of the good/idealized and bad/devalued therapist into the reality of the de-idealized function of the therapist.

In the first phase of the group the underlying fears of dependency are expressed in terms of annihilation—kill or be killed—with the resultant guilt and blame. Murderous rage "turned in" relates to the "over-dependent" depressive, guilty, compliant, passive response to dependency disappointment. Rage "turned out" relates to the "counterdependent", counterphobic, blameful, rebellious, active response to dependency disappointment. In the heat of the barometric transition, these fears are expressed openly. Members in different groups will express the same sentiments, in a varying range and intensity of grief, guilt, and fear. "There is only room for one of us!" "It's either you or me!" This will be familiar to individual therapists in the heat of the negative (essentially paranoid) transference where the belief is that only the patient or the therapist can survive, there cannot be room for both.

Whereas the basic work of recognizing and struggling with defences is done in the earlier stages of the group, it is the authority issue that puts the work to the test. The early work on containment enables the group to regress within its group-generated structure. It is within the safety of this group "surrogate ego" that the regression in the service of therapy is done, with little risk that the group will actually act out the sadism. Typically, of course, the more available and primitive and bloody and savage the primary images, the easier it is for the group to move past the sadistic fantasies, and the more relief the group experiences and the more wholeheartedly they move on to the next phase. This is compatible, of course, with the understanding that the deeper the unconscious access, the less denial, repression, reaction formation, and paranoid ideation will distort the inner experience, and the greater the potential for transformation.

The most difficult experience of the barometric event (more likely in a group-as-a-whole approach that does not include systems training) is when the sadism that underlies the murderous rage breaks through the "containment" in the group-as-a-whole and expresses itself as a group-level paranoid delusion, generating a "real" experience of the therapist as toxic and destructive, with concomitant threats, either of real murder or of symbolic character assassination. This can also take the form of the group unconsciously electing a member with salience for the role to express sadistic virulence for the group without the group being able to subgroup functionally. In both cases, the steady insistence of subgrouping around the issues and a consistent emphasis on the containment of boundaries and a focus on goals increase the likelihood that the group-as-a-whole will, sooner or later, be able to "contain" the dynamics so that they be made conscious and integrated.

The management of levels of regression is an important factor through this phase. As long as the work is contained in subgroups, even the most fragile patient is also "contained", and the different levels in the regressive experience can occur at a pace within which they can be integrated. However, when the pace is mismanaged, or when a member reaches a level of experience from which the group withdraws, a decompensation of the group-as-a-whole can occur. The probability for this increases when the group includes fragile patients who have not yet learned how to work in a subgroup or with whom the subgroups have not achieved valid communication. Both of these conditions are red flags for the therapist. The stability of fragile patients in a group-as-a-whole regression depends upon the supportive environment of a subgroup. In the worst case, the patient who is "too open" to the virulence of disappointment and hatred is split off by the group and "paired" with the therapist, and each becomes the other's paranoid object in a mutual and reciprocal projective identification. For the therapist this experience is very different from the relatively benign and heroic "David-and-Goliath" pairing that the group often sets up in the earlier stages of the barometric event. This is a mutual pairing of assassins!

We have already discussed the role suction for the therapist in relation to the identified patient and the scapegoat and the threat it carries for group fixation. It is through learning not to act out these earlier role relationships that the therapist develops the ability to contain and understand the impulse, and it is therefore some preparation for the powerful role suction of the barometric event. The hatred towards authority experienced in the barometric event springs not only from the object-related defiant and compliant transferences of the first phase of group development, but also from the objectless transferences of the second phase. Thus the therapist's countertransference response is both to the role transferences and to the pervasive transferences. The therapist's own therapy is likely to have familiarized him with his vulnerability to reciprocal role transferences with which he will be challenged throughout Phase I. The sources of pervasive transference responses are, however, always unconscious, and the work of making the unconscious conscious never ends. Thus the therapist will always be more vulnerable to the transferences in the work of the second phase, and never more so than in the crucible of the barometric event.

Working through the vicissitudes of the transition in the barometric event is dependent upon the therapist being able to maintain both the role boundaries in the group and subgroups as containers for the work. It is easy enough for a systems-centered therapist to mistake a "pair" that is a look-alike for a subgroup but is, in fact, functionally a split-off container for a group projective identification. When the therapist is one of the pair, it is even more difficult to maintain objectivity. The way out for the therapist is to rely on the group-level process of subgrouping. With subgroups working around similarities and identifying differences, there is an ongoing opportunity for the group to reabsorb the split-off pair and restore a working environment.

What the group-as-a-whole has to become ready to contain are the regressive, primitive, and often very bloody and violent fantasies of the destruction of the therapist.

> "These many individuals eventually banded themselves together, killed (the father), and cut him in pieces. . . . They then formed the totemistic community of brothers, all with equal rights and united by the totem prohibitions which were to preserve and to expiate the memory of the murder." [quoted by Bennis & Shepard, 1956, p. 425, from Freud, 1921c, p. 112]

Sometimes the therapist is seen as some animal, murdered, thrown into the middle of the group, and savaged. Sometimes the members experience themselves as violent and bloody animals feeding on the carcass, with blood dripping from their faces. At other times the therapist is thrown onto a fire, a pyre, danced around, roasted, and eaten. Sometimes a duality is experienced—the impulse to rend and tear at flesh in savage hunger and, at the same time, to swallow and digest and be satisfied and full inside. Often, the work is followed by a rush of gratitude and love that the therapist can contain so much hate. And afterwards, in the relief, there can be a profound feeling of group communion.

In groups that access less primal levels, seduction or devaluation is used to undermine the authority of the therapist. There can be a symbolic communion around the therapist as an alternative to the underlying savagery. Once a group passed around one small peppermint patty, which the group managed so that each of its members broke off a piece (Agazarian & Peters, 1981). Devaluation can defeat authority by rendering it bumbling and incompetent. One group became convinced that I was aging beyond reason and held no future for them. Another decided that I did not know enough about groups to help and seriously considered the task of trying to train me, and yet another wanted to keep me around affectionately as a pet.

The example that follows illustrates several aspect of the systems-centered approach to the barometric event. The group is much stronger than it was in the earlier illustration, when it joked about "picking on someone bigger than you . . .".

In the first part of the episode there is a transitional quality in which it can be seen how the group builds, through some defensive somatizing, to a collective wish to murder the "battleaxe" with an axe! The second part of the episode illustrates how the subgroup work resonates throughout the group, across the boundaries between the present and the past, and certainly, for Carrie, into an eruption of a spontaneous insight at the end.

Annie: "I think she's a battleaxe, a crazy battleaxe . . ."

Fern: "It makes me so angry." [*To therapist*] "Why won't you help?" [*the voice of the subgroup where active rage has replaced the helplessness of frustrated dependency*]

Annie: "It makes me sad." [*the voice of the subgroup that contains the yearning for dependency*]

Fern: "It makes me so angry. I feel so sick. I feel just sick. Its like if you're not going to help, I want you out."

Adam: "While everybody else has been talking about being sick, I've been sitting here worried that I am the one in the group that's going to have to run to the bathroom and throw up." [*somatic defence*]

Mark: "Feels like I'm going to get rid of something."

[*The group is already familiar with somatizing defences against feelings, and Mark is spontaneously reversing the somatization for the group.*]

Carrie: "Throw up, Yvonne."

Mark: "Like I shouldn't have it inside me, so get it out."

Carrie: "That's the first time I've called her 'Yvonne' instead of 'Dr Agazarian'" [*shift from passive to active—a change in subgroups*]

Annie: "I have such a worry that I have to kill her."

Mark: "Have to?"

Annie: "There isn't going to be any way out. The idea of doing it is really horrible."

And later on in the process:

Sally: "There's only one thing to do it with, with a hatchet."

The group is working closer, with analogy and metaphor.

Mark: "Right."

Adam: "I've turned it into a big long hatchet with about a 20-foot end handle and we all have part of the handle . . ."

Carrie: "We'll do it all together."

Annie: "I can't get that, it feels like shirking. If I hold on to the handle with everybody, then it feels like I'm not doing my job."

Mark: "We could each take a shot."

Annie: "We each all have to take a shot."

Sally: "Murder on the Orient Express."

Fern: "You said there was only one thing to do with a hatchet, though I got confused because the only thing you can do with a hatchet is bury it."

The other subgroup, which turns the retaliatory impulse back on the self, is emerging.

Carrie: "Yeah."

Annie: "Or cut your own foot off."

Carrie: "That's what I was thinking, bury the hatchet."

Fern: "Bury the hatchet and . . ."

Carrie: ". . . and I'm just stuck with whether to bury it in Yvonne's head. Or whether to bury it somewhere else."

[*Group: pause*]

Carrie: "I just had an idea that is sort of scary to me, Adam's idea that we would have a long battleaxe that everyone could hold on to and—this is connected to tightness [*points to her chest*] and I suddenly realized that together we are physically stronger than you are. We *are* stronger, and that just suddenly became real. And that only, like, for a moment the only protection for you is the fact that we can't get together."

Fern: "I feel a little frightened, because I'm sitting so close. Mine isn't the axe, it's just wanting to choke you anytime you say anything." [*shifting from metaphor to direct experience*]

Carrie: "I mean, I mean, it's like, I could just tear this place apart. I could tear the chairs apart. I could tear the furniture apart, I could tear the pictures off the walls, I'm just so mad, just furious, I could . . . It's like this, the feeling that was in my chest that felt like anxiety is just getting bigger. I just really am. I keep seeing my mother's bedroom, my mother's room, and I could just tear it apart. I could tear this room apart, and you're supposed to see it. You're supposed to stop me. If I get really mad, if I get really mad."

Carrie has led the group away from the underlying sadistic fantasies of murdering the leader to the underlying impulses that are fuelling her individual transference to the leader.

Therapist: "What's the experience?"

[*Therapist is encouraging Carrie to contain and complete her experience, both for her individual therapy, and also for the group experience that rage is not dangerous when it is a "contained" experience.*]

Carrie: "If I get really mad. You're suppose to stop me and for once, God Damn, you're supposed to notice me."

Therapist: "Let your experience grow, have your experience. What's it like."

Carrie: "I'm all filled with it."

Therapist: "What's it like, to be so filled with rage, to be so full. What's it like."

Carrie: "I still want to break things. It's now, and it's still up to you . . ." [*still wanting the therapist to contain the acting out*]

Therapist: "What's it feel like inside as you want to break . . ."

Carrie: "I feel something coming all up in here." [*Points to abdomen.*]

Therapist: "Let yourself fill up with it."

Annie: "I'm filled with 'no'." [*Intensely experiences and expresses the impulse that erupts in the "no".*]

Fern: "I felt angry and then I felt this." [*Makes a fist.*]

[*Others in the group are now accessing the physical aspect of their experience. The members' work is deepening in resonance to the deepening of the subgroup work.*]

Adam: "It's like screaming in the middle of the desert, and there is no one there to hear me, and no matter how much I scream its just . . . myself . . . nobody notices, nobody responds, I can go 'Aargh' until I wear out."

Adam has the urge to discharge the anger in a scream and then defends against the urge with an "explanation" that renders the discharge futile—he is now two defences away from his original experience.

Technically, Adam is accessing the objectless alienation, which belongs, not in the object-related experience of the barometric event, but in the partial-object world of the second phase of development. Being out of phase does, in fact, leave him alone in a desert.

Therapist: "How do you feel about me leaving you screaming in the desert and not hearing? Leaving you out there and not responding?"

This is the therapist's attempt to re-connect him to the here-and-now of the object-related world of the barometric event.

Adam: "It feels like beyond rage."

Therapist: "How do you feel about me, leaving you in that state?"

Adam: "I want to strangle you."

Therapist: "How?"

Adam: "By jumping up and grabbing you and grabbing you so hard that we both go right through the window and then just taking you like a rag doll and then beating you and beating you and beating you on the sidewalk. . . .

[*The primary impulse has broken through. Adam's hands are outstretched, and his body charged with energy. He experiences a moment of potency.*]

". . . no matter what I do—scream, rage, grab you, beat you—you are not going to respond."

Adam is now "undoing" his primary experience by making a negative prediction. This then relates his feelings to an explanation, which creates a secondary experience, complete with secondary affect, which then serves as a barrier to continuing to access his primary experience. This is an excellent example of how defensive explanation aborts the experience that is being explored and reinforces the compulsion to repeat—in Adam's case, to repeat both the impotence of his rage and his alienation.

Therapist: "So how do you get even?"

The therapist attempts to re-connect to the primary experience through accessing the primitive affect around the Law of the Talion: "Do unto others what they do unto you."

Adam: "I can't . . . that's the rage . . . that's the frustration, there's nothing I can do to get even." [*a graphic example of the secondary feelings of impotent rage that are generated by the defence against primary affect*]

Therapist: "Find your subgroup." [*Therapist turns to the group, and by putting the conflict back in the group hopes to reconnect Alan to his primary experience through resonance.*] "Get help from your subgroup, the group can help you get even. Its here in the group, the wish."

As you will see, although members of the subgroup carry on the work, Adam does not. It is possible that Adam will resonate more easily with the work of the next phase.

Fern: "Oh I know, I know exactly how you feel. Its a very unusual . . . everything you have described has gone on inside of me—I've never heard it outside—had anyone say it." [*There is subgroup resonance!*]

Sally: "Something's happening, and I really—I need help . . ."

Carrie: "Well, I've got another piece from what Adam said. I've got a sense that it's not . . . that nobody's there . . . it's just *this* room . . . but I'm not very big . . . but it's your legs I'm kicking" [*to therapist*] "It's . . . you've got something . . . you're going to pay attention to me . . . [*with increasing emphasis*] you're going to pay attention to me . . . it's not that you're not there . . . you're gonna pay attention to me . . . Ah! . . ." [*rise in intensity*] "It's a baby! . . . just out of the way . . . it's me! And if tearing up the room isn't enough . . . I'll kick and I'll scream . . . !"

Phase II: group-oriented

Intimacy engenders more complex dynamics than issues with authority in that the dynamics are more primal, and therefore the defences against the primary dynamics are more complex. The major split is into "passive merging" and "actively alienated" subgroups organized around over-personal, counterpersonal, and interpersonal forces. In this second phase, subgroups balance closeness: too far for some, too close for others—enchantment and disappointment, suspicion, alienation, despair, and the emptiness of being together alone!

The experience of paranoid suspiciousness in the second phase of development is not the rationalized paranoid world of the first phase, which is no more or less difficult to endure than the French revolution. The suspicious, paranoid world of the second phase is the objectless world of Kafka—where the location of threat is nowhere and everywhere. It is the world familiar to every adult who remembers what every child forgets: where intuitions of reality make no external sense; where interpretations from reality make no internal sense; and nowhere is the language for making sense spoken.

Taking flight from confusion into a sceptical suspicion or a despairing and isolated alienation and despair is an organized world compared to the nameless dread of this boundless unknown. In the therapy group, the repair of the relationship with the self and the other and the group is the final work of the group: a stark search through the world of the fragmented self.

The inner journey to the lost parts of the self is the challenge to every member and is the challenge to every therapist too. The temptation is to defend against helplessness by "helping", to intervene with therapeutic words, or to interpret the experience in terms of the individual childhood self instead of joining in the transformation experience of the adult membership in the here-and-now: a solo and silent journey. To explain or interpret instead of to accompany is again to contaminate and disconfirm essential reality.

Thus, from the systems-centered point of view, the introjective and projective dynamics of both the first and the second phase of group development are defensive solutions to the annihilation anxiety aroused when the boundary is breached between the undifferentiated world of fragments and the constructs of reality. Just as in the "dependency" first phase, the dynamics of the struggle with authority are influenced by the balance in the conformist (over-dependent) and rebellious (counterdependent) subgroups who contain for the group the split between defiance and compliance, so, in the second "interdependent" phase, the outcome of the dynamics in intimacy are influenced by the balance between counterpersonal and over-personal subgroups that contain for the group the split between blind trust and blind mistrust.

In systems-centered group development, encouraging the group to split into two containing subgroups, one containing the salience for closeness and the other containing the salience for distance, permits both sides of the experience to be explored simultaneously and makes it unnecessary to work through the second phase in two separated phases of enchantment and disenchantment. Thus "blind trust" can be explored in relation to "blind mistrust"; the wish for merging and fusion and togetherness can be explored in relation to the fear of engulfment, the retreat into isolation and alienation. As the exploration of the experiences deepens and differentiates, the different issues can be recognized, contained, integrated, and re-integrated through the many levels of work that are required in this phase.

Subphase IIa: enchantment and blind trust

In the symbiotic ambience of this phase, members experience a euphoric relief. It is as if the dreams of mirroring have become a reality and the group is truly a holding environment. This is the phase in which the group subgroups around learning to experience pleasure fully: to experience it in relation to the self without shame, and to experience it in relation to others without embarrassment or shyness.

It is an interesting fact that the there are many more descriptive words in our language for unpleasure than there are for pleasure. It is perhaps not surprising, therefore, that this is often reflected in the focus of group psychotherapy, where there is often a tendency to encourage a wide range of exploration into the realms of unpleasure and of pain. The exploration of the *pain* of masochism, for example, is "group-syntonic" in most psychodynamic groups, whereas the exploration of the *pleasure* in sadomasochism is not. The same kinds of conflicts around opening the boundaries to spontaneous experience exist, however, whether the experience feels good or bad. For this reason, there is a lot of attention paid, in systems-centered groups, to enabling the full experience of the range of pleasure, with much subgrouping around both the wish for the full experience of good feelings and the inhibitions to it.

Throughout this phase there is also the underlying motif that not close enough for some ("you seem so far away") is too close for others ("a little too gooey"). In the following example, there is a group-as-a-whole solution to the conflict around the experience of pleasure in the "tribe", a metaphor that is apparently acceptable.

Annie: "Well, last week was such a great session for me. I just made all kinds of contact, and it felt wonderful."

Sally: "I feel full, warm. Hi Adam, glad to see you there."

Adam: "Good to be here."

Annie: "You seem so far away." [*too far for some!*]

Adam: "I'm off this kick that going through rough times together is a terrible thing! It's not so bad."

Carrie: "It's like a wagon train going across the plains and the prairies with other people in it and the storms."

Sally: "Yeah!"

Mark: "We haven't seen Indians in months."

Sally: "I was in another desert, actually. It was in Egypt, but it was good that I wasn't alone. It was nice to be with the tribe."

Mark: "The tribe!"

Sally: "Right!"

Mark: "The tribe!"

Carrie: "The tribe!"

Mark: "The tribe!"

Carrie: "That feels great. When the two of you were talking, it was a little bit too close." [*pointing to Sally and Annie*] "A little too gooey. I thought, well, that's you guys." [*too close for others!*] "But a tribe."

Mark: "A tribe!"

Carrie: "But a tribe!"

Annie: "It was hard."

Mark: "A tribe!"

Carrie: "But a tribe, I can get into that!"

Mark: "Tribe is cool!"

Fern: "Tribe is alright!"

The enchanted, merging subgroup above contains the blind trust of the group and each other. For the enchanted subgroup, relationships can never be too close. Differences, when they intrude into the enchantment of similarity, can be experienced with all the pain of a break in mirroring, as is seen below:

Maggie: "This feels real nice for me. I felt myself in the beginning sort of like I'm not sure I want to be part of this tribe—but that's a bunch of bull."

Sally: "God, I really feel good. I mean it . . ."

Mark [*sarcastic*]: "No shit, Sally. You mean you really feel good."

When, in disappointment, the group is "dropped", the pain precipitates the group into the phase of disenchantment, full of despairing mistrust of each other, the group, and the self.

Transition from Subphase IIa to Subphase IIb: enchantment to disenchantment

> "too close to you I disappear
> too far away and you're not here."

Not close enough for some is too close for others, irreconcilable subgrouping that inevitably plummets the group into disenchantment.

There is a relationship between the ability to develop some functional dependency upon the therapist and how virulent the paranoid threshold will be as the group moves into disenchantment. Suspiciousness and the "paranoia" eject the group from its somewhat "manic" heaven of enchantment. Suspicious, persecutor fantasies are also a last-ditch stand against shame and humiliation and the underlying underworld: the dungeons-and-dragons world of half-formed monsters. When the projective defences do not hold, there is the experience of unbearable shame and humiliation, which is retreated from in a painful withdrawal. The group is no longer full of warm interpersonal affective responses. Instead, there is a grim, "responsible" joyless knowledge that survival is at the price of being forever alone.

Depression vs. despair

The systems-centered approach makes an important distinction between the depression that occurs in the first phase of development and the despair that underlies the second. Depression is dynamically related to disappointment and rage in a relationship with another; while in the isolation of despair there is no relationship, there is no other, only the fragmented emptiness that results from the loss of the self.

Depression uses the language of complaining and blaming—a litany bemoaning fate and crying out to God. "Out of the depths I cry to Thee, oh Lord: Lord, hear my voice", says the 130th Psalm—the voice of depression, reaching out in guilt, a sinner in repentance, justifiably abandoned, seeking forgiveness and love and bemoaning fate. But forgiveness and repentance bring, at best, only temporary relief.

The crime of the depressed does not exist in reality. Relief comes only when the depressed gains access to the primitive violence in the retaliatory fantasies that are the reality of the unconscious. In the unconscious, where there is no distinction between thought and word and deed, the crime has already been committed. When the unconscious is made conscious, there is no crime.

Depression is a manifestation of superego pathology: a re-introjection, the law of the Talion turned back on the self—murderous rage denied and turned back on the self. Depression is essentially object-related; despair is not. Despair has no object; there is no God.

Despair is the cry of the hopeless. It is the cry that knows there is no one. Like Thomas Wolfe, in *Look Homeward Angel*, the despairing know that

> naked and alone we came unto exile. In her dark womb we did not know our mother's face. From the prison of her flesh have we have come unto the unspeakable prison of this earth. . . . Which of us has known his brother? Which of us has looked into our father's heart? Which of us has not remained forever prison pent? Which of us is not forever a stranger and alone? . . . Lost! Remembering speechlessly we seek the great forgotten language [Wolfe, 1929]

Despair is not only a matter of accessing unconscious fantasy, it is also a matter of finding the way to the lost self and to the forgotten language. To face the valley of death requires the courage to follow dread's lead through loneliness and alienation and pain, from emptiness into the fear of fragmentation and the fragmented horrors of the underworld, re-experiencing the annihilating memories of shame and the shaming, and finally rediscovering the hidden self and life with spontaneity and joy.

"I thought it was my wish to fly—and now I understand that it was just the wax", said one member who for many years had felt like Accurst, doomed to earth's darkness for the hubris of daring to fly too near the sun and suddenly understanding that it was not hubris, not her essential spirit, that was at fault, but the reality that she needed to develop wings that were held together with something more practical than wax if she was to fly towards the sun.

Subphase IIb: disenchantment, suspicion, despair, and alienation

Adam: "I've had the music of Camelot going through my head—'for one brief shining moment that was known as Camelot'."

Maggie: "Gone so fast!"

Annie: "Yeah!"

Adam: "I think we're all . . . I have a sense that we were a tribe. We were great. We could do anything, and you could pick a person out of a hat and any one of us could lead us anywhere . . ."

Group: "Uh huh!"

Adam: "We were that powerful. That everyone of us had enough resources to lead us anywhere. And that was just a wonderful feeling for us to have together for a while, and now somehow the foundations are, I wouldn't say crumbling, but certainly being shaken . . ."

Sally: "I feel very alone."

Mark: "Well, I'm used to going it on my own."

Disenchantment 1: disappointment and suspicion

First comes the suspiciousness that makes for distance and reduces intimacy—thus requiring the system to shift from the phase of enchantment to the phase of disenchantment. There is great disappointment in the transition work, when the group is working hard to deny the conflicted feelings in relation to each other.

Potentially, the group can take advantage of the emerging feelings of disappointment by learning to own some of the more difficult of the interpersonal feelings, like jealousy or envy, which, when defended against, make for alienation and distance. When this work is kept in focus, as it is in systems groups, then the transition into alienation and despair does not become an overwhelming and alienating experience and can be explored and contained by functional subgrouping.

Suspiciousness disrupts the climate of the group and at the same time increases the need to develop reality-testing mechanisms—thus shifting from the phase of disenchantment to the phase of consensual validation. Suspiciousness "denied" leaves the system doomed to the homeostatic mechanism of blind trust and fixated in the phase of disenchantment. In systems-centered group work, mechanisms of reality-testing have been developed from the inception of the group. Thus, if the salience for suspicion is not too great in the group, this work is done with relatively little difficulty.

Suspiciousness and paranoia protect against shame and humiliation by projection—when this defence does not hold, there is the experience of unbearable shame and humiliation, which is retreated from in a painful withdrawal. The group is no longer full of warm interpersonal affective responses; instead, there is a grim, "responsible" joyless knowledge that survival is at the price of being for ever alone. Suspicion defends, by the projection of blind mistrust, against the bitter, cold, and empty despair of betrayal. When the cohesiveness in the group is strong, the sense of interpersonal betrayal is less but the sense of intrapersonal betrayal more, and suspicion is weighed under by the sense of disappointment. Painful though it is, this is a good time to do interpersonal work. As is illustrated below, the conflict, when accessed, is painfully simple and painfully human: and simply, humanly, acceptable.

Therapist: "And we don't talk about the cynicism that we are withholding right here and now which keeps us running and running in an apparent closeness, but in fact we can't get past that barrier. So what are the feelings that we are not being public about?—that are getting in the way of our being honest with each other?"

Sally: "I have some stuff. I do know that when you started talking, I felt left out, and I didn't want to be left out. I didn't want to be left out."

Therapist: "In what way were you dishonest?"

Sally: "By not saying anything."

Therapist: "What exactly did you withhold?"

Sally: "Jealousy."

Therapist: "So how would you have said that?"

Sally: "Ugh."

Therapist: "Honestly."

Sally: "I don't know."

Therapist: "About the envy and the jealousy that was in your relationship, honestly."

Sally: "I don't know. My heart's racing right now. I wanted to be in on something nice. I didn't want to just watch it. I want to be part of it." [*to Adam and Carrie*] "You were talking to each other—ugh—I just wanted it to be a three-way talk."

Maggie [*to Adam and Carrie*]: "I wanted to break up the contact that you two had."

Therapist: "How?"

Maggie: "How? I wanted to get in the middle. I wanted to be me. I wanted it to be me! I want it with you—just for me—with everyone else out . . . everybody else out. That feels better now its out!"

Carrie: "It's very funny, very uncomfortable. I can only talk to one person at a time right now."

Maggie: "Well, mine was envy and jealousy. Because Adam and I had completed something, and you [*to the therapist*] were wanting to talk to me and Adam at the same time, and I wanted you to talk to me. I want you to talk to me. So . . . I wanted to cut across, that you wanted to talk to Adam."

Adam: "And when you [*to the therapist*] confronted me with reality, my immediate response was, 'Hey, I'd rather live in unreality and enjoy it than settle with reality. Who wants to settle for reality when I can have the solution that I was enjoying so much?'"

Therapist: "What is the cost?"

Adam: "What is the cost for hanging on to the illusion rather than facing the truth?"

Sally: "Empty core."

Adam: "Yeah."

Annie: "The truth that I feel worried and dissatisfied."

Carrie: "The truth . . ."

Disenchantment 2: alienation

Within the schizoid withdrawal there is the association to the black hole—being in outer space without a lifeline—cold—in the ice age—empty—hollow—forever in despair—hopeless. When this defence is threatened, there is a desperate "holding on" so that one does not "disintegrate", "fall apart". When the group is encouraged to regress into and through the feared disintegration, it reaches an understanding at the group level that there is a "shared" alienation—and therefore an existential common experience.

The individual work at this time is the work of "letting go" and "falling into" the black hole", finding the way by following the affective signal of dread. A further retracing step, past the despair, is the original betrayal of the true self by whatever shaming experience created a split between the spontaneous self and the self that was shamed (probably in the process of being socialized). Thus paranoia and despair are the last-ditch defences against the anguish of shame. The consequences of the defences are the permanent absence of that part of the self in intimate relationships, either with the true self or with any significant other, which results in the schizoid feelings of emptiness. (In truth, the self has been "emptied out", and the inconsolable grief is at its absence.)

This work, of course, is greatly facilitated by the resonance of a subgroup. As was illustrated in the episode around the barometric event, one member's work takes the subgroup forward, and when that individual member can go no further, another member picks up and carries on. When one or two members have survived the fear of disintegration and the loss of the self and discover the spontaneous experience behind the original shaming, the map is drawn, and other members can follow. It is in this phase that members learn that they continue to shame the spontaneous experience that was split off in the original shaming. They learn that they are now shaming themselves as they were once shamed.

In one group, for example, where the group was working with inhibitions around sex, two members were building on each other's childhood experience: one caught showing his penis to another boy, and one caught masturbating. It seemed that it was only the first member who was able to move past the memories of his terrible punishment to the original pleasure and pride in himself and in his younger friend's admiration. When, however, he shyly shared his sudden full experience of physical sexuality with the group, the other member was able to join the work and own that she, too, had a full sexual experience and was hiding it behind her shyness.

Working through the phases of leader-centred and group-centred group development, members discover that they are, in truth, self-centred. Confronting the work of membership in themselves, in their subgroups, and in their group systems, they confront the many ways that they have compromised, distorted, or lost themselves. The journey seems easier when the members learn to work in subgroups and learn to be systems-centered.

Transition from Phase II to Phase III: group-oriented to context-oriented

From the understanding that the "whole group" has the potential for an alienated and alone experience comes the gradual testing of reality—the ability to call a spade a spade. In the transition from a developing group to a mature group, the group uses subgrouping as the major developmental force, containing the maturational process of splitting in the group-as-a-whole while the splits are integrated through membership in discriminating subgroups.

The work at the boundary between group-oriented and goal-oriented is the work that affirms individual reality. The following episode illustrates the difficult work of checking out interpersonal impressions, risking that, in spite of one's inner conviction, one has been mistaken.

Fern: "I feel so attached I feel so attached so attached everyone." [*looking around*]

Annie: "To me too?" [*checking her mistrust*]

Fern: "Yeah. I keep feeling you want that answer to be 'no', but I do."

Annie: "Yeah, but . . ."

Fern: "I feel you keep wanting me to say 'no'."

Therapist: "And you feel . . . ?"

Fern: "Angry. I'm angry about that feeling." [*talking directly to Annie*]

Therapist: "So you've got two feelings."

Fern: "I do have two feelings."

Therapist: "And you've only shared one!"

Fern: "Right."

Annie: "Why are you angry?"

Therapist: "Asking for an explanation stops the exploring!"

Annie: "Thank you, because I pick up a different message. I picked up a different message underneath, and didn't realize it until Yvonne said to explore. Now I know that I believe you—that you were giving me a double message."

Therapist: "That's the context. Now for the feelings."

Annie [*looking at Fern*]: "I feel closer to you now that I know you've carried two messages."

Therapist: "That's an explanation of your feeling of right now."

Annie [*still talking to Fern*]: "I feel close. I feel close to you now. I am very grateful that you can be that straight. I feel the release of a lot of pain, a lot of worry, for no reason because I think I know underneath . . ."

Therapist [*interrupts*]: "So how does it feel to know you know something? without having to mask it with a protective 'I think'? How does it feel to know what you know whether you're right or wrong?"

Annie: "A little dangerous."

Therapist: "So how does it feel to own up to what you really feel?"

Annie: "Great!"

Therapist: "So will you do it?"

Annie: "I'm going to do it. I am doing it."

Therapist: "You need to tell Fern what you know, even though you may be wrong about what goes on with you, and what you think goes on with her."

Annie nods her head.

Therapist: "Can you share that?"

Annie: "Yes, sometimes, I think . . ."

Therapist: "Can you tell Fern directly what you know, whether you're right or wrong: how you feel when you think she's sending a double message and only owning one?"

Annie: "When you said you cared, I didn't feel convinced. When you said you thought I was trying to do something, get you to say I didn't like you, I felt trapped. I felt lassoed around the ankles and the rug pulled out from under me. When I owned that you probably had both of those at the same time I feel back in control, and I feel close . . . and I think you were doing it!"

Therapist: "'I think' is a way of not fully owning what you know, whether right or wrong. Can anyone else help?"

Fern: "I wonder if I can! What's happening for me—I have exactly the same feelings to say back to you. I feel like I'm angry, I'm angry because I felt trapped—I felt trapped in hearing from you a question. What I heard was, 'Do you care about me?' and 'I know you don't!' That's what I heard."

Therapist: "And you might be right and you might be wrong. Put your whole self on what you know. Abandon your alibi first."

Fern: "Mm! It's true."

Therapist: "Can you go from there—can anyone in the group help? Does the group understand what the issue is?"

Mark: "Owning the alibi."

Annie: "It's giving up a paranoid world."

Fern: "Checking it out! Boy!"

Phase III: goal- and context-oriented

Phase III introduces the phase of work, goal-, and context-oriented, where the primary goals of survival and development exist in the context of the secondary goals of environmental mastery. Phase III is containment: the inner balancing of the love, the hate, and the many transformations of reality. It is almost as if, once the group has experienced being able to survive, as a group, the descent into the primary experience of abandonment of self and other in the black hole of despair, the transformation occurs. The original fear that to grow separate is to die transmutes to an understanding that to separate is the way to survive and live, in ever-increasing complexity, in the hierarchy of human systems.

There is a major difference between a developing group, developing through the different phases of group development for the first time, and a developed group that can recognize aspects of the developmental phases in the re-experience and re-working of issues that are aroused in group life. It is the difference between the patient in individual therapy who is helplessly tossed on the sea of transference and the one who is familiar enough already with the experience to be able to navigate through its shoals—as is shown in example of Jane.

In a "look-alike" authority issue, Jane was working in a subgroup that was exploring the trap of passivity that she often fell into in relation to the leader. "It's like you are looking at me through the wrong end of the telescope" she said. The leader asked her how that felt when she looked through the wrong end of a telescope, and Jane burst out with "bigger"!—at which both she and the group joined in peals of spontaneous laughter.

The experience of being looked at through the wrong end of a telescope or through a microscope is a frequent metaphor when the group is struggling with the feelings of helplessness and powerlessness in relation to authority (Phase I). Frequently there are sadistic overtones: not only do the members feel small and helpless, like Gulliver with the giants, but they often also feel that they are being scrutinized dispassionately, like bugs under a microscope or, worse, like butterflies being watched fluttering helplessly on the end of a pin.

Reversing the image from small to big is another step of shifting both the self-image and the role relationship towards reality.

The work of the mature group is to enable transactions across the boundaries. In the ongoing group life of work, the issues themselves do not change, but the ability to work with them does. This next episode around fears of fusion illustrates the difference between an anxiety-ridden Phase II subgroup exploration and the deeper yet less frightening work of a mature group.

Exploring their fear of being swallowed up—fused—the group teamed up in subgroups around two sides of an issue: the fear of being swallowed and the fear of swallowing. The group-as-a-whole first distanced itself through talk about the difference between activity and passivity. Next voiced the voraciousness of appetite . . . of greed . . . of the eaters and the eaten. The group was then able to divide into subgroups—the voice of the "eaten" subgroup, saying: "you'll demand insatiably and you'll always complain. . . . I'll never be enough and never do it right enough for you" and the voice of the "eaters" subgroup: "I'll demand and demand and always want more, and there's never enough to fill me up." There was group peace when the work was finished, a sense of completeness and satisfaction and closeness, without fear.

There are some experiences in mature systems-centered groups that are quite marvellous. For example, mature groups are consistently aware that all group work is done in the context of reality: that the first step in any difficult work is to establish a containing reality (of time, place, and person) within which regression to other levels of experience can take place.

In a recent group, "Mac" was urged by the group not to hurt himself by ripping at his hand but to choose another member and talk about why he couldn't talk. He said he could not—a field of energy was keeping him out of the group. There was a startled silence and a moment of group-as-a-whole shock. Then Chris, whose relationships are tenuous at best, said: "Mac is quite right! I've been related to Erica and Betty and that makes a triangle of energy that shuts him out." Claudia, my co-therapist, and I had been unaware of any such connection—and watched with astonishment as Erica and Betty acknowledged the bond. Mac, contained in this reality, was then able to talk to Chris about the explosive force inside him that he was attempting to discharge by ripping at his hand.

Large groups have not been the focus in this chapter, even though, in my personal experience, I observe the same phases of development, whether the developing human system is as small as a dyad or as large as a median to large group of 30 or 100 people (Agazarian & Janoff, 1993). However, the work of one large-group leader has had a great influence on what I look for in the dynamics of developing groups. I look for the dynamic development that de Maré calls "Koinonia" (de Maré, Piper, & Thompson, 1991). De Maré defines Koinonia as follows: "impersonal citizenship and good fellowship . . . a form of togetherness and amity that brings a serendipity of resources". From his many years of work in the large group, de Maré has hypothesized that Koinonia, which can be developed in the large group, can *only* develop in the large group. First, family transferences do not have the tenacious hold on individual experience that they do in the small group. What is more, he says, the large size of the group both elicits and contains the hatred that group experience engenders, but in a less personal focus than in the transference-ridden small group. In his experience, though, even in large groups, he doubts that Koinonia can be developed in much less than ten years.

Pat de Maré's *Koinonia* has been an important book for me. The summer I spent reviewing it brought me to the understanding that it was the containment of hatred without a target that was the nexus of the healing process. This then required me to revise my understanding of the function of the superego. Translating the superego into a defence against human irritability (the basic human response to differences and also the first sign of life!) brought it into isomorphy with the systems-centered hypothesis that "containing" energy within the system was the essential task in the work of integration. This enabled me to make operational a formulation of human system dynamics without pathologizing. This, in turn, led to the current formulation of defence analysis, which is centred around group members taking an executive role in their own therapy (Agazarian, 1992d).

In our training groups for many years we have ended each group with a review period, as a method of formalizing the executive function of the members. We have recently introduced this "review" period to our therapy groups. This requires members to change from their "participant" to their "observer" roles and to focus on the group as the context of their individual experience. After crossing the time boundary, members are asked: "any surprises?" and thus pay attention to what had been the unexpected, and therefore the potentially new, aspects of their group experience that day. We have found that the activity of shifting from one role to another has been particularly useful for our group therapy members, who have taken very seriously

Table 6.1. Systems-centered therapy modifications of restraining forces to group development

Subphase issues	Restraining forces modified	Symptoms modified
Phase I of group development: authority		
FLIGHT SUBPHASE	SOCIAL DEFENCES (Module one)	
	stereotypic social communication	inauthenticity
creating the identified patient	TRIAD OF SYMPTOMATIC DEFENCES (MODULE ONE)	
	1. anxiety-provoking thoughts, ruminations and worrying that divert attention from reality testing	anxiety
	2. tension-generating stress-related psychosomatic defences, which avoid the experience of emotion	tension; psychosomatic symptoms
TRANSITIONAL SUBPHASE BETWEEN FLIGHT AND FIGHT	3. defending against the retaliatory impulse by constricting it in depression or discharging it in hostile acting out	masochistic depression; sadistic & hostile acting out
indirect scapegoating		
FIGHT SUBPHASE	ROLE-LOCK DEFENCES (Module two)	
scapegoating self & other	creating one-up/one-down role relationships like identified patient & helper; scapegoat & scapegoater; defiant & compliant	reciprocal maladaptive role pairing
TRANSITIONAL SUBPHASE BETWEEN AUTHORITY AND INTIMACY	RESISTANCE TO CHANGE DEFENCES (Module three)	
	1. externalizing conflicts onto those in authority: defensive stubbornness & suspicion from the righteous & complaining position	role-suction into interdependent roles of victim, victims' victim, & abuser
scapegoating authority negative transference	2. disowning authority: defensive stubbornness & suspicion of self that blames personal incompetence	crisis of hatred; resistance to reality

Phase II of group development: intimacy		
ENCHANTMENT AND HOPE SUBPHASE	DEFENCES AGAINST SEPARATION (Module four)	idealization, cultism
cultism, idealization	enchantment, idealization, blind trust of others, merging & love addiction as defences against differences	dependency at the expense of interdependence & exploitability
DISENCHANTMENT AND DESPAIR SUBPHASE	DEFENCES AGAINST INDIVIDUATION (module four)	despair and resignation
alienation	disenchantment & blind mistrust of self, others & groups	Independence at the expense of functional dependency & interdependence.
existential despair	alienation, contempt & despair as a defence against similarities	
Phase III of group development: interdependent love, work, & play		
ONGOING PHASES OF WORK IN THE EXPERIENCED GROUP	DEFENCES AGAINST KNOWLEDGE (Module five)	impairment of decision-making & implementation abilities; loss of common sense & humor. Self-centredness at the expense of both self & the environment.
interdependence	defences against inner reality & comprehensive & apprehensive knowledge	
	DEFENCES AGAINST COMMON SENSE (Module five)	
	defences against outer reality & reality testing	

the different goals of the different roles and the different demands that the role shift makes on the way they think and behave. It does, of course, give them an executive function and the challenge of taking personal experience objectively, which is not only often missing in their attitude to their life, but also, unfortunately, too easily undermined in their therapy.

It is in these review periods that we have learned, from our therapy group members as well as from our training group members, the content of those moments of silence that sometimes occur in a group after a completed piece of work: moments that feel so profound and are so seldom discussed. We have found that for training and therapy groups alike, these moments seem to be what Pat de Maré calls Koinonia. In those shared and resonating, though silent, moments members are experiencing some form of existential reality, able to be freed momentarily from family transferences, related yet separate, intimate and differentiated, and experiencing with awe the working fellowship in the work of the group. Communicating across the boundaries in space and time within, between, and among all systems in the hierarchy of human living systems, modifying defences and working functionally in subgroups, has brought into being a structure that has made it possible to deliberately develop Koinonia in small as well as large groups. In the closed system of a workshop this has been accomplished in less than a day. The challenge remains to see how Koinonia can be functionally integrated as an ongoing working property of the individual human system as well as of the group-as-a-whole.

Human responses develop from simple to complex, and so do human systems. Just as the infant responds to excesses of frustration in random behaviour, so do the responses in the early development of groups. Just as the small child kicks the door, so the older child mentally kicks a human object and adults find a scapegoat. Thus, developmentally, human systems change from simple random discharge responses, through behavioural discharge responses, to organizing the frustration in blame: either internalized or externalized. Maturation demands that every human system, when frustrated, must contain the tension, anxiety, and rage while internal and external reality is re-mapped and the problems along the path to the goals of transformation are solved. For example:

The group, with great commitment, were struggling to contain their frustration at how difficult group work is—a frustration that was increased by my asking them to explore the experience of containing their frustration without finding an object to blame. They said: "I don't understand what you mean by 'contain the hatred without an object'" and "How can I be this angry without either hating you or this group or myself?" Just at that moment, the telephone, usually switched off during the group, rang. There was an instantaneous roar of laughter at just how intensely, and with what relief, everybody instantly *hated* the telephone. Almost immediately afterwards came insight: "I need a home for my hatred"—"Now I understand why I keep hating my mother/my parents/my boss/you!" "Now I understand what you mean when you say that if you don't 'contain' frustration, the hatred is fixating!" (Agazarian, 1992c).

It will be clear to theorists that psychodynamically what is entailed in the above example is the ongoing task of separation–individuation. What may not have been so clear before is that the annihilating rage so often aroused in groups is a *natural stage* in the toleration of frustration, and that too much therapeutic emphasis on the frustrating *people* or traumatic events in the past fixates the person in the past rather than directing him to work through the past by developing greater tolerance for crossing the boundary from the past to the present and solving the reality problems in the here-and-now.

In Table 5.1, the phases of group development are presented in a form that makes it easier to compare and contrast some of the dynamic issues that underlie the problems that the group must solve as it travels along the path to the developmental goals.

NOTES

1. At the time of writing I was ignorant of chaos and complexity theory; however, there appears to be an isomorphy both in theory and in the experience of the theorist.
2. The dialogues in this document are taken from the videotape of a training group who put their hearts into "role-playing" the phases of group development in front of the camera. Those dialogues referenced (Agazarian, 1991c) refer to the videotape cited in the bibliography. Where they are not referenced, the dialogues are taken from the original script, which is not yet available on videotape.

CHAPTER SEVEN

Reframing the group-as-a-whole

It is my privilege, at this Ninth A. K. Rice Scientific Meeting, to have been asked to describe the "alternative model" that I have developed. In the organization of this chapter, Section 1 orients the reader to the differences that makes mine an "alternative model" to the more traditional approach. Section 2 begins the discussion of the differences in theory and practice, with examples. For those for whom theory is not a major hobby, Section 2 might be a more practical place to start. The Summary (Section 3) recapitulates the central ideas in this chapter.

Y. M. Agazarian, "Reframing the Group-as-a-Whole". Paper presented on the Panel, "Learning from Experience: Alternatives to the Traditional Conference", Ninth Scientific Meeting of the A. K. Rice Institute, sponsored by the New York Center, New York, 12–14 May 1989). In: T. Hugg, N. Carson, & T. Lipgar (Eds.), *Changing Group Relations: The Next Twenty-five Years in America. Proceedings of the Ninth Scientific Meeting of the A. K. Rice Institute* (Jupiter, FL: A. K. Rice Institute, 1989), pp. 165–181 (by permission of the A. K. Rice Institute, Jupiter, Florida).

1. *ORIENTATION*

The major difference between my "model" and the A. K. Rice Conference model is one of emphasis—a shift in emphasis in practice that reflects a shift in emphasis in theory.

The connection between group behaviour and group goals is made explicit to the working group, as are both the identification of the defensive *behaviours* and their consequence upon task performance. This is a shift in interpretive focus towards underlining the defensive nature and purposefulness of Basic Assumption behaviours.

The defensive function of Basic Assumption behaviour is subsumed under a general assumption that all human behaviour can be described in terms of its approach-and-avoidance character in relation to the problems that must be solved along the path to implicit and explicit goals (Howard & Scott, 1965). Thus the defensive nature of the Basic Assumption behaviour is *interpreted* in relation to the secondary goals and *understood* in relation to the primary goals.

The relationship of Basic Assumption behaviour to the primordial terror of the underlying chaotic group core is also reframed. It is assumed that man has an instinctive compulsion to "make sense" of the unknown. Primary "sense" is primitive sense: archaic, anthropomorphizing, primordial, chaotic, often experienced as psychotic. Thus each new experience arouses "terror" of the unknown, combined with curiosity about it, which fuels the impulse to explore, organize, and master.

The underlying chaos that arouses the group Basic Assumption defences is reframed in terms of "noise" (Shannon & Weaver, 1964). "Noise is the entropic resultant of the ambiguities, contradictions, and redundancies inherent in man's communication with man. Reframing chaos in terms of noise frames chaos as a researchable construct that reflects the universal rhythm of organization and disorganization, matter and mass, entropy and negative entropy.

Noise is assumed to be inherent in the input and output communication transactions that cross system boundaries. Communication transactions occur across boundaries at all levels of the system hierarchy and, on the one hand, reflect the inner state of the system and the primary system goals and, on the other hand, influence the system's relationship with its environment, the environment itself, and the attainment of the systems' secondary goals.

In practice, this means that consultant interventions frame interpretations of Basic Assumption behaviour as but one of the types of group defence that must be modified in the process of group development. The other defences are group tactical defences and the character defences: the particular constellation of defences that characterizes a particular group, much as a particular constellation of ego defences characterizes a particular individual. From the systems perspective, Basic Assumption, tactical, and character defences exist at the individual, subgroup, and group-as-a-whole levels isomorphically, functioning contemporaneously.

All group defences influence the nature of group development, and the nature of the group's development at any one time is reflected in the group's relationship to the system's implicit primary goals of survival and maturation, as well as the system's secondary goals of mediating with its environment. The achievement of explicit task goals is inevitably influenced by the nature of the group compromise at any given moment of maturational time.

The problem-solving skills that the group develops are a function of this compromise. The group's ability to use those skills is a function of the dissonance or congruence arising from the relationship between the group's implicit and explicit goals. The particular style of problem-solving and decision-making that each group develops affects the way the group relates to its work tasks.

In practice, the consultant's deliberate structuring of group boundaries also has a specific meaning in terms of Group-as-a-Whole Systems Theory. The structuring of boundaries implies not only influencing the nature of the boundary permeability of the group-as-a-whole in space and time, but also the nature of the permeability of the boundaries at all levels of the system hierarchy.

Fundamental to this approach is the concept of system isomorphy (Bertalanffy). The dynamics of each system in the relevant hierarchy are defined by constructs that are similar in structure and dynamics that are similar in function. Thus each system in the defined hierarchy is the environment for the system below it and exists in the environment of the system above it, dynamically similar in function, structurally similar but discrete.

The group-as-a-whole system is defined as the environment for the individual system. System-role behaviour serves as the conceptual frame for the behaviour of both the individual and the group: framed as a subgroup containing function when behaviour is viewed as a function of the system "life space" of the group-as-a-whole, and as member-role behaviour when behaviour is viewed as a function of the system "life space" of the individual (Lewin, Agazarian).

This orientation frames consultant interventions as "consultations to system boundaries"—that is, as consultations to the boundaries of the system, within, between, and among systems in the defined hierarchy. It generates the hypothesis that if the nature of the communication contributes to problem-solving rather than to noise, then the system hierarchy will mature along lines in which discriminations can be made and integrated, and the potential for moving in the direction of system primary and secondary goals will be increased.

To this end, all group work, whether large group or small group, is either punctuated by or immediately followed by a period of review.

2. *THEORY AND PRACTICE*

In training groups I introduce the application of theory to practice with the following letter, which is sent to new members of my training groups and workshops.

> *"The orientation of the group is from the perspective of Group-as-a-Whole Systems Theory. The goal of the group is to learn to observe and explain all behaviour in the group as a function of group-as-a-whole dynamics.*
>
> *The proposed format for reaching this goal is that each period of experiential group-work is either punctuated by, or followed by a processing period in which the subjective experience will be reviewed objectively and analyzed from the group-as-a-whole perspective.*
>
> *To this purpose, individual dynamics are relevant only to the extent that they help members to understand the impact of group dynamics upon their individual experience and behaviour.*
>
> *Subgroups are the basic unit of the group-as-a-whole.*
>
> *With the exception of member selection, all decisions that affect the group; like fees, meeting dates and times, holidays, new members, etc.; are the property of the group.*
>
> *Members are reminded that objectively analyzing subjectively experienced behaviour from the perspective of the group-as-a-whole is emotionally frustrating as well as intellectually challenging."*

Thus, the group is the environment in which members experience how their behaviour is influenced by the dynamics of the group-as-a-whole. Through sharpening the skills of participant-observation, they identify how they "contain" and "voice" not only their own dynamics, but also group dynamics, and how the implicit and explicit goals of the group determine the boundaries of their subgroup roles.

The "alternative model" to the traditional conference that I address in this chapter is both the result and the source of Group-as-a-Whole Systems Theory—a framework for conceptualizing group dynamics that I have developed. Below are its basic constructs, and how it is applied in practice.

Group-as-a-Whole Systems Theory

Theoretically, I started with an adaptation of Lewin's hypothesis about behaviour: "Behaviour is a function of the system in interaction with its environment." The basic problem to solve was how to define system dynamics so that the definition would explain behaviour in a group, both when it is defined as a function of individual dynamics and also when it is defined as a function of group-as-a-whole dynamics.

The General Systems Theory principle of isomorphy was the key. The principle of isomorphy requires that the structure and function of the system be defined in such a way that it mirrors the structure and function of other systems in the same hierarchy—ultimately all living systems, from cell to society—but for our purposes we define a very specific hierarchy: the system of the individual member for whom the group system is the environment and the system of the group for which the organization is the environment.

Hypotheses about the dynamics of any of these system levels can be tested at all other levels in the hierarchy: individual, small group, large group, and increasingly complex organizations of different systems. It follows, then, that techniques applied to the management of any one system will carry significance for the management of both larger and smaller systems in the hierarchy. This, then, applies to systems like an A. K. Rice conference. All levels—the conference members, the small groups, the staff group, and the large group—can be defined as systems at different hierarchical levels with equivalent structure and function, whose subgroup roles, goals, boundaries, and communication patterns have similar dynamics but different manifestations.

Borrowed, modified, or reframed

It is important to the presentation of this theory to be clear in what ways I have borrowed, modified, and reframed the work of other theoreticians in the service of Group-as-a-Whole Systems Theory.

I will begin with Bion. Bion's Basic Assumptions of fight/flight, pairing, and dependency are most commonly framed as responses to the anxiety aroused by the psychotic-like group core against which the group defends itself.

Bion and the "psychotic" core

I have reframed Bion's formulation of the group core by emphasizing its chaotic nature in contradistinction to the field's tendency to talk and behave "as if" it is psychotic. De-pathologizing interpretations of everyday human dynamics is basic to Group-as-a-Whole Systems Theory.

All systems develop from simple to complex, and the less sophisticated the system, the more primitive will be the attempts to organize chaos. Thus early phases of group development will arouse the same kind of primitive fears and conceptions of the unknown that characterize the beliefs of primitive societies. There is perhaps a tendency in writing about Tavistock dynamics to dramatize and reify this developmental stage into some "thing" that is terrifying in and of itself and thus to focus more on the aspects of destructive acting out and less on the methods for the organization of chaos.

In Group-as-a-Whole Systems Theory, maturation through the organization of chaos is the primary survival goal of a system: to contain the dissonance that chaos arouses and to maintain system boundaries and system equilibrium. In Group-as-a-Whole Systems Theory maturation is defined as the process of differentiating, organizing, and integrating information.

A. *Bion's Basic Assumptions of flight and fight.* Bion's constructs of flight and fight then, are reframed as behavioural vectors related to the system's goals[1]—both the primary intra-system goals (the implicit goals) and the secondary explicit goals that relate to the system environment.

Thus from a Group-as-a-Whole Systems Theory perspective, Bion's Basic Assumptions of fight and flight are understood as defences against the anxiety aroused by internal chaos, but they are most often interpreted as behavioural vectors that are sometimes oriented in the direction of the relationship between the explicit (secondary) and implicit (primary) goals and sometimes directed to the relationship between either or both the primary and secondary goals and the environment (Howard & Scott, Lewin, and GST).

Consultant interventions serve a dual function: both to help the group identify the dynamics and symptoms of defensive "panic" behaviour and to learn the kind of communication that contains the panic and organizes the chaos.

B. *Bion's Basic Assumption of dependency.* In Group-as-a-Whole Systems Theory, dependency is conceptualized as an existential dynamic common to all living systems and not as a defence.

I define dependency as a dynamic that exists on a developmental continuum with interdependence. Maturational work is an ongoing process and inherently in itself is never a defence. (It is possible that the custom of framing dependency as a defence has contributed to giving this basic human dynamic a bad name in Tavistock work and has led to groups denying the underlying dependency forces that exist functionally in reality.) Defensive functioning comes when the normal maturational conflicts around dependency cannot be contained within the system and are discharged into dependent and counterdependent behaviour that acts out the unresolved conflict.

In practice it is particularly important not to distort the group's attitude towards its dependency or encourage its denial. Phase-appropriate dependency is fundamental to developing appropriate boundary permeability, which is, in turn, fundamental to avoiding fixations in development or a premature maturity.

For example, the management of dependency is in the service of developing intimacy. Intimacy cannot develop unless dependency can be accepted. In psychodynamics terms, dependency is the raw material of later separation–individuation work (see Appendix A). In systems terms, system maturation is dependent upon the ability to open and close boundaries to both similarities and differences.

C. *Bion's Basic Assumption of pairing.* I do not differ with Bion's definition of pairing as an unconscious fantasy that through "pairing" a group saviour will be born. However I see this Messianic fantasy as only one of many unconscious fantasies contained by the group in a "pairing" subgroup. Again, "pairing" is framed as an existential system dynamic, genetically and socially reinforced, that is not necessarily defensive.

In practice, when pairing occurs in a group, it is a signal for a judgement call as to whether pairing is in the direction of fantasy or reality problem-solving in relation to the task required in reaching the explicit and implicit goals.

The principle of discrimination and integration

The maturational process that underlies all systems is defined in terms of the process of discrimination and integration. This concept can be applied to communication . Thus in Group-as-a-Whole Systems Theory, maturation of individual and group systems can be described in terms of the kinds of communication by which discriminations are made. Maturation of a system is a function of the system's ability to integrate information about similarities in the apparently different and the differences in the apparently similar.

In practice, then, group development is facilitated by observing subgroup interactions without intervening, as long as the group-as-a-whole is processing information. Even when the group forms stereotyped subgroups, this in itself is not an intervention point unless the group information flow becomes redundant, ambiguous, or contradictory.

Shannon and Weaver's Information Theory

Ambiguity, contradictions, and redundancy are the source of entropic noise in the communication, according to Shannon and Weaver's (1964) Information Theory. This, then, is the criterion variable I use when listening to group communication.

In the following examples, the interventions are typical group-as-a-whole interventions; it is not to this aspect that I wish to draw attention but, rather, to the specific discrimination and/or integration work in group development that they are designed to encourage.

A. *Ambiguity.* In ambiguity, pointing out first similarities and then differences helps the group to make the necessary primary discriminations.

For example, in a new group relief first comes when members discover that anxiety is shared. This is usually followed by the relief that occurs when a status hierarchy is built, based on the differences in the apparent "expertise" that members appear to have.

B. *Redundancy.* In redundancy, the group is in fixating homogeneity. Pointing out differences in the apparently similar disequilibrates the redundancy.

For example, in a comfortable but repetitive group a functional disequilibrium can be introduced by drawing attention to the fact that a silent voice of the group is expressing an unacknowledged difference: "There have been several yawns in the past two minutes."

C. *Contradictions.* Groups frequently ignore one aspect of contradictory events and behave "as if" there is no contradiction. Bringing the contradictory information to the group's attention is a call for group integrational work.

For example, in a demonstration group in Japan, after an interaction in which the behaviour contradicted the traditional roles, there was a sudden group silence, followed by a shift of attention so abrupt that it was almost as if the group had amputated part of itself in an effort to ignore whatever had just occurred. So I spoke, through Dr Suzuki, and said: "I wish to draw the attention of the group to the last few interactions" (I then retraced the group process for the group). "I wonder if the group work will be helped or hindered if the group agrees to ignore whatever it was that just happened?"

D. *Integration.* One way of facilitating the integration is to point out to the group the similarities in the apparently different and, later, differences in the apparently similar.

In a group that is watching a fight, for example, the first part of the intervention brings the group's attention to the fact that the fighting pair, who are apparently on opposite sides, are in fact in the same subgroup—a "fight" subgroup—and that the rest of the apparently uninvolved group performs the role of a supporting subgroup. Having laid the foundation, a question then directs the group to relate its behaviour to the group-as-a-whole goal—for example, an intervention like: "The fighting subgroup appears to be supported by the group silence. What useful service is this serving for the group-as-a-whole?"

Melanie Klein's "splitting and containing"

Although splitting and projective identification are typically labelled pathological defences, from the perspective of Group-as-a-Whole Systems Theory "splitting" and "containing" are deemed to serve as fundamental mechanisms in maturation. They are mechanisms that "store" information in a subsystem under specific vicissitudes of the normal maturation process. When information is too contradictory, ambiguous, or redundant for the system to integrate into its present organization, then the system "splits off" that part of the information and projects it into a subgroup container.

The system's subgroups then interact with boundaries that are relatively closed to communication transactions that carry projected information until the general system has matured sufficiently to re-integrate it. This is seen in the group in a scapegoating communication pattern when the boundaries to the information are being maintained as closed, and in the form of a communication pattern to the deviant when the boundaries are permeable.

Splitting in this sense is in the service of the maturation process of the system, which is to remain in a viable equilibrium while it interacts with its environment and develops secondary goals. The functions of splitting, projection, and denial are seen as potentially maturationally functional in that they are mechanisms by which differences are isolated and contained in a subsystem within the system until, through further maturation, they can be integrated.

The following example describes how a training group unconsciously created a subgroup to "contain" the scapegoating while the rest of the group became free to create an open communication pattern with the deviant.

Two months before the following event, the group had had a scapegoating experience, and they were still guilty in their relationship to Bill, the scapegoated member. The relationship between Bill and the group was still tenuous. Bill often sat silently with a "chip on his shoulder", and the group trod on eggshells every time it felt punitive, particularly if Bill was involved. The event described started when the group was conflicted about their punitive feeling, not with the silent Bill, but with "Jack". The group acknowledged their struggle with their impulse to scapegoat Jack for "not being honest" and struggled in frustration at feeling so helplessly punitive and "being stuck in scapegoating"!

In the middle of the group discussion of this impasse, "Mary" suddenly attacked Jack. A fight broke out between the two of them about not being honest "*with each other*!" The group immediately relaxed and watched the fight.

When the fight was over, the group worked to understand both sides. An open-communication pattern developed between the group-as-a-whole and its "Jack–Mary" fighting subgroup. The group resonated both with Jack's withholding and with Mary's intolerance. Unexpectedly, this new open-communication climate was interrupted by a second round of the same fight.

I intervened and asked the group what service this second fight was performing for the group. There was a long, bewildered group silence. Suddenly Bill, the original scapegoat, attacked Jack, who attacked back. Again the group watched. In this third fight Bill and Jack fought angrily—but openly—and without any scapegoating blame.

During processing time it was understood that in the previous week's post-session there had been a wish for more feedback and intimacy in the group. The "function" of the above episode was understood as follows:

The group-as-a-whole first projected their unresolved anger into the Mary–Jack scapegoating subgroup, which "contained the deviance". This subgroup was well chosen in that it comprised the two members known to be most comfortable with anger, and who, in this first fight, demonstrated for the group that scapegoating rage could be survived!

Thus "scapegoating" (closed pattern to deviant) was maintained in a "deviant" subgroup while the group-as-a-whole developed an open communication pattern to the "deviant".

When the second fight broke out, it was in the group's new "open communication pattern" environment rather than its previous "scapegoating" one. This second fight again "contained" the scapegoating, but this time in relation to the group role. But the function of this second fight was not available to the group.

Before the first fight, Bill, as one subgroup, had contained for the rest of the group the scapegoated role. Bill, experiencing continuing stress, withdrew into silence. To change Bill's role required both group-as-a-whole readiness and Bill's readiness. When the group-as-a-whole no longer "contained" the "scapegoating", Bill no longer needed to "contain" the "scapegoat" for the group and was ready to give it up for himself.

In this new climate, Bill's group role changed. When he broke the group silence, he also broke his own "chip-on-the-shoulder" silence, and he and Jack modelled for the group an open-communication fight.

This third fight fulfilled the group goal of being able to deal with deviance without scapegoating and to give feedback in such a way that it resulted in increased intimacy. System boundaries increased in permeability at all levels of the hierarchy. When the Bill–Jack fight was over, the group-as-a-whole experienced an integrative intimacy and talked of the experience of disagreeing, being different, and still being intimate.

This event is framed in terms of a group-as-a-whole systems understanding. A more detailed description of the theoretical orientation follows.

Group-as-a-whole development

From the individual system perspective, groups are made up of individual members—but from the systems perspective, both the group system and the individual system are made up of components.

Thus, whereas looked at from the individual perspective individual group members are seen as the basic building blocks of the group, from the group system perspective the basic building blocks are subgroups, which exist independent of the individuals whose subgroup membership may overlap or change from instant to instant. (This same frame can, of course, also be applied to individuals. It is relatively easy to experience the many and different subgroup "voices" that "talk things over" inside oneself and to become aware of how they perform a successful defensive function that both keeps one's system in equilibrium and reflects the conflict between, shall we say, the competing id, ego, and superego goals.)

Thus subgroups are the raw material of system development and contain the group potential. They are self-generating and regenerating. Subgroups are the source of the integrating blueprint, the basic container for similarities and differences. Through subgroup interaction, systems develop through predictable phases towards maturation.

Subgroup roles in group-as-a-whole development

Subgroups come together around similarities and separate on differences. Each matures by the process of differentiating and integrating similarities and differences within its subgroup system and between subgroup systems in the environment of the group-as-a-whole.

At each moment of group life, the group-as-a-whole system integrates all subgroup discriminations that are within its integration ability.

Individual and group isomorphism in the group-as-a-whole

When an individual member of the group serves in the "container" role for the group, he is acting out in his member role a set of behaviours that express an internal conflict. In other words, he sets up an old, familiar, stereotype role relationship that expresses an unresolved conflict externally, thus discharging the tension which would otherwise have to be experienced, contained and integrated internally (within his individual system).

Isomorphically, from the group system perspective, the member is performing a subgroup role and containing for the group-as-a-whole a "difference" that the system has split off and projected. This mechanism serves, at the group level, to discharge disequilibrating tension into a boundaried subsystem, which permits the group-as-a-whole to continue in a maturational process that can lead to reintegration of the difference at a later time. In the process of splitting, projecting, containing, re-introjecting, and reintegrating, developmental change can occur at all system levels.

Primary and secondary group goals

By "containing" in separate subgroups those differences that the group-as-a-whole is not yet sufficiently differentiated to integrate, the primary goal of the system—to maintain a viable equilibrium—is met. And so the differentiation between primary and secondary goal behaviour is created. The primary system goals of survival and maturation take precedence over the secondary goals of mediating with the environment.

The maturational task of the group is to develop sufficient maturity to reopen the boundaries between subsystem roles and integrate the information (resolution of projective identification).

When subgroup boundaries are impermeable to different information and an individual is assigned a deviant containing role, the stage is set for an identified patient, a hero, a saviour, a group mascot, or a scapegoat. Creating a deviant role does maintain the group system in equilibrium, unless or until the group-as-a-whole becomes developmentally ready to open the system boundaries to the dissonant information. Most leaders are alert to the "deviant" solution when it is allocated to a scapegoat, because of the nature of the scapegoating climate; but they are less easily alerted when the solution takes the form of creating an identified patient, a hero, a saviour, or a group mascot.

In practice, then, the deviant solution is most reliably recognized by the group's communication pattern: the wheel pattern, with group members at the rim and the deviant in role at the hub. When this pattern is observed, it is important to make a differential diagnosis between a closed, fixating pattern and an open communication pattern to the deviant. Although the patterns are similar, the climate changes when communication to the deviant is in the service of scapegoating and when it is in the service of open communication. There are two criteria for a differential diagnosis: (a) the scapegoating pattern carries a one-way information flow, and the open communication pattern is two-way; (b) the character of the verbal behaviour that is used in the communication process. (See Appendix B, "SAVI: An Instrument for Coding Information".)

In open communication to the deviant, the behaviour is characteristically descriptive, data-gathering, and problem-solving, and the subgroup boundaries are permeable to both similar and different information.

In scapegoating, the verbal behaviour is characteristically coercive: either dominant or persuasive, with contradictions, yes–buts, "oughtitudes", opinions, accompanied by discounts, sarcasm, attack, and blame in the case of the hard sell, or by personal questions, agreement, support, and proposals in the case of the soft sell.

You will note that the hard sell is a caricature of the Tavistock consultant and the soft sell of the humanistic group therapist. This is no accident, in that both lead a group by setting up a relatively impermeable boundary between the subgroups of "leader" and "group" and therefore do in reality employ behaviours that function to maintain a pattern to the deviant with one-way communication. In the case of the Tavistock consultant, the leader boundaries are relatively impermeable—characteristic of the scapegoating pattern—and it is also true that many small groups do feel scapegoated by the communication style of their consultants. In the case of the humanistic consultant, the boundaries are permeable to selective information, which is characteristic of a reinforced dependency relationship.

Group-as-a-whole leadership style

It is for this reason that group-as-a-whole consultancy has no pre-set role boundaries. Group-as-a-whole leadership behaviour is related to the aspects of the developmental phase that the group is in and is oriented to the relationship between the system equilibrium and the primary and secondary group goals. There is, however, a general guideline for the form of an intervention.

1. Whenever possible, the words are selected from the group vocabulary, reinforcing the task of consensually validating group language (Bennis & Shepard, 1956).
2. Whenever possible, a description of the group events that form the

data base for the consultant's hypothesis are included in the intervention.

3. The target of the hypothesis is to influence the process of discrimination and integration of group information.
4. Certain skill-building interventions "train" the group in communication and problem-solving skills and in certain dynamics like the process of "taking back" projections. Learning how to take back what the group has projected into the "container" role is essential to the group-as-a-whole method in that it is the group work of undoing the containing split and is essential to the development of the group ability to change scapegoating communication to an open communication to the deviant.
5. Consultant interventions are conceptualized as consultations to the transactions across the boundaries of systems.

Consulting to boundaries

The task of the group-as-a-whole leader can be conceptualized as that of "consulting" to the dynamics of the group-as-a-whole and monitoring the noise in the communication transactions across the boundaries between and among all systems in the relevant hierarchy.

A general criterion for consultation to boundaries is that the information itself should mirror a problem-solving communication—in other words, it should contain as little noise as possible. Whenever feasible, this is done by grounding the communications in here-and-now reality, which exists at both the primary and secondary goal levels.

The language that relates to the primary goals in the here-and-now reality of the group-as-a-whole is the language of emotion, condensations, metaphor, and paradox. Primary goal communication organizes chaos in ways that can be integrated without isolating thought from affect. It is the language that every consultant recognizes and uses intuitively—and is very difficult to code or teach.

The language that relates to the secondary goals is the language of problem-solving. This language is relatively easy to teach.

Much of the thinking behind the understanding of communication as a series of input and output transactions between systems and of consultation as acts of influence directed at these communications transactions at the boundaries of systems has its roots in the development of SAVI, a "System for Observing Verbal Interaction" that Anita Simon and I started to develop in 1965. (See Appendix B.)

3. SUMMARY

Framing consultation as acts that are designed to reduce the noise in the transactions across boundaries is an operational definition of Group-as-a-Whole Systems Theory. I have applied this predominantly with small groups: to the therapy groups that I lead; to supervision groups of those interested in using this orientation with their groups, to experiential training groups for both group therapists and organizational consultants and in a modified form as a consultant to the Tavistock conference at Temple University and at Minster Lovell.

A major difference between this orientation and that of the more traditional Tavistock small group is that the task is consistently and explicitly kept in focus and related to the explicit sub-goals and to the implicit goal.

A major difference in leadership style in general, and therapy group leadership in particular, is that group management is gradually transferred from the leader to the group. Thus both my training groups and my therapy groups decide when a new member will enter the group, based on the criteria of determining what work has to be completed and what preparation work has to be done first. The group-as-a-whole decides raises in fees and in the process learns how to note the criteria for the decisions and to differentiate between primary and secondary goal criteria. (See Appendix B.)

The maturation process of a group in the group-as-a-whole systems orientation is conceptualized in terms of subgroup transactions. Subgroups form around similarities and separate on differences; they tend to be stereotyped "good" when similar and "bad" when different. Groups attempt to get rid of the "bad" by scapegoating. The dynamics of scapegoating essentially mirror splitting into good and bad, projecting out the bad and maintaining the good. The more immature the group, the more simplistic the stereotyping, and the more primitive the projection.

Keeping clear boundaries between subgroups depends upon differences being over-emphasized. When similarities in the apparently different are noted, new beginnings of integration and maturation take place. As the group matures, so does the capacity to integrate greater differences, and thus more sophisticated functioning develops.

Whenever the group or individual system is confronted with differences that are too different, too disequilibrating to integrate and too overwhelming to project, the difference is split off and isolated within a "containing" subsystem. It is thus that the system meets its primary goal of maintaining a viable equilibrium. The secondary goals that exist in relation to reality are literally secondary to these primary goals.

In Group-as-a-Whole Theory, goal achievement and individual change is explained as a function of group dynamics. In a developing group, the dynamics of each phase of development are available as a major force that impacts upon the individual experience. Within each member, salient developmental issues are aroused that resonate with the issues that the group is in the process of mastering. It is the group-as-a-whole leader's function to relate the developmental arousal to the explicit goal of the group—to the goals of therapy, when a therapy group is involved, to the specific training in a training group, to the conference task in conferences. Traditionally, in Tavistock conferences the leader behaviour tends to highlight the fight/flight phase of development, which arouses regressive dependent and counterdependent behaviour. This arousal is congruent with the conference goal of exploring relationships with authority.

APPENDIX A
Dependency

Dependency is defined as a natural maturational phenomenon that exists on a continuum of growth through independence to interdependence. The nature of the system's boundary permeability changes along this continuum. In dependency, boundaries are selectively open only to mirroring information, and intra-system homogeneity is maintained by projecting differences out. In independence, inter-system heterogeneity governs boundary permeability. In interdependence, boundaries are relatively permeable to all information. Thus the location of the system on the dependence–interdependence continuum is a diagnostic for the nature of the permeability of intra- and inter-system boundaries to the selection of input and output information.

Separation–individuation takes place as a function of intra-system dependence and the cross-fertilization (transactions of difference) of inter-system information that leads to interdependence. Separation is a function of being able to contain both similarities and differences (good and bad) within the boundaries of each system and in the information transactions between systems; it is a function of intra-system dependence and the development of appropriate boundary permeability that leads to interdependence.

Dependency can, therefore, be conceptualized as a maintaining of the good and bad split. Separation is a function of being able to contain both similarities and differences (good and bad) within the system. Dependency can be defined as the splitting of good and bad, the projection of "bad" into another subsystem in an attempt to maintain "good" within the projecting subsystem. However, this is a crippling solution that fixates the system in a symbiosis that no amount of closing boundaries can cure.

Thus the primal wish to merge in bliss with the "good" when frustrated by the conflict of good–bad arouses great grief and a murderous rage, generated by the experience that there is no solution to the noxious symbiosis except to kill or be killed.

Hence scapegoating rage: the experience of primal aggression, which, when it cannot be "contained", is then denied, repressed, and expressed in defensive sadism—the acted-out sadistic rage of scapegoating behaviour. This is a phenomenon that occurs at all levels of the system hierarchy—as masochism, or sadomasochistic relationships at the individual level; as social stereotyping, witch-hunting, or persecution at the social level; the "feeding frenzy" of scapegoating rage "group-as-a-whole as a mob".

APPENDIX B
SAVI: an instrument for coding communication

SAVI is an observation instrument that defines nine classes of verbal behaviour characterized by differing potential for introducing ambiguity, contradiction, and redundancy into the communication process. The patterns of communication that result from a SAVI analysis serve as an operational definition of the dynamics at both the individual and group system levels and operationally define the behavioural vectors in the system as approaching or avoiding the problems reacted to the achievement of primary and secondary system goals.

SAVI data can be coded in ways that picture the direction of information flow and chart the behaviours that influence changes in the communication patterns at all levels of the system hierarchy. It has been an ongoing task to use SAVI to learn practical and testable methods for consulting to the boundaries of the system.

Communication patterns can provide powerful information. For example, one fixated group that we studied demonstrated that no matter how individuals in the group changed the way they communicated, the pattern of the group remained the same—thus confirming the hypothesis that the implicit goal of the group-as-a-whole (to flight) was stronger than any individual goal, including the goal of the small-group consultant, who unwittingly reintroduced flight into the communication pattern when the members briefly worked!

Successful consultation results in a group communication pattern that solves problems that relate to its task. The advantage of thinking in terms of communication behaviour as it is organized by SAVI is that it provides a tool for diagnosing the potential for information transfer in a communication pattern and also maps a strategy for intervention. SAVI can also be used as a training tool for consultant interventions and as a tool for observing their impact upon the communication pattern of the group.

NOTE

1. Lewin's force field is a useful construct for mapping these.

CHAPTER EIGHT

Book review of *Koinonia: From Hate, through Dialogue, to Culture in the Large Group* by Patrick de Maré, Robin Piper, & Sheila Thompson

It will be of great significance to every group therapist who has wondered how large a therapy group can be that the authors of *Koinonia* propose a "median" group (of 20 to 40) as the ideal "container" for hatred and paranoia. The "median group", they argue, is the ideal arena for social resolution through "koinonic" dialogue, which requires the transcendence of individualized narcissism and the development of impersonal and interdependent friendship/citizenship. Thus "Koinonic dialogue" carries a potential highly relevant to all group work—and a potential particularly relevant to therapy

Koinonia is a remarkable and milestone book.

> Koinonia . . . communion, fellowship, intercourse . . . from the common carthorse of a language Koin . . . which united pre-classical Greece . . . belonging to everybody because it belonged to nobody . . . Koinonia . . . implying not personal and individualistic but impersonal friendship . . . a "democracy" . . . a form of togeth-

---

Y. M. Agazarian, "Book review of *Koinonia: From Hate, through Dialogue, to Culture in the Large Group* by Patrick de Maré, Robin Piper, & Sheila Thompson". In: *International Journal of Group Psychotherapy, 42,* No. 3 (1992). New York: The Guilford Press (by permission of the Guilford Press, Inc., New York).

> erness and amity that brings a serendipity of resources . . . "communion" as it is understood in the Greek Orthodox Church. [de Maré, Piper, & Thompson, 1992, pp. 1 & 2]

Of the co-authors, Pat de Maré is the pioneering giant in the field of the large group. Robin Piper and Sheila Thompson are (as yet!) less well known. Robin Piper is the co-conductor of the median group with Pat de Maré, and Sheila Thompson is a founding member of the Large Group section of the Group Analytic Society. Their book is a communion of writing that is a marvellous representation of its basic Koinonic theme.

Koinonia is not necessarily an easy book to read, but it is an important one, not for its scholarship and references, which are impressive, nor for the "Koinonic" experience awaiting the readers—but for a single, significant reframing of the understanding of the dynamics of aggression that may permanently change the practice of group work.

> It has become . . . clear to us that *hate,* arising out of the frustrating situation of the larger group, . . . provides the incentive for dialogue and becomes transformed, through dialogue, into the impersonal fellowship of Koinonia. [p. 4]
>
> The primary problem of large groups centres around primal hate . . . [p. 114]

The authors reinterpret the experience of hate in groups from a destructive affect into a natural, inevitable response to frustration—an energy that carries high potential for both destructive and constructive transformation.

> Hate . . . which in Greek also means grief . . . then constitutes the basis for psychic energy, which is transformed and expressed in the form of thinking dialogue and learning as distinct from an instinctual process. [p. 141]
>
> Working on the basis that hate is the energy and the result of frustrated instinct, we have arrived at the conclusion that the (median) group constitutes a structure large enough to contain and transform hate for cultural purposes via the system of dialogue. Such a structure is not evident in either psychoanalysis or in small group situations. [p. 174]
>
> Whereas the small group, particularly the psychoanalytic and Foulksian group, evokes family transferences and repetition meanings in terms of the inner lives of the past, the large group requires, through the containment of hate . . . the transformation of energy

> into the socializing process of impersonal friendship and dialogue. [p. 98]

The common psychodynamic understanding of hatred is closely linked to Freud's concept of the death instinct and the destructive superego. In *Koinonia* the authors reframe both:

> the energy of the superego is said to be derived from the Id, but we emphasize again that this energy is not direct and biological, but as the frustrated energy of hate (not superego guilt! [p. 122]
>
> which can become transformed into mental energy. [p. 125]
>
> Hate, then, is not the adversary of Eros but the inevitable irreversible outcome of the frustration of Eros: if there is any adversary to Eros, it is . . . ananke . . . external necessity. We have to cope with ananke, and thereby we evolve dialogue, mind and culture. [p. 62]
>
> [The] . . . structuring of hate through dialogue constitutes transformation. [p. 108]

Thus the authors transform Freudian pessimism into optimism by contrasting

> [the] passive renunciation of instinctual gratification, on which civilization is built (Freud) and the active frustration of hate to which the evolution of culture owes it origins. [p. 61]

It is a major contribution to group work to recognize that the frustration inevitable in all groups generates hatred, which dialogue and communion resolves. In this way, Koinonia in the median group is framed in terms of a process that is universal to all human beings. If there is a weakness in the authors' argument it is that, although the work is approached from a systems "group-as-a-whole" point of view, they overlook the essential systems concept of isomorphy—that is, the equivalence of structure, function, and dynamics for all systems in the same hierarchy. Thus the Koinonic potential for resolving hatred is seen as a property of the median group rather than as a property of Koinonic dialogue. I would question whether the development of the Koinonic group is a function of group size. Is it the variable of size or the state of the art that it can "take more than ten years to create a culture in which people can begin to talk to each other without violation" (p. 94)? The development of group boundaries, norms, goals, and structure is a system dynamic affected by, but not determined by, size or time. Perhaps a more relevant influence on the development of Koinonia is leadership?

Critically, I would say that the authors have a sense of group-as-a-whole forces without requiring group-as-a-whole consciousness of those forces and, perhaps, without consciousness of the potential for deliberately managing those forces. A "conductor" conducts both by providing the structure (the score) and by influencing how the orchestra will behave within that structure! A leader can disown personal leadership but never the influence of the leader role! For example, in the large-group report, when members dropped out, either in dissatisfaction with the group or in discord with the leader, the group-as-a-whole was not "led" to ask itself what dynamics those leaving members "contained" for the group, nor why the group had exported them.

Any criticism pales, however, before the implications of reframing hatred as potential creative energy in the service of the ego rather than as a destructive, guilty, death-focused superego force, and that therapy could (nay, should!) take place in groups of 20 to 40! This is a particularly challenging reframing in this era of psychotherapy where we are at the threshold of paying attention to which of the dynamic aspects about which we write are issues generic to treating human ills and which are iatrogenic, regressive, or defensive constellations elicited by our treatment context and methods. For example, if we were to focus less on transference in small groups and more on the socializing requirements underlying the development of Koinonia, would we in truth be looking to a new future rather than to the expected repetitions of the past? Can one envisage groups of the future (whether groups of one, two, three, or many) saying: "I am in hate with you, don't take it personally, let us use the energy to develop Koinonia!"

CHAPTER NINE

A systems approach to the group-as-a-whole

In viewing the group as a system, I begin, not with Bion (1959) and Bertalanffy (1969), who are the true forethinkers of group-as-a-whole and systems theory, but with Korzybski (1948), who wrote passionately of the prison that Aristotelian logic has created for our Western minds. Whatever you say a thing is, it is NOT, says Korzybski, striking at the heart of our either/or splits. The map is not the territory, says Korzybski, forcing us to notice that our theoretical maps simultaneously both represent and misrepresent our reality as well as create it! All our observations are self-reflexive, says Korzybski—an important point for us as therapists who so often talk about the group as if we are not part of it. Finally, only when our use of language reflects both the structural and the dynamic aspects of reality, says Korzybski, will we understand that there is both space *and* time, as well as a relationship between space/time; individual *and* group, as well as the individual/group relationship.

It is rare that the development or consolidation of a theory is done in isolation. Thus, although I have devoted my theoretical self to devel-

---

Y. M. Agazarian, "A systems approach to the group-as-a-whole". *International Journal of Group Psychotherapy, 42,* No. 3 (1992). The Guilford Press, New York (reproduced by permission of Guilford Press, New York).

oping an organized and integrated set of principles for thinking further about group psychotherapy, it is inconceivable that this conceptual journey was in reality taken in isolation, or that there will not be many people who, on reading these pages, do not immediately recognize developments of their own.

I began with every group therapist's Sisyphus: the need to think about individuals in group in a psychodynamic way, and to somehow think about the group itself in a group dynamic way. My first attempted solution (Agazarian & Peters, 1981) was to conceptualize individual psychodynamics and group dynamics as two discrete but compatible systems, both of which could be understood and influenced by applying the constructs of Lewin's (1951) Field Theory. In this way I integrated Freudian psychodynamics, Bion, and the group-as-a-whole theoreticians (Agazarian, 1989d), the heritage of Korzybski (1948), and the riches of social science theory and research (Agazarian, 1986b; Cartwright & Zander, 1960; Coleman & Bexton, 1975; Coleman & Geller, 1985; Miller, 1978). After working with Helen Durkin (1972) and the members of the General Systems Theory committee (James Durkin, 1981), I was able to apply the principle of isomorphy to the problem and develop operational definitions for the structure and dynamic function of human systems.

There are many in our field who intuitively sense that there is a group-as-a-whole perspective (Horwitz, 1977) or who intuitively apply General Systems Theory principles (Anzieu, 1984). For example, individually oriented group therapists "know" that the group influences the individual and the individual influences the group; they "know" that interpretations speak differently to the systems of the conscious, pre-conscious, and unconscious and serve a similar (isomorphic) function for all. Intuition, however, is different from explanation and definition. Leading a group intuitively creates one kind of group reality, leading a group from theory, another. Systems equifinality sets out many roads to Rome.

Group-as-a-whole thinking differs from more traditional thinking about groups in that it is group-centred, not individual-centred (Agazarian, 1989d). Members' behaviour is therefore understood in terms of group dynamics rather than in terms of individual dynamics. General Systems Theory, stemming more from social psychology than from individual psychology (Ackoff & Emery, 1972), adds the heritage of scientific thinking with a potential for providing a meta-theory of human behaviour (Klein, Bernard, & Singer, 1992). Thinking of group as a system of systems in a hierarchy of systems is a meta-shift in thinking from both the individual-centred and group-centred approach (Agazarian, 1992a).

Group as a system is an abstraction. It is not a place in which people live. It "appears" when you think it and disappears when you do not! This chapter introduces the reader to thinking "systems-centered": to thinking about group as a system that exists in a hierarchy of systems and is itself a hierarchy of systems, self-reflexively isomorphic in structure and function.

I have developed systems-centered theory to enable systems-centered thinking. Whether it will prove to be a useful meta-theory for human systems in general, and the systems relevant to psychotherapy in particular, is in the hands of those who will apply it. To date, it has enabled me and my colleagues to generate hypotheses and to test them informally as interventions in live training and psychotherapy groups.

Systems-centered group therapy

Systems-centered group therapy is a new discipline in several ways, based on some different constructs. First and most important to understand is that the *subgroup*, not the individual member, is the basic unit of the systems-centered group. The subgroup exists in the environment of the group-as-a-whole and is the environment for its members. It follows, then, that the subgroup is the fulcrum. Subgroups form around similarities and separate around differences. Functional subgroups contain differences in the system while the system develops sufficiently to integrate them.

Dynamics of systems are *isomorphic,* as is system structure and function. Therefore a change at any system level influences a change at all system levels. The structure of a system is defined by its boundaries. The condition of the systems' *boundaries* in space, time, reality, and role contain the energy available for work. The system functions to remain in quasi-stationary equilibrium in relation to its *self-correcting goals* (Bowlby, 1969, chapter 3), of survival, development, and environmental mastery. For a system's *energy* to be directed in relation to its goals, potential energy must be transformed into active energy (Miller, 1978). Active energy will either be contained in a freeze or be directioned in fight/flight or work. The behavioural output of the system—individual member, subgroup, and group-as-a-whole—implies the internal and external goal orientation of the system.

The *developmental principle* of all living systems can be formulated as a function of discrimination and integration of information

(Agazarian, 1989d). Systems-centered therapy takes place by facilitating the process of discriminating, communicating, and integrating perceptions of differences in the apparently similar and similarities in the apparently different.

Communication takes place at the boundaries between systems at all levels of the hierarchy: the group, the subgroup, and its members. The major focus of intervention is thus not level, as in the group-as-a-whole, but system boundaries (Agazarian, 1989a). All content is potential information. All content is conveyed in communications that occur in time and space. System change occurs when the boundaries of the system become appropriately permeable to communication and a flow of energy is released. Content in the communication indicates which boundary is involved: time–space boundaries, fantasy–reality boundaries, functional role boundaries, or subgroup boundaries.

Every communication across a boundary carries both a potential for being a flight or fight from the current task and/or in service of the current task. Shifting the ambiguity, contradiction, and redundancy balance in the communications will change the problem-solving potential of the communications (Simon & Agazarian, 1967). The boundary that is being crossed gives information as to the direction of energy. The content of the communication gives information as to the kind of resource it is to the problem being solved. It is not the content in and of itself that is important, but the nature of the communication conveyed by the content. Increasing the problem-solving nature of communication across system boundaries increases the probability that all systems in the hierarchy will solve problems inherent in goal-directed behaviour. The systems-centered leader attends to the systems communication process across subgroups rather than to the content conveyed in the individual member communications. How this looks in practice is introduced in the following section.

The difficult member

In both *group-as-a-whole and systems-centered therapy*, difficult members are difficult in group, not because of their pathology, but because of their deviance from the group norms. From the group-as-a-whole perspective, difficult members are not simply those members who are the fight/flight or pairing Basic Assumption leaders, leading the group away from work, but those whose role suction is so great that the group-as-a-whole institutionalizes them in a scapegoat or identified patient role. *Group-as-a-whole work* is as powerful as it is because it utilizes the mechanism of projective identification at the group level as a major therapeutic force by making it the group task to take back projections from the member who is containing them for the group. When, in spite of the leader's best efforts, the group is simply not able to successfully undo the projections, the group is developmentally fixated and has, by definition, failed in its fundamental purpose. Thus the very strength of the group-as-a-whole is its weakness. A patient, acting out an oft-played role, can become more than anyone bargains for when the role contains not only their individual dynamics but also the dynamics of the group-as-a-whole. This is how, when group-as-a-whole interventions fail, members can become casualties. Even if, in their familiar role of scapegoat or identified patient, the member leaves safely and re-integrates outside the group, the work of taking back and reintegrating is not done in the group, which is a deprivation for both the member and the group. There is a significant difference in the level of experience and insight when group members are able to engage in a live, here-and-now, interdependent process of recovering and re-integrating projections.

The systems-centered approach to the group-as-a-whole introduces the technique of functional subgrouping, which increases the probability that splits will be contained at the group-as-a-whole level rather than displaced into a stereotype containing role. A member then becomes "difficult" not because of his role salience, but because he cannot work in a subgroup. Subgrouping requires being able not to be the centre of the group, to understand that work in the group requires joining others' work and allowing them to join yours. It requires some understanding of the advantage of not taking things personally, volunteering to serve as a projective screen for each other, and, most important, it means being willing to give up self-defeating roles. It doesn't matter that the member who enters the group cannot do any of these things, as long as he can see in them a value for him and something that he will want to learn. Without this willingness, it is inappropriate to place him in a systems-centered group. Thus, for example, members do not join until they have stopped taking drugs. Members who are very self-centred have a very hard time, but it is not impossible for them to learn how to work. Psychotics are perhaps better in a systems-centered group of their own, unless their medication makes them available at a more complex systems level.

Subgrouping in a systems-centered group is a technique for putting the systems developmental process into practice: the ability to discriminate and integrate. Subgroups are therefore used deliberately to split the two different sides of a conflict, so that each side can be contained and understood separately as a discriminatory step towards developing whatever ability the system needs to develop in order to contain, accept, and integrate the conflictual differences. Borderlines, whose basic mechanism is to split the good from the bad and who are accustomed to feeling alone, tend to feel less alien in a systems group, where splitting is deliberately fostered, deep undifferentiated feelings are valued, and everything is legitimized so that it can be overtly contained and explored.

The difficult member in a systems-centered group is the one who must learn how to work at the individual system level before he can benefit from the subgroup work in the group-as-a-whole. In systems-centered group work, unless a group is still working through the stages of group development, it is highly unlikely that the group will maintain stereotype roles as a solution to group disequilibrium. Therefore, patients who arouse the extremes of compassion or murderous rage in the group are rarely supported in the role of identified patient or scapegoat. As we will see in the section on subgrouping, the very requirements of becoming a subgroup member make the split conscious and integrate the inherent differences, which is the obverse of solving the conflict through projective identification.

The techniques for working with the difficult patient mirror the same techniques that the systems-centered therapist uses to help the group move through the phase-appropriate defences that coincide with the stages of development of the group-as-a-whole. If the difficult patient is a member of a developing group, then this entails particular difficulty for the group on the one hand and an experience of how much it costs the group to react with group defences on the other. If the group is able to contain the patient, then the particular difficulties that the patient brings into the group will contribute significantly to the strength of the group's mastery of the phase. It is in this sense that the natural group scapegoat is the patient who benefits most from group therapy in the resolution of the fight stage in which he inevitably plays a significant role.

Mac, a new and impossible member, is the one I have chosen to illustrate how the difficult patient is absorbed into a systems-centered group. His difficult behaviour could equally well represent a difficult group or a difficult subgroup. Claudia, my co-therapist, and I had admitted Mac under pressure from his current individual therapist, who was impressed by his motivation, and from Mac himself, who, although clearly a lifelong patient and the victor of many spoiled therapies, had managed, in the last year, to wean himself off drugs. Mac arrived in the group and conquered, putting into practice all the different constellation of skills he had learnt in how to drive each of his many therapists crazy.

Mac was not able to subgroup: the appropriate level of intervention was, therefore, to his individual system. Claudia and I became containers for the good/bad conflict inside Mac, and each of us "joined" one of Mac's internal subgroups. I joined his harsh superego subgroup, which I modified by "teaching" him some practical methods of managing himself. Claudia joined his ego subgroup, giving him encouragement and empathy for his courage in striving towards his goals. We both praised every positive response we could find, ignored his pathology, and kept him connected to an achievable goal: "Your job, Mac, is to learn how to work in this group, that is your only task, and we will all help."

I sat next to Mac. I pointed out that his "shaking with anxiety" was generated by vibrating his foot on the floor, and I insisted that he make eye contact. Whenever he spoke, I said (and soon so did the other members): "Who are you talking to, Mac?" "It's against the group rules to talk or work by yourself alone, Mac." "Choose someone and tell them what you want to say." Mac's initial reaction was an outward compliance, with many protestations of how much he wanted to get better and how he would learn, while he consistently sabotaged every effort to relate to him. The group subgrouped around their frustration with him, one subgroup feeling that we, the therapists, were being too tough, the other feeling that we were not tough enough. As they subgrouped, they experienced their range of responses to Mac and identified and shared with Mac, as fast as they could, what defences he was using and why they wouldn't work. Over and over again, one or another member would say: "I used to do that, Mac, when . . . and it didn't work any better for me than it is working for you".

Mac and the group survived four group meetings, making some progress, but with much uncharacteristic quarrelling as one or another member became frustrated past endurance. By the fifth session the tide turned, and the group learned to feel some empathy for Mac's determined destructiveness. Mac was no longer able to get a reaction from the group even with threats of suicide: "Yes, Mac, I also used to threaten suicide until I realized I might as well be dead if I was going to try to relate to people like that." He walked out of his fifth session and missed the next. He came back and sulked in silence. He sulked for four more sessions, and the group neutrally, without hostility, paid no attention and continued with their work.

In the middle of his tenth session the "difficult" subgroup made contact with Mac. It was certainly Mac's natural subgroup. First Bob, much given to violent fantasy, said " Mac, what work have you been doing during your silence in here?" thus asking the question that was his own task in the group. Mac continued to sulk. Chris, whose group life is terrorized by anxiety, which scatters the thoughts in his brilliant mind and leaves him inarticulate and stumbling, and whose group task is to say whatever he can, whether or not he judges it appropriate, spoke up for Mac. "I'm so afraid to say this . . . I'm sitting here, and I feel so different. . . . I'm not frustrated with Mac. . . . I'm different from the whole group . . . it's like this is my whole life. . . . I don't want to be so different. . . ." At this point, on the criterion that no member should have to work alone, I, the therapist, as the only one in the group at that moment resonating with Chris's position, joined his subgroup. The "self-disclosure" intervention I made next is a good example of how "putting theory into practice" sometimes requires me to reverse a previous orientation and take a leap of faith. With feelings more appropriate to leaping off a bridge, I said: "I know what that is like, Chris. I have just been to a weekend conference, and I felt like the only Martian there . . . don't give up." Chris didn't. "I do not understand why you all can't see that Mac doesn't understand something." The group supports Chris, wanting to know what he sees. Championed by the group, Chris struggles to communicate what he understands to Mac. Predictably, Mac evades and changes the subject and answers questions that were not asked and picks up the wrong end of every stick. In the middle of his efforts, in a rare moment of connection, Chris is able to turn to Paula in delight and say: "I'm in your subgroup! Now I understand what you feel like—how frustrated you get." At this point both therapists join Chris's work with Mac. I keep Mac in eye contact with Chris, Claudia encourages him not to mount a legalistic defence. The group, in the meantime, is rooting for us all. Like a flash that has gone almost before it appears, a micro-moment of communication takes place. Chris knows it. The group sees it. Mac tries to undo it. Both therapists pounce and insist that Mac give a straightforward paraphrase of what Chris has said. Mac gives in and does. An "official" transfer of information between the group and Mac has publicly taken place. The group cheers. Mac is congratulated, and he actually smiles. Chris is lauded: "You have done such an important thing for the group . . .

none of us could do it . . . we couldn't manage the frustration . . . you reached him . . ." The group was moved and moving, triumphant, tearful, exultant. Chris, enveloped in positive feeling, turns pink with pleasure. No longer white-faced and withdrawn, free from depression and anxiety for the moment, Chris is pleased and relaxed and moved and in contact with the group and with Mac.

What happened next? Within a month of this episode, the following work took place in the group when Mac backed away from an interchange and started to sulk:

Paula: "Don't give up!"

Linda: "Don't back down!"

Mac: "She . . ." [*complain/blame*] . . .

Bob: "Don't fight!"

Mac: "I've got to fight!"

Paula: "This is what you need to know. You can't do anything until you hear this. Don't fight! Nobody here is going to hurt you!"

Chris: "Drop your guard! That's what we're all here to do. Find out what's underneath. I have the same trouble you do about keeping my guard up."

Mac: "I have to keep my guard up to be able to work."

Bob: "No! Work in here is learning how to let your guard down."

Mac had just graduated to his next group task!

Functional subgrouping

Traditionally, in the group-as-a-whole, the first subgroups to appear represent the most obvious and simplest "containment" of differences in a group, like sex, age, colour, race, and status. Stereotype subgrouping is one of the first ways the group-as-a-whole structures itself to contain its differences and maintain group stability. Later in dynamic development, the group-as-a-whole uses the roles of "benevolent leader"/"malevolent leader", the scapegoat and the "identified patient", as containers for its unintegrated splits around differences. This dynamic is so dramatic in group development that the less obvious dynamic of "functional subgrouping" can go unnoticed in the developmental process. Stereotype subgrouping is the simplest level of subgrouping (Agazarian, 1990b). Subgroups naturally come together around similarities and separate around differences, thus mirroring the developmental process of discriminating and integrating. Thus the dynamic that underlies the function of subgrouping mirrors the dynamics of system development and can be deliberately harnessed in the service of containing and integrating group splits. Explicitly encouraging the group to do subgroup work interrupts the spontaneous fight response to differences and replaces it with the discipline of "functional subgrouping".

The most efficient method for facilitating the subgroup work of discrimination and integration is to encourage the exploration of experience within each individual subgroup before there is any cross-subgroup communication. Thus, by the very process of development, the internal process shifts from the cohesion around similarities to seeing differences in the cohesively similar. This process increases differentiation within each subgroup and increases the permeability potential of the boundaries between the subgroups. When boundaries become appropriately permeable to a transfer of information, similarities between the differing subgroups are perceived, and new subgroups can form. This is the process of system integration and the ongoing task of crossing from irreality to reality (and from the unconscious to the preconscious to the conscious).

Some functional subgroups appear as obviously balanced dichotomies in the group that the leader can easily encourage the group to explore: cognition and affect; compliance and defiance; closeness and distance. Others are less obvious and have to be "believed" before they are seen: like seeing that fighting members belong to the same subgroup and are one of two subgroups balancing the groups' fight-and-flight response. When the systems-centered therapist manages conflict through functional subgrouping, the group is encouraged to first identify and then to "take sides" in the conflict, and to do their individual insight work in the supported context of the subgroup. This bypasses ambivalence—the common defence against the experience of being pulled two ways by the forces of both sides of the conflict. The therapist encourages a conscious splitting into subgroups and, by so doing, discourages defensive splitting within individuals. The conflict is *contained* within the group-as-a-whole rather than within each individual. Through membership in a subgroup, individuals are supported in their work of exploring one single side of their version of the conflict instead of denying, projecting, or acting out in the struggle to contain both at once.

An example of intervening to promote functional subgrouping follows. It also contains a good illustration of the dilemma of choosing the level of intervention. The episode occurred in a group that had worked hard to surface their sadomasochistic conflict. One milestone day, the worm turned, and Annette, usually quiet and passive, startled the group by energetically confronting Celia as a "bully". This was particularly poignant as Annette experienced much of her life as the passive, bullied victim, while Celia was in a terrible struggle with herself, systematically destroying her relationships by treating people the way she had treated Annette.

The whole group mobilized around Annette. It was so unusual for Annette to be fight leader rather than isolated that I, too, wanted to take her side! But scapegoating Celia, though progress for Annette, was a regression for the group. I was thus in conflict between different levels of intervention: whether to encourage the group to work with Annette as a representative of the subgroup "learning to stand up for oneself"; whether to encourage the subgroup to do the work of "taking back" their projections into Celia; or whether to orient the group-as-a-whole to functional subgroup work in which both sides of the sadomasochistic split could be explored. The group-as-a-whole energy was so actively mobilized that I decided to intervene with the group-as-a-whole. I said softly, several times, that I thought it would help if the group divided into subgroups and deepened their own individual subgroup work before they tried to talk across to each other. Finally, I raised my voice over the hubbub and said: "You can fight if you want, and I'll sit here and watch. Or I'll help you to contract to do subgroup work so that you can explore both sides of the fight. I'll sit and watch the fight, or I'll help you to subgroup. It's up to you. Either way is OK with me."

A criterion of successful subgroup work is when, at the moment of group re-integration, individual insight "erupts" group-wide. Dramatically, as the group experienced their subgroups as two halves of the same whole, so spontaneous cries came from Celia and Annette: "I see . . . by victimizing you, I stay safe from the unbearable humiliation of being a victim like you." "Yes, and I'd rather be the victim than experience how vicious I'd be if I ever got started."

Levels of intervention: group, subgroup, member

Systems are isomorphic. Influencing one system level influences all. Levels of intervention in both the group-as-a-whole and the systems-centered approach have the characteristic of vectors with a direction, a velocity, and a point of application. Both are primarily concerned with the defensive process in the group rather than the content. *Group-as-a-whole interventions* are primarily targeted at the Basic Assumption behaviours with the intention of bringing the group's attention to how fight/flight, dependency, and pairing are defensive reactions to the underlying group chaos that the group must learn to master in the service of here-and-now work. Chaos, *in systems-centered thinking*, is unorganized and disorganized information—the "entropy" in the group. Chaos is potential energy that, when organized in communications across the boundaries between, within, and among systems, becomes active working energy. Successful interventions increase the appropriate permeability of the boundaries between systems so that the problem-solving potential in the communication is increased. In this sense, a more relevant way of thinking about systems-centered interventions is in terms of the boundaries: time and space boundaries, role boundaries, and reality/irreality boundaries.

In the example of Annette and Celia's group above, *the group-as-a-whole leader* would encourage the group to understand the fight reaction in relation to the underlying group issues. For the group-as-a-whole leader, Annette and Celia are the "voice" of the group issue, as well as "containing" for the group split-off and projected parts of the group members. These "containing roles" of the group-as-a-whole approach are the subgroup leaders of the systems approach.

The appropriate level for the *systems-centered intervention* is not simply whether to intervene at the level of the subgroup, member, or group-as-a-whole, but which boundary to influence. Influencing the permeability of the boundary between, within, or among systems at any level of the hierarchy influences the balance of driving and restraining forces in relation to the goal. Influencing the system through Celia would be influencing the boundary permeability between the group and the scapegoat. Influencing through Annette would be influencing the boundaries within Annette's "member system" so that her changed communication "output" would serve as a change "input" with the potential for influencing other member systems and the group-as-a-whole. Subgroup boundaries are often the target of choice because subgroups are the fulcrum system. As we have seen, subgrouping seemed to me to be the appropriate level to influence, and in this case it paid off.

Boundaries: here-and-now, there-and-then, reality–irreality

Both the group-as-a-whole and the systems-centered approach have a primary concern with group defences. *In the group-as-a-whole,* the Basic Assumption defences are the fight/flight, dependency, and pairing reactions in relation to the here-and-now of group work. In addition to these Basic Assumption defences, *systems-centered interventions* attend to the defences that reduce communication across the boundaries between, within, and among the group-as-a-whole, the subgroup, and the member systems. There is a direct relationship between defences at the boundary and the permeability of the boundary to information. Systems-centered interventions are, therefore, intended to reduce defences at the thresholds of the boundary. Reducing defences increases the potential for boundary permeability, which increases the probability that relevant information can be exchanged. A crucial boundary to monitor and influence in this respect is the boundary in time.

Boundaries in time define the existence of the group, not only in space/time but also in the realities and irrealities of the psychological time that exists in the past, present, and future, all co-existing without contradiction in the unconscious: a significant determinant of the state of the system existence, experience, and productivity in the present.

Lewin's (1951) model can be a useful way for the therapist to image the boundary relationships and the direction of communication flow in the group. Work can only take place in the present, but, as Figure 9.1. illustrates, the source of information that is relevant to work may be in the past or the future as well as the present: the reality of the present, the reality of the past, the probability in the future, or the irreality of any one level. Creativity, innovation, and tomorrow's discoveries exist in the irrealities of yesterday and today.

	Past	Present	Future
irreality			
reality			

FIGURE 9.1. Lewin's (1951) model

Communications: process and content

From both the group-as-a-whole and the systems perspectives the content of what is communicated is not important by itself: it is important for what it communicates about the conflicts of the system and how they are being contained. Conflict is generated by the inherent opposition to differences. When differences are not too great, the work of integration is not too hard. When the oppositional forces pull in different directions, then the tendency is for the system to split and to isolate the conflicting "too different" behind impermeable boundaries in a containing subsystem. The most familiar, but perhaps not the most obvious, is the tendency for groups to manage the basic good/bad split by projecting it into the good/bad leader. Equally familiar and more obvious is the creation of the "scapegoat" as the container of deviance and the "identified patient" as a container for conflict.

Thinking about groups from a systems-centered perspective, I was once again confronted with a need to question an approach that I had long practiced with conviction and comfort. Left to itself, a group "grows like Topsy", and, charming though this often is, it is not likely to be the most efficient way to a therapeutic environment. Functional subgrouping and other systems-centered skills are made, not borne. For the systems-centered therapist, the purpose of interventions in the group process are primarily related to teaching the group to recognize and put into practice the skills that systems needs to survive, to mature, and to reach environmental goals. Therefore the process work of a systems-centered leader is to teach the fundamentals of systems-centered group work from the very beginning of group life: the monitoring of boundaries in space and time that contain the work energy in the group, functional subgrouping, group roles and problem-solving communication, defence reduction, and goal orientation. To date, this has not appeared to coerce dependency: rather, by reducing defensive dependency, functional dependency is legitimized and not shamed.

Group–system communication crosses system boundaries at all levels of the hierarchy. Every person who speaks in a group plays an individualized role for themselves at the individual system level and for a subgroup and the group-as-a-whole at the group-role level. The major leadership task of the systems-centered group therapist is to influence the patterns of communication that emerge from the transactions across the boundaries so that the group-as-a-whole develops the ability to solve the problems that are relevant to its survival, to each phase of its maturation, and to the achievement of its environmental goals. In this way, as the work of developing mature communication in the group requires increasing maturity from the group members, individual therapy takes place.

There are three major interventions, targeted at the content, that the systems-centered therapist makes, particularly in the early stages of group development. These interventions are derived from the hypothesis that there is an inverse relationship between ambiguity, contradictions, and redundancies in the communication and the probability that the information contained in the communication will be received (Shannon & Weaver, 1964). These interventions can be directed either to the subgroup, the member, or the group-as-a-whole:

1. point out similarities in apparently different content when the group is in fight, too contradictory, full of should-nots or yes-buts, or too full of "differences" to work;
2. point out differences in apparently similar content when the group is in flight, too vague or intellectual or too ambiguously "similar" to work;
3. introduce new differences and new similarities into the content, which will require new integrations, when the group is too predictable, too cohesive, complacent, or redundant to work.

Defence and resistance: restraining forces relating to system goals

Group-level defences are the restraints that interfere with the group's ability to solve the problems that lie on its path to its goals. Whether the work of modifying defences is done directly with a member, with a subgroup, or with the group-as-a-whole will depend upon where the restraining forces can be most easily weakened. Thus the systems orientation is not group-problem-oriented as much as it is group-defence-oriented. In other words, the primary task in the group is not to solve problems! Instead, the primary task is oriented towards reducing the restraining forces in the communications across system boundaries so that group communication will result in solving problems. This rests on the hypothesis that reaching the secondary goals of environmental mastery is dependent upon the relationship of the system to the primary goals of system survival and development.

Therapeutic systems "learn how to work" by autonomously learning to recognize and modify defences (McCullough, 1995). There is not space here to go into the "training" of a systems-centered group. Sufficient to say that the first line of defence that groups learn to take in charge for themselves are the tactical defences, particularly critical superego language and tendencies to pathologize, vagueness, ambivalence, rationalization, yes–buts. Next comes the struggle with the character defences: compliance and defiance, passivity, blind trust or suspicion, isolating mistrust, acting out, retreating into suffering victim or victimized bully; and, finally, there are the barrier defences: shame, guilt, humiliation, and shyness, which guard the threshold of the core self and on the other side of which are the forbidden experiences of love and hate, rage and pain, grief and joy. In a systems-centered group, what is important is to find a way through the boundary, past the defences, not to become fascinated by them or spend more time than necessary in them.

Defence analysis is central to the work of a systems-centered group. Figure 9.2 is an adapted version of the force field (Lewin, 1951), which illustrates the state of defensive communication in a group (Agazarian 1991a). It shows how group defensiveness in communication can be analysed. The balance of goal-related driving forces and defensive restraining forces function keeps the group in quasi-stationary equilibrium. It is intuitively obvious that to the extent the defensive restraining forces to communication are reduced in the group, so its driving forces increase in strength. For example, asking and answering questions is a powerful method of enabling the transfer of information in communication. Indirection or avoidant behaviours will not only interfere with the flow of information, they will also introduce ambiguity and contradictions into the communication process itself. Thus, by "weakening" these restraining forces, not only do the driving forces "drive" against less resistance, but the communication process pattern itself also serves as a driving force.

Perhaps it will also be apparent, for those who take a second look, how a force field can serve as a diagnostic of the group's implicit goals and the relationship between its resistance and its drive. A goal of "opening boundaries to communication" can be heuristically inferred from the driving forces, just as a goal of "closing boundaries" can be inferred from the restraining forces. The force-field model can always be used to delineate dynamic equilibrium from which the heuristic group can be inferred, no matter what style of therapy group is under analysis. Only the labels for the forces, the conceptual framework, and the language of analysis will change (Agazarian, 1986a).

Force field of driving and restraining forces in influencing boundary permeability to communication

→ DRIVING FORCES →	← RESTRAINING FORCES ←
asking direct questions →	← indirect questions ← leading questions ← sarcastic questions
answering questions →	← avoiding answering ← changing the subject ← answering a question with a question
building on ideas →	← pre-empting ideas ← yes-butting ← interrupting
proposing →	← blaming & complaining
owning own feelings →	← putting self down
supporting self and others →	← oughtituding
Goal opening boundaries to communication →	**Goal** ← closing boundaries to communication

FIGURE 9.2. Adaptation of Lewin's Force Field Model demonstrating the quasi-stationary equilibrium of communication in a self-correcting system (Agazarian, 1991a)

Transference and countertransference

In the *group-as-a-whole,* the blank screen of the therapist's stance induces strong negative and positive transference to the leader. It is this strong transference reaction that exacerbates the fight/flight and pairing reactions and increases the strength of the projective identifications into the scapegoat, the identified patient, and the benevolent/malevolent leader roles. The group-as-a-whole leader uses countertransference resonance to gauge the depth and readiness for group interventions to transform transference into insight in the group. Here is another instance where *systems-centered theory* requires a reframing of the basic construct. Transference and countertransference are framed as input and output communications at the boundary.

For example, the more Claudia and I applied systems-centered tenets, the less we were protected by our distancing analytic neutrality and interpretations, and the more we experienced the impact of being "silent partners" resonating with subgroups even though we did not (in the earlier stages of applying systems) work explicitly in them. For a period of about six months we experienced ourselves acting out, being unable to keep time boundaries, running over as much as ten or fifteen minutes, group after group. In addition, although the group did obey the spirit of the "no socializing" rule, both we and the group were aware that the group itself often continued on the pavement outside the door for as long as half an hour and sometimes 45 minutes, so that often we waved goodbye to it when we left after our de-briefing. We would bring this up in the group, but clearly our hearts were not in it. This was particularly paradoxical in that it coincided with the time in developing systems-centered theory that I was increasingly convinced that it was the management of boundaries that enabled the energy to be contained and focused on the group work. In our dilemma, we repeatedly analysed our "countertransference" in our review after group. The best that we could come up with was that as the group work deepened, so it became increasingly clear to us that we did not suffer as they did. Resonating with their pain left us with pain, and often we would do the after-group work of understanding the system dynamics through our own tears. We interpreted to ourselves that we felt so badly for them that we were trying to make up to them by "running over" in group.

It was the group that initiated the work around acting out. Discussing the pros and cons of its impact on their therapy, the group decided that although they would not make it a hard-and-fast rule, it was probably better if they stopped meeting regularly after group. They reduced their after-group contact to waiting for everyone before going down in the lift, and they dispersed once they reached the street. Then, in one session, the members focused on our acting out: saying that acting out was bad for everyone. My co-therapist was confronted with her passivity, I was confronted with my difficulty in keeping the bills straight, and we were both confronted with not keeping the time boundary, which had made a patient late for an appointment. After that, the group ended itself on time with our cooperation.

The next major work that the group did was experiencing reality helplessness—acknowledging that offering sympathy or solutions, interpretations, opinions, exhortations, and explanations not only failed to help, but were distancing and created identified patients. Without these defences, the group confronted the grim work of crossing the boundary from wish and magic into the reality of how hard it is to accept the problems that they could not change. We made no connection, initially, between the re-established the time boundaries and this important work. We were not even aware of the "coincidence" until one day we recognized that it had been a relatively long time since we had cried through our co-therapy review. It then became clear that it had been our own reluctance to confront how little we could help our patients in the way we wished. Rather than helping, "giving" the group extra time had in fact deprived it of the structure it needed to do the work that followed. That as we opened up to the depth of the pain of our own helplessness as our part of the group work, we stopped crying. True for us as well for our patients, our real pain was more bearable than our defences against it!

In conclusion

In *group-as-a-whole* therapy people learn that they avoid their problems in the same way the world does. What they find unacceptable in themselves, they split off and project into others, whom they then treat as unacceptable. By taking back these parts of themselves, they feel whole. In the group-as-a-whole people learn that the roles they play in the group are determined more by the group than by themselves, and sometimes the group requires them to contain, for the group, more than they can bear.

They learn that when it is too hard to approach and solve the many problems on the road to their goals, they will avoid and fight or flight or enter a political relationship with another instead. That in their groups at home and away, the goals that are implied by the way they behave are the goals that they are working towards—and that these implicit goals are often destructively different from the goals that they think or say they are working towards. They learn that envy of others costs them their competence, that idealizing or devaluing authority makes it impossible for them to have authority.

In addition, in systems-centered therapy groups people learn that they do not work alone—they work in subgroups. They learn to join a subgroup in deed and not just word. One good self-disclosure deserves another. Joining is not saying "I'm in your subgroup, so tell me more about that", which is more like pushing the boat out to sea. Joining is jumping in and rowing. When one member of a subgroup gets stuck, others carry the ball until the subgroup work is done. The work of subgrouping is to deliberately split the group into two sides of a question so that each side can be thoroughly explored. Coming together in the same-side subgroup and exploring the meaning of the experience results in discovering differences. When the subgroup work is done, when the two sides of the question do not seem so different after all, a new integration has taken place for the subgroup members and for the group-as-a-whole: differences are acknowledged and accepted, whether or not they are liked!

The systems-centered therapy group is a system that develops from simple to complex for all its members. People in a systems-centered group learn that the here and now is the place of work: that boundaries in space and time keep the energy for work in the group. That goals can be reached if they know what next steps they need to take to reach their goal. The group-as-a-whole has the responsibility for monitoring the boundaries so that work can take place, and boundaries are always the therapist's responsibility when the group drops the ball.

The systems-centered therapist consults to the boundaries, reduces the redundancies, ambiguities, and contradictions in communication so that boundaries remain permeable and information is exchanged. In practice, this means weakening the defences (within and between the members and the subgroups and the group) that interfere with work towards the goal. People in systems-centered groups know that patients and therapists are allies and have the same personal tasks: to relate authentically to the problems in group life, to alert to their own and each other's defences, and to make intimate contact with themselves and each other. This work is frustrating, enraging, terrifying, humiliating, shaming, painful and sad, full of grief and disappointment and love and hope.

Subgrouping encourages the confrontation of conflict and discourages an escape into ambivalence, depression, somatization, stubbornness, passivity, or other solitary defences. Subgrouping helps each individual to experience both sides of the conflict and to bear together the anxiety that contradictory impulses engender. Subgroup norms value the work of experiencing and containing feelings and learning how to express them rather than to turn them in or discharge them in acting out.

Members of a systems-centered group learn that work is the struggle to recognize defences against authenticity—to make defences ego-alien with the others' help. Each person learns their own symptoms of anxiety—the beating heart, breathlessness, feeling spacey or faint, headaches or stomach-aches, obsessions, ruminations, predictions of doom—and learn to accept their symptoms as a signal of the problem and not mistake their symptoms for the problem. It is a goal for the group to know the internal difference between experiencing and containing a feeling and expressing it. The difference in experience between impulse and feeling, between feeling and anxiety, between feeling and its discharge into tears or tantrums or diatribes, between feelings and the turning in on the self in guilt, self-recriminations, and despair. Each person learns their favoured tactical defences: the verbal skills that create a safety curtain between oneself and another, between oneself and oneself, evading and avoiding and dodging, deflecting and contradicting, half truths and vagueness, rationalizations and intellectualizations, answering questions with a question, yes-butting, criticizing, judging others or oneself.

When a member deports himself into a rationalized world of negative predictions, fear and pessimism and persecution, other members remind him that living there is instead of confronting a hurt or angry feeling and a wish to get even. The group knows how easy it is to defend against real helplessness by becoming or making a victim, blaming and complaining, educating others instead of themselves. They know the doors to the prisons where members retreat: choosing depression instead of the experience of murderous rage, living in righteous indignation instead of bearing the helplessness and the hurt, entering the bondage of stubbornness, volunteering as victim or bully. They cry together in grief for the time spent behind their own bars.

Members come to know their particular character tendencies: towards compliance or defiance with people in authority, the particular bricks they use to build a wall between themselves and intimacy, blind trust or suspicion, the wish to merge or isolate. The work in a systems-centered group is in the here-and-now of the group and the reactions to the issues that the members are struggling with in their relationships with each other, or with the difficulties of living their lives. They do not spend much time talking about their past or the events of their childhood—understanding how their past influences their present usually occurs spontaneously after a flash of insight. Therapy in a systems-centered group is training in an ongoing task of recognizing defences from moment to moment, against sharing and working and playing together. A forever here-and-now goal is to feel alive as a system in a hierarchy of systems.

A final word for systems isomorphy: working on the difficult task of traversing the barriers of shame and humiliation into the core self, first one and then another group member hesitantly expressed a wish to be the centre of the group's attention and also expressed concern that if any one member got all the attention, there would be none left for anyone else. During the subgroup work of separating out "wanting" and "getting", the exhilarating freedom of being *able* to want broke through: "I want to be the centre!" ... "Me too!" ... "I want to be grandiose!" ... "I want to be narcissistic ... I want it all!" In the delighted pause that followed the euphoria, the group noticed that there had been plenty of room for everyone: "The more we want to be, the more room there is!"

Systems-centered theory was developed in the process of defining and making operational General Systems Theory constructs: systems in the same hierarchy are isomorphic in structure and function. Below are the definitions of these theoretical constructs, which have generated guiding principles for systems-centered interventions, which, when tested in group and individual psychotherapy (not without many moments of self-doubt and dread) have resulted in the systems-centered practice described above. Is this a meta-theory? Are subgroups the fulcrum for change? Will these constructs be useful to therapists in deliberately reducing the restraining forces to communications across the boundaries of the group, its subgroups, and its subgroup members and, by so doing, increase the drive towards the goals of therapy? For those therapists who wish to take systems-centered thinking into their own groups, the theoretical constructs and their operational definitions are presented below.

Hierarchy: Each system exists in the environment of the system above it and is the environment for the system below it.

Isomorphy: Systems in the same hierarchy are similar in structure, function, and dynamics.

Structure: Each system in the hierarchy can be described in terms of similar structural elements: structural boundaries in space and time contain the energy in the group.

Function: Each system in the hierarchy can be observed to function by remaining in quasi-stationary equilibrium in relation to self-correcting goals. This can be modelled in a force field of group behaviours that imply the system goals: primary goals of survival and development and secondary goals of mastery. Goals can be both explicit and implicit—goals explicit for the system, and goals implied by the direction of the system behaviour.

Dynamics: System dynamics are a function of the system's organization of information by discriminating and integrating transactions across all system boundaries in the hierarchy. System development is a function of the system process of discrimination and integration: discriminating between similarities in the apparently different and differences in the apparently similar. System development is a function of communication in the system hierarchy: within each system, among systems at the same hierarchical level, and between systems at different hierarchical levels.

In Figure 9.3, the discriminatory and integrative principles of human self-correcting systems in particular are related to the ambiguities,

Force field of driving and restraining forces to system development discriminating and integrating communications across boundaries

DRIVING FORCES →	← RESTRAINING FORCES
discriminating differences and similarities →	← ambiguity
discriminating similarities in the apparently different and differences in the apparently similar →	← contradictions
integrating information in new ways →	← redundancy
system development →	← system fixation
system development →	← system fixation

FIGURE 9.3. Force field of the quasi-stationary equilibrium of the self-correcting system showing the balance of forces between entropic and negentropic communications (Agazarian, 1990a)

contradictions, and redundancies characteristic of life in general (Agazarian, 1990a). In the table, a summary model of systems-centered theory is presented in a force-field model. This model can be applied to the practice of systems-centered group psychotherapy. As the group-as-a-whole learns to weaken its own defensive restraining forces, so the potential increases for the member, subgroup, and group-as-a-whole systems to become autonomously self-correcting.

CHAPTER TEN

A systems-centered approach to individual and group psychotherapy

Systems-centered therapy (SCT) is an innovative approach to individual and group psychotherapy. It is different from most approaches to therapy in that the theory about the dynamics of systems was developed first (a theory of living human systems, Agazarian, 1991b), and the practice of systems-centered therapy was developed from putting the theory into practice (Agazarian, 1997).

This systematic approach to therapy was introduced based on some important characteristics of system thinking. The most important implication for therapy is the idea that all living human systems exist in a hierarchy and function in the same way, develop in the same way, and have a common structure. This is called "system isomorphy". Thinking about therapy isomophically is revolutionary. It means that once the structure (how a system is constructed) and function (how a system works) are defined for one system, they are defined for all systems. Therefore, although individual therapy, couples therapy, marriage

---

Y. M. Agazarian, "A Systems-Centered Approach to Individual and Group Psychotherapy". In: L. Vandecreek & T. Jackson (Eds.), *Innovations in Clinical Practice: A Source Book, Vol. 20* (Sarasota, FL: Professional Resource Press, 2002), pp. 223–240 (reproduced by permission of Professional Resource Press, Sarasota, Florida).

therapy, and group therapy do not seem the same, whatever one learns about the dynamics of one will, because they can all be defined as living human systems, generalize to all the others.

This means that intervening at any one level of the system will influence all the other levels! Thus, in individual therapy, interventions to the patient influence the therapeutic system, and interventions to the system influence both the patient and the therapist; in group therapy, intervening to the subgroup will influence both the member and the group-as-a-whole (Agazarian 1992c)!

SCT argues that what kind of therapy can be done depends more upon the system that is developed than it does on either the individual potential of the patient or the skills of the therapist. Therefore, systems-centered therapy develops a therapeutic system first as the prerequisite for any therapeutic treatment.

Every different style of therapy influences the way the therapeutic system develops. Most of the time, this is done informally, sometimes unwittingly. In contrast, systems-centered therapists deliberately introduce a series of methods and techniques that influence how the system develops (structure) and how the system directs its energy towards the goal of therapy (function). This is why all systems-centered therapy starts by building a therapeutic system first.

The practice of systems-centered therapy is standardized. SCT therapists learn the SCT protocol, which is the blueprint for developing a therapeutic system by using a series of methods and techniques. As each of these techniques is derived from theory, each intervention tests both whether the theory can be put into practice in the real world (validity) and whether the techniques introduce change in the direction that is predicted (reliability). These methods and techniques are introduced in a specific sequence and are simple to learn. They introduce specific innovations to the practice of psychotherapy, some of which are described in this chapter.

INNOVATIONS IN THE PRACTICE OF SCT

The patient–therapist partnership

The first major innovation brings the therapist and patient into partnership, recognizing their different roles and different responsibilities as they work together to reach the goals of the therapy.

For example, the therapist immediately brings it to the patient's attention if he or she enters the therapy in a submissive role (one way to tell a submissive role is when a patient sits looking up at the therapist from under his or her eyebrows.) The SCT therapist may then say something like: "I get the impression that you think I know more about you than you do. That is not true, however. You know more about yourself than I do, and I know more about how to help you understand yourself better than you do. So together we have a good partnership." The intention is to lay the groundwork for functional dependency at the beginning of therapy, so that patients can safely explore their impulses to act out their dependency or counterdependency.

Maintaining eye contact

Nonverbally, the SCT therapist also reinforces this message by making authentic eye contact with the patient and maintaining it in attunement. We discovered that learning how to maintain attuned eye contact is perhaps one of the greatest challenges for SCT trainees, and perhaps one of the most therapeutic of the SCT skills.

Reframing instead of interpreting

Another major innovation is that, wherever possible, SCT therapists refrain from directing the patient with overt interpretations. Interpretations tend to suggest that the therapist knows and the patient does not, and patients can easily feel that there is something wrong with them. SCT therapists substitute reframing a patient's experience in terms of common human dynamics. This is a more subtle redirection, away from pathology and towards legitimizing and normalizing human experience. For example, anxiety at the beginning of the session is normalized by pointing out that everybody is always somewhat anxious in a new situation when they do not know what is going to happen next, and it helps to become curious. Patients are encouraged to explore all their experiences within the frame of common human experience, thus not only depathologizing their symptoms but also legitimizing the exploration of those dynamics which may otherwise be embarrassing, humiliating, shaming, or frightening.

Common human dynamics

The universal reality of experience is brought home to SCT therapists in their own training, as they discover their own sadistic or masochistic impulses, their tendencies towards merging or alienating, the difficulties they have in managing frustration, and their tendencies to turn their retaliatory impulses out on others in blame or inwards on themselves in depression. Perhaps one of the most significant outcomes of SCT training is that SCT therapists become tolerant of their own aggressive impulses and can therefore be good containers when their patients explore theirs.

The fork in the road

The substitute for interpretations is the "fork-in-the-road" technique. The fork in the road that is presented to the patient is always between two sides. Separating two sides of an issue enables patients to choose which side they wish to explore first. The first fork in the road presented in SCT therapy is between *explaining* and *exploring*. The SCT therapist points out that *explaining* difficulties takes us to what we know already, while exploring difficulties takes us to what we do not know, and discovering what we do not know is the purpose of therapy.

There is a paradox here. Patients are free to choose between exploring their experience or exploring their impulse to explain it. But they do not have a choice about whether or not to choose! The fork-in-the-road technique reduces the time that is otherwise spent in "talking about" problems instead of exploring what is problematic.

Discriminating and integrating

Requiring patients to explore both sides of every issue is based on the assumption that all living human systems survive and develop through one (and only one!) dynamic process: the process of discriminating and integrating differences. Discriminating involves recognizing both the differences in the apparently similar and the similarities in the apparently different. Integrating new information contributes to transformation. The fork-in-the-road technique implements this principle in individual therapy. In group therapy it is implemented by the technique of functional subgrouping. Functional subgrouping requires members to come together and explore similar issues that resonate as important to them. Members with differences are asked to wait until after the first subgroup has finished their exploration and to then form a new subgroup and explore their issues. In this way, the group contains, discriminates, and integrates differences. Functional subgrouping is probably the most important innovation that SCT has introduced into group therapy. (For those who are interested in learning more, the best reference is the Agazarian, 1997, text.)

What do defences defend against?

SCT takes if for granted that every defence defends against something. The patient is therefore encouraged to choose whether to explore the defence first, or whether to explore what they are defending against. When patients explore the alternative to the defence, they discover some aspect of internal or external reality that they were distracted away from by paying attention to their defence: some internal impulses, thoughts, emotions, or some conflicted responses to the here-and-now. For example, anxiety-provoking thoughts are framed as an "explanation" that substitutes for managing the uncertainties of reality. Brought to the patient's attention as a defence, patients discover that as long as they are involved in anxiety-provoking thoughts they are not aware of the reality of the here-and-now.

When patients do not know what is being defended against, they are asked if they are curious. The advantage of curiosity is that it shifts patients from being passive victims of their thoughts to active explorers at the edge of the unknown, which is a good place to be if one wants to discover here-and-now experience. (SCT calls mobilizing curiosity "turning on our researcher self".)

Emphasis on the here-and-now

Based on the reality that the present here-and-now is the only place in which we can make changes, patients learn to deliberately shift from the past to the present, from the future to the present, and from the wishes and fears of the present into present reality. The underlying assumption is that although neurological pathways to the past or the future are laid down early and reinforced obsessively, the tendency towards dysfunctional thought patterns can be modified by developing new neurological pathways that process information in the context of the present. Patients are told not to worry when they are hi-jacked by their old self-critical thoughts, but to gently take their energy away from the thought and to pay attention to what is present in reality. SCT points out that they cannot undo the old patterns, but they can lay down new ones as an alternative route.

Returning to the present

There are some simple techniques that SCT therapists use to redirect thinking away from "habit" to becoming aware of the present. When, for example, a group member associates to a family event in the past to escape from managing a difficult moment in present of the group, the therapist asks: "How is the group different from your family?" This draws the patient's attention back to the present. When a patient flees to the future, worrying whether the therapy will work, he or she is encouraged to gently take their energy away from their fears and come back to the present to see what, in the here-and-now, they did not pay attention to because they were worrying about the future.

The difference between feelings from thoughts and feelings from experience

SCT patients are also encouraged to recognize that the feelings that they generate from their thoughts are different from the feelings that arise from their direct experience. Guilt, for example, is a conflict between a thought "I should not" and the reality experience that "I did" or "I want". When the feelings generated by the thoughts (should) are separated from the feelings that are generated by the experience (want), there is room to recognize the conflict. (We return to this when we address the undoing of anxiety in the beginning of therapy.)

Driving and restraining forces to change

SCT therapists assume that it is easier to reach the goals of change if one reduces the things that are in the way of change rather than trying to increase the drive. This idea originated with Kurt Lewin's force field (1951), with which he demonstrated that if one reduces the restraining forces, the drive towards the goal is automatically released. There is a simple way to test this out for yourself. Place your right fist against your left fist (knuckles to knuckles) and push as hard as you can. You will see that neither fist moves. (The system is stalled!) Now reduce the pressure in your right fist, and you will see that your left fist automatically drives forward. You have now experienced how much easier it is to move in the direction you want to go by reducing the restraining forces rather than trying to increase the driving forces. It is for this reason that SCT therapists systematically reduce the defences, releasing the innate drive in all of us towards health.

It was in the process of modifying defences that SCT developed what is called the "hierarchy of defence modification". The hierarchy evolved from recognizing that defences cannot be reduced randomly. Only those defences that the system is ready and able to reduce can be reduced, otherwise the act of reducing the defences becomes a restraining instead of a driving force.

The hierarchy of defence modification

The hierarchy of defence modification outlines the sequence by which defences can be reduced systematically. Each defence is reduced by introducing the SCT skills for modifying that defence. These skills then prepare the patient to reduce the next defence, during which the patient again acquires skills to address the next defence. For example, reducing anxiety-provoking thoughts restores the patient's ability to use common sense: "to turn on their researcher". When defensive tension takes the place of anxiety (as it will!) the patient discovers that tension is like a strait-jacket, restricting an experience. Because the patient has already modified the tendency to escape into anxiety-provoking thoughts, they can explore the experience they were constricting rather than interpret it as threatening. Next, the patient recognizes that frustration and tension lie on two different forks in the road. Frustration without tension is a very different experience from frustration with tension. Thus the patient's frustration tolerance increases, and so on. (More is said about this when we come to the phases of system development.)

The next discovery that was made as SCT was put into practice is that each phase of development is characterized by certain defences. When the defences that characterize the phase are modified, not only are the restraining forces to individual development reduced, but so are the restraining forces to system development. Isomorphy again: the restraining forces that inhibit system development are common to all levels of systems.

For example, "flight" defences are reduced in the "flight" subphase, and the system moves into the here-and-now, with its frustrations, which, in turn, mobilize "fight" defences, which, when reduced in the fight subphase, permit the system to move on again to the next subphase. What SCT discovered in this process is that when defences are explored rather than acted out, certain group therapy experiences that I had always taken for granted as part of the process did not occur. For example, in the flight phase, both the impulse to take care of someone and the wish to be taken care of by someone were explored instead of being acted out by creating the identified patient. Similarly, in the fight phase, when the impulse to project differences into a scapegoat were explored instead of acted out, scapegoating did not occur.

The social defences

The first defences to be addressed, at the very beginning of the first phase of development, are the social defences. These are reduced by reducing the aspects of social communication that say a lot but mean little. The second are what is called "the triad of symptomatic defences" in that they are the defences that create the symptoms of anxiety, tension, and depression—the three symptoms that most often bring people to therapy. Symptoms are like restraining forces that, when reduced, release the drive towards development, both long-term and short-term. SCT is therefore particularly suited to short-term therapy in that the most frequently presented symptoms are immediately addressed and modified as the defences are modified.

Anxiety

Anxiety is reduced as soon as it surfaces. The SCT techniques for reducing anxiety are similar to cognitive therapy, with an important difference: SCT techniques not only highlight the cognitive distortions that generate anxiety but also point out that by taking the fork in the road towards worrying, people have left the present. When they release the energy bound up in anxiety, people can re-direct their attention to their conflicts in the present. Undoing anxiety restores a functioning intelligence with which to address reality.

Tension

In the process of developing SCT practice, we discovered that when anxiety-provoking thoughts are reduced, it seems that tension automatically increases. Undoing tension (and deconditioning somatic symptoms when necessary) restores a relationship to the body and its natural responses to the here-and-now. SCT techniques for undoing tension have many similarities to behavioural modification techniques. The difference lies in the emphasis on discrimination: for example, discriminating the discomfort of tension from the discomfort of frustration and making room for the energy of the feeling in the body.

Frustration

Frustration without tension is discovered to be an energetic alertness and readiness. It is not until frustration tolerance is exceeded that the next defence surfaces: defences against the retaliatory impulse. SCT encourages people to recognize that it is normal to have the impulse to retaliate when people, things, or situations are annoying. Techniques for making space for recognizing, exploring, and accepting the retaliatory impulse include learning to contain it instead of acting on it.

Depression and the retaliatory impulse

A surprising discovery is that rageful behaviour, tantrums, complaining, blaming, and moral outrage are not anger but, rather, a defensive discharge of the energy in the retaliatory impulse. A second surprising discovery is that depression, withdrawal, and sulking are a defensive implosion that turns the energy of the retaliatory impulse back on the self. These discoveries are in line with the pioneering work done by Habib Davanloo (1987).

Undoing anxiety restores the relationship to common sense. Undoing depression and hostility restores the relationship to the emotions. These are initial steps that pave the way for work with the conflicted love/hate relationship, to each other, to authorities outside the self and inside the self. This, in SCT, is called the "crisis of hatred" and is the final step in Phase I as well as the transition between Phase I (authority issues) and Phase II (issues with intimacy).

Below, the phases of system development, as the context for defence modification, are discussed as they apply to the real world of individual and group psychotherapy.

The phases of system development

Most of the work identifying phases of development has been done on groups (Agazarian, 1994, 1997, 1999; Agazarian & Peters, 1981; Beck 1981; Bennis & Shepard, 1956; Brabender, 1997; Buzaglo & Wheelan, 1999). SCT applies the developmental sequence to systems. Phases of system development apply to all systems—to individual therapy as well as to group therapy. SCT argues that each of the phases and subphases of system development is the *context* in which therapy takes place, and the context determines what work can be done successfully. Doing only work that is phase-appropriate bypasses the frustrations and regressions that arise when work is attempted that patients are not ready to do and sets up a potential win–win situation, in which the patient succeeds step by step, each step paving the way for the next.

If each phase of system development presents a different context and if it is the context that determines what therapy can take place, then it is important to know how to recognize the phases. The process of therapy is not linear: it is more like a spiral with many therapeutic issues presenting simultaneously. The therapist who can recognize the phase of development that a person is working in can encourage the patient to focus on those issues in the spiral that are phase-appropriate.

This synchronicity between individual defences and restraining forces to system development is attributed to the theory that all systems in the same hierarchy share the same structure and dynamic function (system isomorphy). The payoff is that by reducing those individual defences that are phase-appropriate, not only do the individuals who come for therapy systematically weaken their defences against therapy, but the driving forces that are released serve to move both the individuals and the system-as-a-whole towards the goals of therapy.

Phase I: relationship to authority

The first phase of system development is divided into three subphases: fight, flight, and the "crisis of hatred" (which is fuelled by the negative transference). This first phase is oriented around the patient's relationships to society and his own and others' authority. This reflects the fact that people enter therapy as already socialized human beings who have learned to relate to their life in the world in both adaptive and maladaptive ways. In the process of becoming socialized, people learn to discipline the way they think and speak, the way they behave, and they way they feel.

In this first phase of therapy, the SCT goal is to restore the patients' natural connection to the mind, the body, and the emotions and thus to regain fuller access to both verbal and emotional intelligence. This is done by systematically reducing the defences that interfere or constrict people's access to their self-knowledge.

The subphase of flight

"Flight" is the label for the first subphase, because at the beginning of any new situation—and therapy is no exception—people tend to flee from the reality that they do not know what is going to happen next. At the edge of the unknown, everyone is somewhat wary and apprehensive. Some people take flight from their apprehension by leaping before they look. Others become wary and frightened and can only perceive the new situation through a filter of anxiety-provoking thoughts. In both cases, people are not fully present in the situation and do not have access to their common sense. And in both cases patients look to the therapist to help them find their way.

It is not possible in one chapter to introduce all the methods and techniques that guide the steps that describe of the whole of SCT therapy. Nor is it possible to go into the dynamics of each phase of development in detail. (For those who are interested, the best reference is Agazarian, 1997, for the textbook on SCT process and Agazarian, 2001, for the full script and comments of a first session of an SCT group on an inpatient unit.) However, it is important to give the reader a flavour of how this work is accomplished. Therefore, wherever possible, examples of how the therapist addresses the different phase issues are given. Immediately below, in the discussion of "flight", two important techniques are outlined at some length: (a) the methods by which social defences are modified right from the start, and (b) both the rationale and the protocol for undoing anxiety, which is the first symptom that is addressed in SCT therapy.

The language of social defences

The modification of defences against valid communication is the first restraining force to be modified in systems-centered work—whether it is in an initial interview, a first session, or the beginning of an ongoing individual or group session. Shannon and Weaver (1964), in their Mathematical Theory of Communication, demonstrated that the less noise in the communication, the more likely it is that the information it contained will get across. They identified as noise the ambiguities, contradictions, and redundancies that we introduce into language when we are not sure it is safe to be clear. The following examples illustrate how.

Ambiguity: Vague, obscure language acts like a smokescreen in which the meaning of the communication is lost. For example:

Patient: "I'm not quite sure why I'm here . . ."

Therapist: "What was happening when you first decided to come?"

Patient: "I kind of think that on the whole things are not going well—er—well, some things seem to be going all right, but I don't know what to do about others—you know, all the things I worry about, though everybody worries sometimes, and I don't know if I worry more than others, maybe its all the same, but its all the things that may not be right that . . ."

In the example of ambiguous communication above, the message is not clear, frustrating both the therapist and the patient. If this communication pattern is allowed to continue, it will establish a frustrating therapeutic system. Therefore the SCT therapist addresses the ambiguity immediately.

Therapist: "Do you notice that you are being somewhat vague in the way you are describing your difficulty? Would you see if you can be more specific please? It is very important that I understand why you are here, so that together we can decide the best next steps."

Contradictions. These say one thing but mean another, thus making it difficult to know where the reality is. The most socially acceptable of these is the "yes . . . but . . ."—an important distancing communication frequently used in defensive climates. The speaker sounds "as if" she is in a dialogue, when actually in a monologue.

Therapist: "You are telling me that your husband wanted you to come here. Did you, yourself want to come?"

Patient: "Yes, of course, but whenever there is a problem he always wants me to fix it."

Therapist: "Do you notice that it will be more difficult to discover what you want to get for yourself if you focus on your husband?"

Patient: "Yes, but I wouldn't be here if it wasn't for him."

Therapist: "You are telling me about the impact that your husband has on you. Do you know how you feel about the fact that you are here, because he wanted you to come?"

Patient: "Well, that's an interesting question, but what can I do when he always gets his way?"

Therapist: "I'm wondering if you notice that you are talking about your husband and leaving yourself out again? Do you notice that when I ask you a question about you, you talk about your husband instead? Is there anything about you that you want me to know?"

Redundancy. Saying the same thing over and over in different ways is another frustrating way of saying a lot while communicating very little.

Patient: "I think that my relationship with my mother is an important problem for me, certainly one I should pay attention to. My mother is central, I think, to my difficulties. As I've told you, she was controlling in ways that left me no room to do anything new or different. She did this in so many ways: I can remember one example—perhaps I've already mentioned it—when she said . . ."

Patients tend to go over and over the same ground when they are explaining themselves. The SCT therapist will point out simply that they are explaining their experience rather than exploring it. When patients repeatedly talk about their history, however, the redundancy often goes unnoticed due to the therapists' expectation that talking about the past is, in itself, therapeutic. When patients talk about their past, SCT therapists ask themselves the question: Is the patient taking flight to the past in order to avoid some "look-alike" conflict in the present? Or is the patient going to the past to collect information to better address some conflict in the present?

Patient: "I think that my relationship with my mother is an important problem for me, certainly one I should pay attention to. My mother is central, I think, to my difficulties . . ."

Therapist [*interrupts*]: "Do you know what, in the here and now, may have triggered your association to your mother?"

Patient: "Well . . . yes . . . I think you remind me of her."

Therapist: "How am I different from your mother?"

You may notice that asking "How am I *different* from your mother?" brings the patient's attention to how the *present* is different from the past. When, later in therapy, the therapist encourages the patient to explore the past, the therapist will change the question in an important way: "How am I *similar* to your mother?" In the first question, the answer is in the present; in the second, the answer lies in the past. This small change in words is a good illustration of how simple many of the SCT techniques are and how significantly they can alter the course of therapy.

The superficial transferences

Transference and the repetition compulsion are the two most likely dynamics to be operating when the patient goes to the past. Undoing superficial transferences (like "you remind me of my mother") are undone in the early phases of SCT therapy, so that when the deeper underlying transferences emerge, the patient is better prepared for insight. This approach makes it less likely that therapy will end prematurely on the unresolved negative transference or perpetuated because of the unresolved positive transference. For example, in the early phases of therapy, redundancies around childhood memories or repetitions from the past into the present are addressed by bringing the patient back to the unknown of the present rather than the known of the past. Asking the patient "how I am different from your mother" is an example of addressing the superficial level of transference, leaving the deeper transference implications for later in the therapy.

Ambiguity, contradictions, and redundancy as a diagnostic in the initial interview

One of the advantages of immediately modifying ambiguity, contradictions, and redundancy in the initial interview is that the therapist can get a good idea, from the patient's responses, whether or not the patient will be a good candidate for SCT therapy. Another advantage is that recognizing the characteristic defences that the patient uses is useful in thinking about the treatment plan as well as about the differential diagnosis.

For example, ambiguous communication may alert the therapist to the patient's probable difficulty in understanding themselves or others or the world and in setting goals and planning how to meet them. Ambiguity, as in the first example, is important to address immediately, otherwise the interview may end without any clear understanding of what the problems are and without any thoughts about a treatment plan. Asking the patient to be specific is also an important initial step for future therapy. Discovering that they may not be able to be specific is important information for the initial diagnosis.

Contradictory communications can imply that the patient may be difficult to influence and perhaps either actively or passively controlling of others and the environment (as the patient certainly is in the example above). Yes-but communications successfully shut out the therapist—and also, unfortunately, shut out the patient from the patients' own self.

Redundancy may imply that the patient is wedded to his or her own explanations of reality and will tend to maintain it through storytelling. However compelling the stories may be, there is always a risk that they are not being used in a way that is therapeutic but, rather as a defence against exploring the relevance they have to the present, and thus become a substitute for therapy.

Anxiety-provoking thoughts

Anxiety-provoking thoughts are another form of cognitive defence that intervene between the person and reality. Negative predictions about the future, pessimistic predictions from the past, and self-consciously thinking about what others are thinking are all cognitive distortions that create anxiety. They are also a common restraining force shared by both patient and therapist. They are thus important restraining forces to modify in the process of building a therapeutic system, both in the system as-a-whole and within the system of all its members. (There is a strong emphasis on undoing anxiety-provoking thoughts in the training and supervision of SCT therapists.)

SCT discriminates between anxiety and apprehension as the expected response to uncertainty and the unknown. Apprehension is often confused with anxiety. Labelling apprehension as anxiety interprets it as unpleasant. Reframing it as normal apprehension around "not knowing" makes it easier to turn on curiosity. SCT understands anxiety about uncertainty as a signal that curiosity about the unknown has been pre-empted by anxiety-provoking thoughts.

Techniques for undoing anxiety

In undoing anxiety, the first step is to alert the patient that anxiety does not come out of the blue. It has three sources (and only three!): (a) anxiety-provoking thoughts; (b) misinterpreted sensations, emotions, and impulses; (c) uncertainty and the unknown. The most usual source of anxiety is thoughts. The SCT protocol for undoing dysfunctional thinking goes like this:

Therapist: "Are you are having a thought that is making you anxious?"

Patient: "Yes."

Therapist: "What is it?"

Patient: "That I'm never going to learn how to undo anxiety."

Therapist: "Well, that is certainly an anxiety-provoking thought . . . and as you know, anxiety-provoking thoughts provoke anxiety! The first thing to do in undoing anxiety-provoking thoughts is to bring in your common sense. Turn your researcher self on! Do you believe you can tell the future?"

Patient: "No!"

If the patient says he or she can tell the future—engage their common sense. For example, say something like: "Are you accurate 100% of the time?" The answer is probably "No". "So ask yourself whether this particular time could be the one in a hundred when events do not go as you predicted? Making predictions is an attempt to have more predictability and control in our lives." Turning on our common sense rather than jumping to conclusions about the future actually gives us more control of our lives, not less!

Therapist: "And if you bring your attention away from the future and back into the here-and-now, does your experience change?"

Patient: "Yes."

(Almost always the patient will discover a significant difference in feeling, and anxiety will be lowered).

Therapist: "So do you see that your experience was coming from your thoughts about the future? Now that you are experiencing the present, do you feel better, worse, or the same?"

Patient: "Better!"

(If the answer is "worse" or "the same", ask if there is another negative prediction. If so, repeat exercise.)

Therapist: "Next time you get anxious, will you remind yourself that negative predictions are on the fork-in-the-road that leads away from the here-and-now. Do you know what, in the present, you defended against by taking flight into anxiety-provoking thoughts?"

We have already emphasized that SCT assumes that there is always a trigger for a defence: a thought, a sensation, a conflict, an emotion or impulse that is experienced as threatening. If the patient cannot identify the trigger, it is important to reassure the patient that the first step is to know that there was a trigger and that the anxiety did not just come out of the blue.

The final step in all SCT techniques is to normalize the defence and reframe the experience so that the patients can be involved in the process of learning how to use the techniques for themselves.

Therapist: "SCT assumes that there is a strong pull in everyone to go to anxiety-provoking thoughts and worrying. The way to make a change is to build a new neurological pathway to compete with the old, by repeatedly and gently taking the energy away from your thoughts about the future or the past and redirecting it into your experience of you're here-and-now present."

Anxiety-provoking sensations

When anxiety is provoked by sensations, impulses, or emotions that are being interpreted as dangerous, SCT encourages patients to allow themselves to make room to have their experience: "Allow yourself to fill up with your feeling, let it be the size that it is, and see what you experience."

Anxiety and the uncertainty of the unknown

When anxiety is provoked by the uncertainties of the unknown, SCT encourages patients to mobilize their curiosity about what is going to happen next in the here-and-now. Mobilizing curiosity is a simple technique that has great significance: it shifts the relationship between the person and the surrounding environment from passive to active—from potential victim of the unknown into active explorer!

Therapist: "Everyone is anxious at uncertainties of what is going to happen next at the edge of the unknown. It helps to mobilize your curiosity—see if your experience changes if you turn your curiosity on."

Undoing "mind-reading"

The other cognitive distortion that is addressed as soon as patients are familiar with the techniques for re-establishing contact with reality is the painful tendency to worry about what others are thinking about you. SCT calls this "mind-reading". Undoing mind-reading is more challenging than undoing anxiety in that it requires checking with the person whose mind you are reading. One advantage of group therapy over individual therapy is that it is a little easier for patients to check their mind-reads with other patients than it is with their therapist. In either case, the protocol is the same. "Mind-reads" are checked out by asking a question that can be answered with a "yes" or a "no":

> *Patient:* "I have a mind-read that you are thinking that I am silly. Is that true?"

The answer to the question will be either "yes" or "no". SCT members (including the therapist) are encouraged to give a simple, neutral "yes" or "no" (no explanations, in either case). This reinforces their training in not taking other people's projections personally.

There are two more steps to this process, depending on whether the answer is "yes" or "no":

(a) If the answer is "no", the leader asks: "How do you feel when you discover that the world isn't the way you thought it was? This question brings the patient's attention to the cognitive dissonance that occurs when their picture of the world does not match the reality (Festinger, 1957).

If the answer is "yes", the leader asks: "How do you feel now that your worst fears have turned out to be true?" (Typically, a reality answer is a relief, even when it isn't the answer one wants!)

After the patient has heard the answer, the therapist will ask whether or not they believe the answer. Sometimes they don't believe the answer, or are doubtful, and it is important to have an established climate in which they can say so.

If the patient does not believe the answer, the therapist asks: "So what is it like working with a patient (or with your therapist) that you do not believe?"

Anxiety, frustration, tension

As we mentioned earlier, anxiety, tension, and frustration are often confused. It is the work of the flight phase to discriminate between them. Signals of anxiety are a beating heart, cold hands, butterflies in the stomach, and sometimes confusion in the mind. Tension is a tightness in the muscles—sometimes a painful tightness. Frustration is energy.

SCT addresses tension by framing it as a "strait-jacket that constricts one's experience", and the patient is encouraged to let the tension go. It is at this point in SCT work that patients discover that the experience of frustration is significantly different when not mixed with tension and is often a simple experience of arousal and readiness.

Projection

The underlying flight dynamics are the same, whether the developmental issues are addressed in individual or group therapy. However, they manifest differently. In individual therapy the therapist is used as the container for projection. In the group, a group member can be used by the group-as-a-whole as a container for group projections. For example, group members will project their wishes to be taken care of into one patient and elect the patient to take the role of the identified patient for the therapist to cure. Part of the power of group therapy is that though many members unconsciously volunteer for the role, only one is chosen! In individual therapy, the same dynamic is acted out when the patient becomes increasingly helpless and symptom-oriented. In both cases, if the therapist responds to the helplessness, the patient's own abilities are undermined, and a dependency relationship is established, which will have serious implications for the therapeutic process (Agazarian, 1994). In both individual and group therapy, the "solution" of the identified patient is forestalled by immediately addressing the anxiety that is driving the helplessness.

Tension, frustration, and the retaliatory impulse

The advantage of the SCT method of exploring experience is that patients in group and individual therapy (and trainees in training groups) collect information about the changes that occurred for them as defences are modified. Thus, we discovered that there appears to be a natural sequence to defences. We discovered that tension and anxiety are often experienced together, that as patients and trainees modified their anxiety, they became more aware of their tension, and that when frustration is experienced without tension, it becomes a pleasant fizz of excitement, energy, and readiness. When people experience frustration simply as potential energy, they discover themselves not only alert and aroused, but also confident and symptom-free. In other words, there has been a break through to a free ego—an experience of the undefended self. There is no mistaking it: there is a spontaneous change in posture. People looked grounded and powerfully "full of themselves".

Frustration, however, is an inherent part of all experience. Although there was a marked increase in frustration tolerance when the experience of frustration was separated from tension, sooner or later frustration returned. It came as no surprise that at a certain level of frustration people become irritated, and at a certain level of irritation people have the impulse to retaliate against the frustrating situation, person, or thing. This initial work with the retaliatory impulse was done in systems-centered training groups, pioneering the process of systems-centered techniques before they were used with patients. The SCT technique of functional subgrouping greatly increased the potential for exploring dynamics rather than either defending against them or acting them out. These training groups discovered two clear forks in the road: one led to depression, the other to hostile acting out.

Depression and masochism

Understanding depression as a defence in which the retaliatory impulse is turned back on the self is not a new idea, but it is a significant one (Davanloo, 1987). In exploring the road to depression, it became clear that depression is fuelled by the masochistic side of the self. Once depression is undone (using the SCT techniques for undoing depression), the energy that has been bound in depression automatically redirects towards the sadistic impulses to retaliate. This made the transition in the groups from the more passive subphase of flight to the more active subphase of fight.

The transition between the subphases of flight and fight

In the years that followed, we saw that how the transition between the subphases of fight and flight play out will depend on the particular mix of the dynamics. The underlying processes are always the same, but how they manifest and which aspects of them are in the background or forefront will reflect the makeup of each particular therapeutic system. The transition between fight and flight is accomplished when the system is geared towards exploring aggression rather than depression. This is also the transition between projecting dynamics into an identified patient and projecting dynamics into the scapegoat.

The subphase of fight

The simplest discovery of the retaliatory impulse is the discovery how strong the impulse is to retaliate over even apparently quite trivial events. With the support of the therapeutic system, people discover that retaliation is often accompanied by a murderous rage. It requires an encouraging and supportive system to enable people to experience fully the energy of rage without becoming afraid that they will act out destructively. This is a good example of how important it is to understand the difference between the fears that come from negative predictions and those that come from not having made sufficient internal space to experience the rage without constriction.

Aggression and rage

Specific SCT techniques are designed to enable people to reach a good relationship with their rageful impulses so that they can contain the anger rather than acting it out. The discussion below applies only to those patients who can tell the difference between the impulse and action; for those who have serious difficulty with impulse control or who do not know the difference between thinking and doing, these techniques must be used with extreme caution and skill, if at all.

Undefended access to murderous rage requires learning how to contain both the experience and spontaneous fantasies:

> *Therapist:* "Allow yourself to make a little more space inside yourself, just like you did when you were getting to know the experience of frustration without tension. As you make a little more space, what is your experience?"

This technique paces the person's ability to experience the energy of the aggression without being overwhelmed by it. For those with poorer impulse control, this stage of conditioning is done very, very slowly.

The retaliatory impulse

The next event is a recognition of retaliatory fantasies. These are often signalled by physical intention movements:

> *Therapist:* "Do you notice that you are making a fist with your right hand? Do you know what you are experiencing?"

If the patient is not aware of the fist, the therapist comments:

> *Therapist:* "Your body knows more about your impulse than you know! Are you ready to let yourself explore the experience that your body is already having?"

If the patient allows the experience, he or she will nearly always have a full experience, together with a spontaneous fantasy of how he or she wants to retaliate. Sometimes the patient is shocked at the violence; at other times there is an experience of satisfaction and completion, and the person is restored to a full experience of energy and understanding. Accessing the reality of the impulse almost always goes hand in hand with an understanding of how to respond appropriately to the reality that triggered the reaction.

When the patient is shocked by the violence, the therapist reminds the patient of the difference between impulse and action:

> *Therapist:* "You have just had an experience of your impulse. Do you notice the difference between acting on your impulse and experiencing your impulse without acting on it—as you just did? You had the full experience of the impulse, but no one got hurt.

It is particularly therapeutic when the patient reaches the stage when they can turn their retaliatory impulse towards the therapist. Being able to bring the recognition of the impulse into the therapeutic relationship leads to an understanding that a good relationship contains both aggression and affection, both love and hate. Once again, the fork in the road leads to an experience of the free ego and access to emotional intelligence and insight.

Aggression and sadism

The alternative route to the free ego leads through sadism. Once again, it requires an encouraging and supportive system to enable people to explore their sadistic fantasies. In the earlier days of discovering the common dynamics that human beings are heir to, discovering the extent of the sadism, the fantasies of torture, and the experience of triumph and satisfaction that accompanied them often aroused shock, horror, and even nausea, sometimes in the person, sometimes in other group members, and sometimes in the therapist. In all therapies, this is a stage at which people are in great danger of being punished severely by the superego. In some therapies it is even commonly accepted that to access sadism without horror means that the person is basically flawed. However, innovative techniques lead to innovative understandings. Further exploration of the road through sadism led to understanding that horror and nausea, when it occurs, is a defence against one's own sadistic impulses and fantasies, with the concomitant relief when they are acknowledged.

Projective identification

Even more important is the insight that the torture fantasies are a code for what the person experienced as having been done to them. The tortures then become a symbolic communication to the original torturer, with the wish that if the torturer knew what it was like, then they would stop, and in the shared experience the relationship would re-establish and communication could take place. With this insight came compassion for the sadistic responses available to the human race, and the determination to fight against the impulses to treat others, or be treated by others, in sadistic ways. Once again, the fork in the road led to the energy of the life force.

The crisis of hatred

Insights into the dynamics of masochism and sadism that are aroused in the retaliatory impulse have great therapeutic implications. Most importantly, there is insight into the way projections reduce the experience of the world to a series of political win/lose relationships. In business and social relationships they are experienced and acted out in exploitive inequality. In families they are experienced and acted out in exploitive relationships with parents and siblings. In therapy, they are experienced in terms of an exploitive relationship with the therapist.

As most therapists know, therapy most often founders on the negative transference. It is for this reason that SCT pays full attention to preparing both patients and trainees to work with the depth of the hatred that is aroused when the negative transference surfaces in group and individual therapy. What makes it particularly difficult is that the underlying dynamic in the crisis of hatred is paranoid rage. How the paranoia will be manifested depends partly on the dynamics of the individual and partly on how well people have integrated the earlier work in Phase I—particularly the undoing of cognitive distortions. However well prepared, however, the therapist or trainer must be ready to be the target of paranoid rage and also to contain the deep projective identifications that characterize this phase. This phase is particularly difficult for everyone, whether in the role of therapist or trainer, or whether in the role of patient or trainee.

What is innovative in SCT is the preparation for work with the negative transference, as described above. Less intense experiences that contain important elements of the subphase are experienced in the cognitive distortions that generate anxiety (particularly mind-reading) and in undoing the projective identifications in sadomasochistic role-locks. Managing the crisis of hatred is a matter of containment by the therapist within the therapeutic system. All successful therapies need a good-enough containment of the hatred aroused in the negative transference if the system is to move past it.

Transference

The major discovery for people as they develop through the first phase of development is that a major motivation for us all, when we work, is to get approval, praise, and even love from the people for whom and with whom we are working. It is the frustration of these wishes that arouses Phase I defences. SCT discriminates between two kinds of transference. The superficial transferences, which SCT calls the secondary transferences, are addressed immediately. Thus the simpler compliant or defiant transference responses are brought to the patients' attention and explored. Recognizing these transferences paves the way for ultimately recognizing and containing the negative transference when it emerges at the end of the first phase. The deeper primary transferences, though present, are not elicited and are not addressed until the second and third phases of system development. The issue is never whether or not transference exists, but which are the levels of transference that are addressed, and when.

Thus, in undoing the cognitive distortions in the process of undoing anxiety and depression, the SCT therapist recognizes that the roots of the distortions go deep, but he pays attention only to those aspects of the transference manifestations that can be managed by common sense, as in the example of deliberately bringing the patient back to the present by asking: "In what ways am I different from your mother?"

Similarly, in working with the sadism and masochism that surface around the retaliatory impulse, the therapist works at the level of dominant and submissive relationships as they manifest between the patient and other group members, or (in individual therapy) between the patient and the therapist. Group members do this work in functional subgroups. In individual therapy, transference is managed by immediately surfacing it whenever it is implied. Thus the therapist might say: "It seems as if you believe that I know more about you than you know yourself? Is that true?" Or in the subphase where role-locks are the focus: "Do you notice that you have taken on a submissive posture and voice tone? (thus discouraging people from taking on the postures and attitudes of the roles that they learned in childhood, which return under stress.)

Thus in the first phase people come to recognize their tendency either to volunteer or to be volunteered as an identified patient or scapegoat, and thus to relate to the world as helpless, as helpful, or as rejecting and hostile. Therapeutic work comes a long way when people observe, recognize, and experience the behavioural cues that signal others to respond to them in a reciprocal ways. However, observing and modifying behaviour does not address the depth of the dynamics of the repetition compulsion. Nor does it address its roots. This is the work of the second and third phases, which are the context for insight into transferences.

The negative and positive transferences

Most of the techniques and skills of SCT developed as patients and trainees discovered them in the process of the phases of development. It was repeatedly brought to our attention that intimacy, in the first phase of development, occurred as a defence against the work of understanding the underlying hatred of the disappointing authority (in the self, in the other, and in the therapist). Once again, of course, this does not mean that transient excursions into the positive transference in the first phase cannot be used therapeutically. Nor should the genuine positive feelings that belong to the therapeutic relationship be confused with a positive transference. It means that therapy works best if work on the negative transference occurs before work on the positive transference.

The conclusions that we did draw were, in fact, that the negative and positive transferences actually belong to two different phases of development. The negative transference belongs in the first phase because it is fuelled by a basic split between good and bad, in which the bad is projected out onto the hated object in an attempt to keep the good in the self. Thus the negative transference denies the good in the other. The positive transference, on the other hand, denies the bad in the other. The work with the negative transference leads to a recognition and acceptance of the murderous hatred and rage in human beings. The work with the positive transference leads to increasing the ability to endure differences in the loved one.

In the work of the first phase, undoing anxiety, tension, depression, and the defences against the retaliatory impulse restores the experience of the energy of the true self (often referred to as "a free ego"). Undoing role-locks reduces the tendency to create dominant or submissive relationships. Paranoid hatred is muted when hated objects become people like us rather than hated objects. This phase ends in the grief at the cost of our defences on our life and relationships. Poignant as this insight is, it serves as a driving force to becoming ourselves and ready to relate to others. Thus patients and trainees who enter the phase of intimacy are open to the group therapist and other members in group therapy, and to the therapist as a facilitator in individual therapy.

Phase II: intimacy

The second phase of development builds upon the insights into projective identification that occurred, at a greater or lesser depth, in exploring the dynamics of the repetition compulsion. The work of the second phase of development is recognizing the driving and restraining forces to separation and individuation.

SCT work with intimacy is based on the work of the first phase, where people came to recognize that one cannot relate to another until one can first relate to oneself. In this second phase the focus changes to how to make relationships with others. It is then that people come to understand that one can never have the relationship one wants, one can only have the relationship one can make! Relationships one can make require, of course, coming out of the fantasy of the perfect relationship and into a world where one can bear, and accept, the differences in the other.

The SCT approach to defences against intimacy is both simpler and more profound than work with the defences in Phase I. The dynamics are profound in that they have roots in the basic good–bad split, a primary discrimination made by all of us before we have developed the ability to integrate. This pre-integration level is available in all of us, and we regress to it under sufficiently stressful conditions. On the good side, all is all right with the world as long as we experience a mirroring and attuned relationship; on the bad side, nothing is ever good enough, and we reject mirroring, attunement, and empathy.

Intimacy is the phase in which SCT therapists have more in common with psychodynamic therapists than in the first phase of active intervention. Dependency dynamics are explored both as they relate to the dependency impulses to be as one with others in enchanted blind trust (the good side of the split) and as they relate to the counter-dependent impulses to be distant from others in disenchantment and blind mistrust (the bad side of the split).

The basic SCT methods for explicitly recognizing differences in the apparently similar and similarities in the apparently different are essential to this phase. Recognizing differences in what is apparently similar between oneself and others enables us to separate. Recognizing similarities in what is apparently different between oneself and others enables us to individuate without the fear that we will lose our identity in relationships.

SCT methods for managing the dynamics of intimacy are highly containing. The two most challenging experiences to explore in the phase of intimacy are the experience of emptiness and the fear of falling apart. The therapist reframes these experiences so that patients and trainees can explore them with the natural apprehension about going into the unknown rather than believing them to be dangerous or pathological. For example:

> *Therapist:* "You are becoming anxious about your experience of emptiness. Stay at the edge of the unknown and see if you can become curious enough to go into it, just like the way you go inside your tension, to discover what is there."

And another example:

> *Therapist:* "You are afraid of falling apart. We all have to let the old self fall apart to make room for the new. Think of the chrysalis before it emerges as a butterfly. Can you stay at the edge of the unknown and allow yourself to fall apart and see what you can discover about what emerges?"

And in the experience of falling (which appears to be part of "falling apart"):

> *Therapist:* "Let yourself go. Of course you are apprehensive, you have not done this before. Stay curious, like Alice, as she fell

down the rabbit hole, not knowing what she would find along the way."

Phase III: integration

The goals of SCT in this third phase are to increase the capacity to use one's verbal and emotional intelligence and access one's existential understanding. Work in the third phase includes understanding what it means not to take things just personally, increasing the ability to cross the boundaries into reality, changing roles as the context requires it, and maintaining access to both a personal and an existential sense of humour. This work can be done in therapy or out of therapy, in a group or by oneself. This phase requires the ongoing development of one's capacity to experience or respond to reality without defending against it, and when defensiveness occurs—as of course it does—to reduce the defences using the SCT techniques acquired in therapy.

The ongoing work of the third phase of SCT system development is to continue to recognize and modify the various forms of transference, particularly the pervasive transference.

The pervasive transference

Work with transference, as with all SCT work, moves from the simpler to the more complex. Work with the social transferences in the first phase reduces the compliant or defiant acting out towards authority and the identification with being the victim or aggressor in a world perceived as exploitative. In the second phase, understanding the deeper transferences from preverbal and just-verbal childhood attachments reduces the tendency to over-react to the everyday failures in attunement and empathy. It was not until we followed the work of SCT patients in the third phase that we came to understand that there was a much deeper, more subtle and pervasive experience that we called the pervasive transference.

The pervasive transferences colour one's experience of the world without our being aware that it is the colour of the pervasive transference rather than the colour of the world. In this third phase the previous glimpses of the existential experience, and the understanding that comes with it, become more visible as the screen of the pervasive transferences become more transparent.

With every insight into the pervasive transference, the experience of the world transforms. For example: pervasive pessimism (or optimism) resolves into understanding that the world simply is. Recognizing that judgements about good or bad are context-related develops the ability to see the world from more than one perspective at once.

Innovation in Phase III: the systems-centered context

SCT assumes that it is easier to understand the world from its many perspectives if we recognize that we have shifted contexts. We shift contexts all the time without being explicitly aware that we are doing so. When we go to work, we shift our context from home to work. When we go home, we again shift our context back to home. Why does SCT emphasize the importance of context? Because thinking about work and home as different contexts allows us to recognize that two important things change as we change our context: one is our role, and the other is the goal. The way we play our role depends not just on us ourselves but on choosing those aspects of us (our role behaviours) that are appropriate to the goal of the context.

Why does SCT translate this kind of awareness into systems language? Because thinking systems make it easier for us to think about all the different levels of system that co-exist in every context. Let us take the context of "home" as an example. When we marry, we become part of the system of "marriage". In every marriage there are subsystems: the system of parent, spouse, and person (not to mention pre-existing systems in the extended family or previous marriages). Each subsystem also has subsystems. For example the system of parent has the subsystems of mother and father; the system of spouse has the subsystems of husband and wife. And every level of system is a different context, has different goals, and requires different behavioural roles. The goal of the husband and wife, for example, is to manage the business of the marriage, and the way the husband and wife take up their roles determines the manner in which the goals are reached in reality and our roles in it.

Applying systems thinking to couple therapy

An example from couple therapy follows, illustrating how SCT uses context. Let us say that a couple, in a conventional marriage with children, comes to therapy because they are frustrated and angry with each other. In presenting the couple with a systems framework, the SCT intention is to turn their attention away from the frustrations of trying to change each other to the challenge of changing the system of their marriage.

The frustration and anger that each feels for the other is generated from taking each other personally: to members of the system "marriage", these frustrations are not "just personal"—they are also a conflict of system roles.

For example, in the role of mother and father, there is the goal of bringing up children (importing babies and exporting adults!). For the husband and wife, there is the goal of managing the finances and business decision of the marriage (where and how to live). For the man and woman, the goal is intimacy (and satisfactory sex). And for each, in the role of person, the goal is personal and interpersonal development (which happens if the couple cooperates successfully in all the interdependent roles!).

How well the conflicts within and between these subsystems are resolved will determine the stability of the system-as-a-whole.

Looking at their marriage from the perspective of roles, it becomes easy for the couple to understand one of the most common sources of conflict in marriage: approaching each other from incompatible roles. If one partner approaches the other romantically while the other is trying to balance a chequebook, for example, it is easy to get into a conflict that is then blamed on dynamics that are much more serious than incompatible role behaviours. Another major advantage of focusing on role conflicts is that it refocuses the couple away from blaming each other and onto reframing the marriage as a system that, as they developed it together, they can choose to change together. In the service of this goal, they are asked to notice which of their interdependent roles works best—and to identify how to generalize from what they do that leads to their success so that they can generalize to other roles. (SCT constantly orients towards the positive to weaken the restraining forces of the negative.)

CONCLUSION

The most important implication of this systems approach is that what kind of individual and group therapy can occur depends more upon the "system" that the therapist and patients develop together than it does on either the individual potential for therapy of the patient or the skills of the therapist! This is why all systems-centered therapy starts by building a therapeutic system first.

The goals of systems-centered therapy are no different from the goals of psychodynamic therapy: that people will change in a therapeutic direction by coming to recognize, understand, and contain their conflicts and impulses rather than acting them out. However, how these goals are achieved is different.

Based on the reality that the present is the only arena in which problems are solved, systems-centered techniques deliberately shift energy from the past to the present, from the future to the present, and from the wishes and fears of the present into present reality. The underlying assumption is that although neurological pathways to the past or the future determine familiar thinking patterns, the maladaptive aspects of those patterns can be modified by developing new neurological pathways that process information about the past and predictions about the future in the context of the present.

In the systems-centered approach, systems-centered therapists build a therapeutic system by establishing norms that reduce the "noise" in communication and resolve conflicts and undo splits by discriminating and integrating differences. This approach applies to both individual and group therapy. The advantages of the systems-centered approach is that people learn not to take their experiences just personally, to explore their experience instead of interpreting or explaining it, and to redirect their energy away from their defences towards discovering what they are defending against. Systems-centered therapists are both active and directive in the first phase of system development while SCT norms are being established. Once established, the SCT norms provide the containment and support for the therapeutic system.

REFERENCES AND BIBLIOGRAPHY

Ackoff, R., & Emery, E. (1972). *On Purposeful Systems*. New York: Aldine Press, Atherton.

Agazarian, Y. M. (1969a). The agency as a change agent. In: A. H. Goldberg (Ed.), *Blindness Research: The Expanding Frontiers*. University Park, PA, & London: Penn State Press.

Agazarian, Y. M. (1969b). A theory of verbal behavior and information transfer. In: *Classroom Interaction Newsletter, 4* (2): 22–33.

Agazarian, Y. M. (1972a). Communication through the group process: An approach to humanization. *The Devereux Papers, 1* (1): pp. 1–7.

Agazarian, Y. M. (1972b). A system for analyzing verbal behavior (SAVI). Applied to staff training in milieu treatment. *Devereux Schools Forum, 7* (1).

Agazarian, Y. M. (1982). Role as a bridge construct in understanding the relationship between the individual and the group. In: M. Pines & L. Rafaelson (Eds.), *The Individual and the Group: Boundaries and Interrelations. Vol. I, Theory*. New York: Plenum Press.

Agazarian, Y. M. (1983a). Some advantages of applying multi-dimensional thinking to the teaching, practice and outcomes of group psychotherapy. *International Journal of Group Psychotherapy, 33* (2).

Agazarian, Y. M. (1983b). Theory of the Invisible Group applied to individual and group-as-a-whole interpretations. *Group: The Journal of the Eastern Group Psychotherapy Society, 7* (2).

Agazarian, Y. M. (1986a). Application of Lewin's life space concept to the individual and group-as-a-whole systems in psychotherapy. In: E. Stivers & S. Wheelan (Eds.), *The Lewin Legacy: Field Theory in Current Practice.* New York: Springer-Verlag.

Agazarian, Y. M. (1986b). "Towards the Formulation of a Group-as-a-Whole Theory: The Lewin Legacy—Application of Modified Force Field Analysis to the Diagnosis of Implicit Group Goals." Paper presented at the Second International Kurt Lewin Conference, sponsored by The Society for the Advancement of Field Theory, Downingtown, September.

Agazarian, Y. M. (1987a). "Bion, The Tavistock Method and the Group-as-a-Whole: Three Reactions to a New Member—An Interpersonal Tale Retold from the Perspective of the Group-as-a-Whole." Paper presented as Guest Lecture, Group Psychotherapy, Harvard Medical School, Department of Continuing Education, sponsored by the Massachusetts General Hospital Department of Psychiatry, Boston, MA, April 3–5.

Agazarian, Y. M. (1987b). The difficult patient, the difficult group. In: *Group: The Journal of the Eastern Group Psychotherapy Society, 2* (4) [chapter 3, this volume].

Agazarian, Y. M. (1987c) "Group-as-a-Whole Theory: Framed in Terms of Field Theory and General Systems Theory." Paper presented at the "The Lewin Legacy Symposium", 95th Annual Convention of the American Psychological Association, New York City, August.

Agazarian, Y. M. (1987d). "Group-as-a-Whole Theory Applied to Scapegoating." Paper supplementary to the workshop on "Deviance, Scapegoating & Group Development", EGPS Annual Conference, New York, 31 October [chapter 1, this volume].

Agazarian, Y. M. (1987e). "Re Viewing Yalom: An interpersonal tale retold from the perspective of the group-as-a-whole." Guest Lecture, Group Psychotherapy, Harvard Medical School, Department of Continuing Education, sponsored by Massachusetts General Hospital, Department of Psychiatry, April 3–5 [chapter 2, this volume].

Agazarian, Y. M. (1987f). "Theory of the Invisible Group: Group-as-a-whole Theory Framed in Terms of Field Theory and General Systems Theory." Paper presented at the "The Lewin Legacy" Symposium, 95th Annual Convention of the American Psychological Association, New York, August.

Agazarian, Y. M. (1987g). "Three Reactions to a New Member: An Interpersonal Tale Retold from the Perspective of the Group-as-a-Whole." Paper presented at Friends Hospital Speaker Series, Philadelphia, 11 December.

Agazarian, Y. M. (1989a). Group-as-a-Whole Systems Theory and Practice. *Group: Special Issue on the Group-as-a-Whole, Journal of the Eastern Group Psychology Society, 13* (3/4: Winter): 131–155 [chapter 4, this volume].

Agazarian, Y. M. (1989b). "Group-as-a-Whole Theory and Practice." Panel presentation for "The Group-as-a-whole Perspective: Tool for Understanding". Tenth International Congress of Group Psychotherapy, Amsterdam, August.

Agazarian, Y. M. (1989c). "The Invisible Group: An Integrational Theory of Group-as-a-whole." Twelfth Annual Foulkes Memorial Lecture. *Group Analysis: The Journal of Group Analytic Psychotherapy, 22,* (4).

Agazarian, Y. M. (1989d). "Pathogenic Beliefs and Implicit Goals: Discussion of 'The Mount Zion Group: The Therapeutic Process and Applicability of the Group's Work to Psychotherapy'." Slavson Memorial Lecture, presented by Harold Sampson & Joseph Weiss, AGPA, San Francisco, February.

Agazarian, Y. M. (1989e). "Reframing the Group-as-a-Whole." Paper presented on the Panel, "Learning from Experience: Alternatives to the Traditional Conference." Ninth Scientific Meeting of the A. K. Rice Institute, sponsored by the New York Center, New York, May 12–14. In: T. W. Hugg, N. M. Carson, & R. M. Lipgar (Eds.), *Changing Group Relations: The Next Twenty-five Years in America. Proceedings of the Ninth Scientific Meeting of the A. K. Rice Institute.* Jupiter, FL: A. K. Rice Institute [chapter 7, this volume].

Agazarian, Y. M. (1990a). "A Flip-chart of Systems-Centered Thinking and Its Application to the Practice of Group Therapy." In: *Collected Papers: Systems-Centered Workshop I.* Philadelphia, PA: Systems Centered Press.

Agazarian, Y. M. (1990b). Systems-Centered Thinking Applied to Human Systems in General and to Systems-Centered Therapy in Particular. *Collected Papers: Systems-Centered Workshop II.* Philadelphia, PA: Systems Centered Press.

Agazarian, Y. M. (1991a). "Application of a Modified Force Field Analysis to the Diagnosis of Implicit Group Goals". Paper presented at the Third International Kurt Lewin Conference, sponsored by the Society for the Advancement of Field Theory, September, 1988. In: *Collected Papers: Theory I.* Philadelphia, PA: Systems-Centered Press.

Agazarian, Y. M. (1991b). Systems theory and group psychotherapy: From there-and-then to here-and-now. *The International Forum of Group Psychotherapy, 1* (3).

Agazarian, Y. M. (1991c). Videotape introduction to group-as-a-whole dynamics, presented by Yvonne M. Agazarian. *Agazarian Videotape Series: Systems-Centered Group Psychotherapy, Module I.* Philadelphia, PA: Blue Sky Productions.

Agazarian, Y. M. (1992a). Book review of "Koinonia: From Hate, through Dialogue, to Culture in the Large Group" by Patrick de Maré, Robin Piper, & Sheila Thompson. *International Journal of Group Psychotherapy, 42* (3) [chapter 8, this volume].

Agazarian, Y. M. (1992b). "Contrasting views of a Representative Group Event." Discussion of a 10-minute videotape of a psychotherapy group led by Irvin Yalom, Forty-ninth Annual Conference, AGPA, February 20–22, New York.

Agazarian, Y. M. (1992c). A systems approach to the group-as-a-whole. *International Journal of Group Psychotherapy, 42* (3): 177–205 [chapter 9, this volume].

Agazarian, Y. M. (1992d). "Systems-Centered Group Psychotherapy: How to Get through Group Defenses." Paper written for Friends Hospital Training Series on "The systems-centered approach to Group-as-a-whole therapy". Philadelphia, PA: Friends Hospital.

Agazarian, Y. M. (1994). The phases of development and the systems-centered group. In: M. Pines & V. Schermer (Eds.), *Ring of Fire: Primitive Object Relations and Affect in Group Psychotherapy* (pp. 36–85). London: Routledge, Chapman & Hall [chapter 6, this volume].

Agazarian, Y. M. (1997). *Systems-Centered Therapy for Groups*. New York: Guilford.

Agazarian, Y. M. (1999). Phases of development in the systems-centered group. *Small Group Research, 30* (1): 82–107.

Agazarian, Y. M. (2001). *Systems-Centered Therapy for Inpatients*. London: Jessica Kingsley.

Agazarian, Y. M. (2002). A systems-centered approach to individual and group psychotherapy. In: L. Vandecreek & T. Jackson (Eds.), *Innovations in Clinical Practice: A Source Book, Vol. 20* (pp. 223–240). Sarasota, FL: Professional Resource Press [chapter 10, this volume].

Agazarian, Y. M., Boyer, G. E., Simon, A., & White, P. F. (1973). *Documenting Development* (*Vols. 1–3*). Philadelphia, PA: Research for Better Schools.

Agazarian, Y. M., & Carter, F. (1993). The large group and systems-centered theory. *The Journal of the Eastern Group Psychotherapy Society, 17* (4): 210–234.

Agazarian, Y. M., & Gantt, S. (2000). *Autobiography of a Theory*. London: Jessica Kingsley.

Agazarian, Y. M., & Janoff, S. (1993). Systems theory and small groups. In I. Kaplan & B. Sadock (Eds.), *Comprehensive Textbook of Group Psychotherapy* (3rd ed.). Baltimore, MD: Williams & Wilkins.

Agazarian, Y. M., & Peters, R. (1981). *The Visible and Invisible Group: Two Perspectives on Group Psychotherapy and Group Process*. London: Routlege & Kegan Paul.

Agazarian, Y. M., & Simon, A. (1989). "An Analysis of Excerpts from the Chicago Group Script of a Psychotherapy Group by SAVI, a Behavioural Observation System." AGPA, San Francisco, February.

Anzieu, D. (1984). *The Group and the Unconscious*. London: Routledge & Kegan Paul.

Ashbach, C., & Schermer, V. (1987). *Object Relations, the Self, and the Group: A*

Conceptual Paradigm. International Library of Group Psychotherapy and Group Process. London: Routledge & Kegan Paul.

Bateson, G. (1972). *Steps to an Ecology of Mind*. New York: Ballantine Books.

Beck, A. P. (1981). A study of group phase development and emergent leadership. *Group, 5* (4, Winter).

Beck, A. P., & Lewis, C. M. (Eds.) (2000). *The Process of Group Psychotherapy: Systems for Analyzing Change*. Washington, DC: American Psychological Association.

Bennis, W. G., & Shepard, H. A. (1956). A theory of group development. *Human Relations, 9* (4, November): 415–437.

Bertalanffy, L. von (1968). *General Systems*. New York: George Braziller.

Bertalanffy, L. von (1969). *General Systems* (revised edition). New York: George Braziller.

Bion, W. R. (1959). *Experiences in Groups*. London: Tavistock.

Bion, W. R. (1985). Container and contained. In: A. D. Colman & M. H. Geller (Eds.), *The Group Relations Reader, 2*. A. K. Rice Institute Series, Washington, DC: A. K. Rice Institute.

Bowlby, J. (1969). Instinctive behaviour, an alternative model. In: *Attachment and Loss, Vol. 1: Attachment*. New York: Basic Books.

Brabender, V. (1997). Chaos and order in the psychotherapy group. In: F. Masterpasha & P. Perna (Eds.), *The Psychological Meaning of Chaos* (pp. 225–253). Washington, DC: American Psychological Association.

Buzaglo, G., & Wheelan, S. (1999). Facilitating work team effectiveness: Case studies from Central America. In: *Small Group Research, 30* (1): 108–129. New York: Sage Publications.

Cartwright, D., & Zander, A. (1960). *Group Dynamics Research and Theory* (2nd ed.). New York: Elmsford, Row, & Peterson.

Coleman, A. D., & Bexton, W. H. (Eds.) (1975). *The Group Relations Reader, Vol. I*. Washington, DC: A. K. Rice Institute.

Coleman, A. D. & Geller, M. H. (Eds.) (1985). *The Group Relations Reader, Vol. II*. Washington, DC: A. K. Rice Institute.

Davanloo, H. (1987). Clinical manifestations of superego pathology. *International Journal of Short-Term Psychotherapy*, 2: 225–254.

de Maré, P., Piper R., & Thompson, S. (1991). *Koinonia: From Hate, through Dialogue, to Culture in the Large Group*. London: Karnac Books.

Durkin, H. E. (1972). Group therapy and General Systems Theory. In: C. J. Sager & H. Singer Kaplan (Eds.), *Progress in Group and Family Therapy*. New York: Brunner/Mazel.

Durkin, J. E. (Ed.) (1981). *Living Groups: Group Psychotherapy and General System Theory*. New York: Brunner/Mazel.

Festinger, L. (1957). *A Theory of Cognitive Dissonance*. Evanston, IL: Rowe, Peterson & Co.

Foulkes, S. H. (1948). *Introduction to Group Analytic Psychotherapy.* Maresfield Reprints. London: Karnac, 1983.

Foulkes, S. H. (1964). *Therapeutic Group Analysis.* Maresfield Reprints. London: Karnac, 1984.

Foulkes, S. H. (1973). The group as a matrix of the individual's mental life. In: L. Wolberg & E. Schwatz (Eds.), *Group Therapy: An Overview.* New York: Intercontinental Medical Books.

Foulkes, S. H., & Anthony, E. J. (1957). *Group Psychotherapy: The Psychoanalytic Approach.* Maresfield Reprints. London: Karnac, 1984.

Freud, S. (1921c). *Group Psychology and the Analysis of the Ego. Standard Edition, 18.* London: Hogarth Press & Institute of Psychoanalysis, 1957.

Ganzarain, R. (1989). *Object Relations Group Psychotherapy: the Group as an Object, a Tool, and a Training Base.* Madison, CT: International Universities Press.

Hinshelwood, R. D. (1989). *A Dictionary of Kleinian Thought.* London: Free Association.

Horwitz, L. (1977). Group centered approach to group psychotherapy. *International Journal of Group Psychology, 27*: 423–439.

Horwitz, L. (1983). Projective identification in diads and groups. *International Journal of Group Psychology, 33*: 259–279.

Howard, A., & Scott, R. A. (1965). A proposed framework for the analysis of stress in the human organism. *Journal of Applied Behavioural Science, 10*: 141–60.

Klein, R. H., Bernard, H. S., & Singer, D. L. (1992). *Handbook of Contemporary Group Psychotherapy.* New York: International Universities Press.

Korzybski, A. (1948). *Science and Sanity: An Introduction to Non-Aristotelian Systems and General Semantics* (3rd ed.). Lakeville, CT: International Non-Aristotelian Library.

Lewin, K. (1935). *A Dynamic Theory of Personality: Selected Papers.* New York: McGraw Hill.

Lewin, K. (1951). *Field Theory in Social Science.* New York: Harper & Row.

Malan, D., Balfour, F. H., Hood, U. G., & Shooter, A. M. (1976). Group psychotherapy: A long-term follow-up study. *Archives of General Psychiatry, 33* (11): 1303–1315.

McCullough, L. (1995). Short term dynamic psychotherapy: A cross theoretical analysis of change mechanisms. In: R. Curtis & G. Striker (Eds.), *How People Change.* New York: Plenum Press.

Miller, J. G. (1978). *Living Systems.* New York: McGraw Hill.

Rothman, M. A. (1992). *The Science Gap, Dispelling the Myths and Understanding the Reality of Science.* Buffalo, NY: Prometheus Books.

Sampson, H. (1989). "How The Patient's Sense of Danger and Safety Influence the Analytic Process." Slavson Lecture, AGPA, San Francisco, CA.

Shannon, C. E., & Weaver, W. (1964). *The Mathematical Theory of Communication.* Urbana, IL: University of Illinois Press.

Simon, A., & Agazarian, Y. (1967). *S.A.V.I., Sequential Analysis of Verbal Interaction.* Philadelphia, PA: Research for Better Schools.

Weiss, J. (1989). "The Nature of the Patient's Problems and How in Psychoanalysis He Works to Solve Them." Slavson Lecture, AGPA, San Francisco.

Winnicott, D. W. (1951). Transitional objects and transitional phenomena. In: *Playing and Reality.* Harmondsworth, Middlesex: Penguin, 1974.

Wolfe, T. (1929). *Look Homeward Angel.* London: Charles Scribner.

Yalom, I. D. (1970). *The Theory and Practice of Group Psychotherapy* (4th ed.). New York: Basic Books.

INDEX

For Product Safety Concerns and Information please contact our EU
representative GPSR@taylorandfrancis.com
Taylor & Francis Verlag GmbH, Kaufingerstraße 24, 80331 München, Germany

www.ingramcontent.com/pod-product-compliance
Ingram Content Group UK Ltd.
Pitfield, Milton Keynes, MK11 3LW, UK
UKHW022205190926
475702UK00003B/206
* 9 7 8 0 3 6 7 3 2 7 2 9 3 *